VISUAL QUICKSTART GUIDE

PAGEMILL 3

FOR MACINTOSH & WINDOWS

Maria Langer

 Peachpit Press

Visual QuickStart Guide
PageMill 3 for Macintosh & Windows
Maria Langer

Peachpit Press
1249 Eighth Street
Berkeley, CA 94710
510-524-2178 • 800-283-9444
510-524-2221 (fax)

Find us on the World Wide Web at: http://www.peachpit.com/

Peachpit Press is a division of Addison Wesley Longman

Editor: Nancy Davis
Indexer: Emily Glossbrenner
Cover Design: The Visual Group
Production: Maria Langer, Lisa Brazieal

Colophon

This book was produced with Adobe PageMaker 6.5 on a Power Macintosh G3/300. The fonts used were Kepler Multiple Master, Meta Plus, and PIXymbols Command. Screenshots were created using Snapz Pro on a Power Macintosh 8500/180 and Hijaak Capture on a Gateway 2000 GP6-266.

Notice of Rights

Notice of Liability

Trademarks

ISBN 0-201-35443-8

9 8 7 6 5 4 3 2 1

Printed and bound in the United States of America.

 Printed on recycled paper.

Dedication

To my friend Fred Showker,
designer and Web publisher,
for his outstanding work
with the user group community

Thanks!

To Nancy Davis, for her sharp-eyed, long-distance editing skills. It's always great to work with you, Nancy!

To Nancy Ruenzel, for letting me write this revision to my two *PageMill 2 Visual Quick-Start Guide* books. Doing a cross-platform VQS proved to be quite a challenge, but I think I did okay.

To Lisa Brazieal, for letting me be a little stubborn about the layout. I know the book doesn't look *exactly* the way you wanted it to, but I think it's fine. To really appreciate the layout, take a look at my first VQS. Ick!

To the rest of the folks at Peachpit Press—especially Gary-Paul, Trish, Hannah, Paula, Zigi, Jimbo, and Keasley—for doing what they do so well—and being so nice about it!

To Adobe Systems Incorporated's PageMill development team, for putting together a nice revision to what I'll always think of as the easiest, most intuitive Web authoring tool around. But next time, can you make the menus and shortcut keys on the Mac and Windows versions the same?

And to Mike, for the usual bunch of reasons.

http://www.gilesrd.com/mlanger/

TABLE OF CONTENTS

Table of Contents

TABLE OF CONTENTS

INTRODUCTION TO WEB PUBLISHING

Before You Begin...

If buying PageMill was your first big step into the realm of World Wide Web publishing, stop right here. There may be gaps in your understanding of the Web and how it works. It's a good idea to fill those gaps with basic background information before you go any further.

This introductory chapter was written for people who are brand new to the Internet and the World Wide Web. It explains what the Internet and World Wide Web are. It tells you about HTML and how it is interpreted by a special kind of software called a Web browser. It explains what PageMill does for you so you know exactly why you should be glad you use it. Finally, it provides a list of things to keep in mind when planning your Web site. All along the way, it defines important terms that will be used throughout this book.

You won't find many pictures in this introduction, but you will find lots of good, useful information. If you're new to the Internet or Web publishing, don't skip this introduction. The few minutes you spend here could save you hours in the future.

The Internet

The Internet is a global network of computers. It's a lot like the network you might find in an office environment—but instead of the networked computers being separated by walls or cubicle partitions, they may be separated by miles, mountains, and oceans.

The Internet has been around since the 1960s, so it isn't new. What is new, however, is the boom in Internet interest and access. More people access the Internet today than ever before. And with access getting cheaper and easier all the time, the Internet will continue to grow long into the future.

The Internet offers access to many features. Here are just a few that interest most Internet users:

◆ **E-mail.** Electronic mail makes it possible to exchange written messages with other people all over the world, quickly and cost effectively.

◆ **Software.** FTP (file transfer protocol) sites offer the latest and greatest shareware and freeware files.

◆ **Discussion groups.** Newsgroups and mailing lists let participants join in topical discussions with people who share their interests.

◆ **"Published" Information.** Gopher, WAIS, and World Wide Web servers make it possible to publish and retrieve information from a wide variety of sources.

✔ Tip

■ A lot of people think the phrase *World Wide Web* is the same as *Internet*. This isn't true. The World Wide Web is only part of the Internet. The Internet is far more than just the World Wide Web.

THE INTERNET

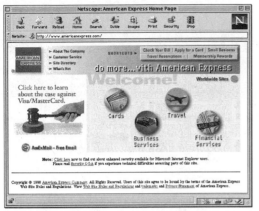

Figure 1. The home page for American Express,...

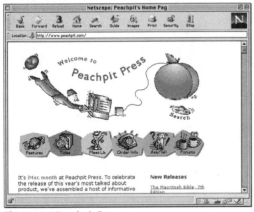

Figure 2. ...Peachpit Press,...

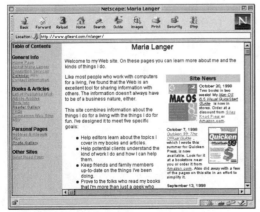

Figure 3. ...and yours truly.

The World Wide Web

The World Wide Web is the fastest growing part of the Internet. Often the first part of the Internet that new users explore, its popularity is due primarily to its graphic user interface and ease of use.

Each week, thousands of new Web pages appear on the World Wide Web. Web publishers include:

◆ Major corporations interested in global exposure (**Figure 1**).

◆ Small, medium, and large businesses interested in advertising (and selling) products and services (**Figure 2**).

◆ Individuals interested in sharing information about themselves (**Figure 3**).

The truth is, *anyone* can publish on the World Wide Web. If you've got something to say, the Web is a good place to say it—especially if you're ready for millions of people to get your message.

Web Pages & Sites

A Web *page* may include any combination of the following elements:

◆ **Formatted text.** Headings, bold and italic styles, indented lists, and other kinds of formatting can make text easier and more interesting to read.

◆ **Graphics and Multimedia.** Whether images, colorful lines, background patterns, QuickTime movies, or Java applets, graphics and multimedia can make pages visually appealing or convey information that cannot be expressed in words.

◆ **Hyperlinks.** Clicking a text or graphic link can display another page, download a file, or open a mail form.

◆ **Forms.** Edit boxes, radio buttons, check boxes, and pop-up menus are some of the form elements that can collect information from a Web page viewer.

◆ **Tables.** Displaying text and graphics in table layout keeps page appearance neat.

◆ **Frames.** By splitting a browser window into frames, more than one Web page can be displayed at a time.

Figure 4 shows an example of a Web page with many of these elements.

A Web *site* is a group of related pages. Most Web sites have a *home page*—a main starting point for accessing the rest of the pages on the site. **Figures 1**, **2**, and **3** are home pages for three different Web sites.

✔ Tip

■ Don't let the word *page* confuse you. In Web lingo, page is the same as document or file. A Web page can be any length—it has nothing to do with the size of a printed piece of paper.

Figure 4. Here's an example of a Web page with many commonly used elements.

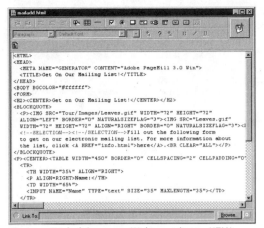

Figure 5. Underlying every Web page is raw HTML code. Here's what the code for the page in **Figure 4** looks like in PageMill's Source mode.

HTML

One of the benefits of publishing on the World Wide Web is that Web pages can be read by any kind of computer using any kind of Web browser. (I tell you more about browsers on the next page.) This is possible through the use of a programming language called *HyperText Markup Language* (HTML). Plain text documents written with HTML codes can be interpreted by Web browsers, which display the codes as formatted text and graphics.

Figure 5 shows an example of what the HTML document for the Web page in **Figure 4** looks like. If you look closely, you can find and read the text that appears on the page. Everything else is an HTML code or tag that tells a Web browser how to format text, where to find graphics, and how to make form elements.

Fortunately, you don't need to deal with HTML code. PageMill writes the code for you automatically as you enter and format text, graphics, links, and other Web page elements.

✔ Tips

■ PageMill supports HTML version 3.2 codes, along with some Netscape Navigator and Microsoft Internet Explorer extensions. **Appendix D** lists the codes PageMill supports.

■ If you know HTML, you can enter raw HTML codes in the Source mode of a PageMill document window. If entered correctly, these codes will be read and understood by browsers that support them. If PageMill does not support them, it will ignore them.

■ If you're looking for a good guide to HTML, be sure to check out *HTML 4 for the World Wide Web: Visual QuickStart Guide* by Elizabeth Castro.

HTML

Web Browsers

Web browser software is what makes HTML code work. Programs like Netscape Navigator and Microsoft Internet Explorer read HTML code, interpret it, and display it the way the Web page designer intended.

Well, not always. Unfortunately, not all Web browsers interpret HTML codes the same way. And not all Web browsers support all HTML codes. The only way to see exactly how your Web page will look when viewed with a specific browser is to open the page with that browser.

The good news is that the most commonly used browsers—Navigator and Internet Explorer, which account for more than 90% of the browsers in use today—can interpret all the HTML codes that PageMill supports.

✔ Tips

- Each major computer platform—Macintosh, Windows, and UNIX—has its own collection of Web browsers. Because of this, your Web pages can look very similar from one platform to the next. This makes the Web a perfect cross-platform environment for sharing information—even if that information is accessible only within an organization's intranet and not the Internet.

- Throughout this book, the term Web browser refers to a *graphic* browser—one that is capable of displaying formatted text and graphics on Web pages. A *text* browser is another kind of browser that displays Web pages as unformatted text documents. Although text browser users will not see the graphics and formatting of your pages, they will see the textual content.

WEB BROWSERS

Planning Your Web Site

If you're creating a Web site from the ground up, you can create an effective site and save yourself a lot of aggravation by planning ahead. Here are a few things to consider:

◆ **What do you want your pages to look like?** If you plan on having multiple pages, you may want to use consistent formatting, colors, background patterns, logos, or other elements to give your site its own identity and set it apart from the others.

◆ **Will your pages be long or short?** Long pages make it possible to provide more information with fewer hits to the site. Short pages load more quickly. Each approach has its pros and cons.

◆ **Will your pages rely heavily on graphics?** Not all people who browse the World Wide Web do so with graphic browsers. These people won't be able to see your pictures. And even though most of your site's visitors will see your graphics, not all of them are willing to wait for large graphic images to load and appear on screen.

◆ **How do you want to organize your pages?** Create an outline showing the relationship between pages so you know how the pages will link to each other.

◆ **How do you want to store your pages and other files on disk?** Take advantage of the hierarchical file system to organize files in folders and subfolders.

These are just a few things to think about before you even launch PageMill. Browse the World Wide Web to see what other Web publishers are doing. Examine the sites that appeal to you and figure out what makes you like them more than others. Anyone can create Web pages, but it takes creativity and planning to put together *effective* Web pages—the ones people visit regularly and share with their friends.

GETTING STARTED WITH PAGEMILL

Introduction

PageMill is an Internet authoring tool that makes it easy to create Web pages. You can use PageMill's word processor-like interface and drag-and-drop editing techniques to enter, edit, and format Web pages; add graphics and links to other pages; and create forms for gathering information from the Web "surfers" who browse your pages. With PageMill, there's no need to struggle with HyperText Markup Language (HTML) codes. PageMill does all the HTML coding work for you, behind the scenes.

This Visual QuickStart Guide will help you master PageMill 3 by providing step-by-step instructions, plenty of illustrations, and a generous helping of tips. On these pages you'll find everything you need to know about PageMill—and more!

This book is designed for page-flipping. Use the thumb tabs, index, or table of contents to find the topics for which you need help. If you're brand new to PageMill, however, I suggest that you begin by reading at least this first chapter. In it, you'll find important introductory information about PageMill's interface.

The World Wide Web has opened the world of publishing to anyone with something to say. PageMill is one of the best tools around to get your message out on the Web with the least amount of effort.

Running PageMill

The PageMill installer places a number of files on your hard disk in a folder called Adobe PageMill® 3.0 (Mac OS) or PageMill 3.0 (Windows). One of these files is the PageMill application or program (**Figures 1a** and **1b**).

To launch or start PageMill

1. Using the Finder (Mac OS) or Windows Explorer (Windows), locate and open the Adobe PageMill® 3.0 (Mac OS) or PageMill 3.0 (Windows) folder on your hard disk.

2. Double-click the Adobe PageMill® 3.0 icon (Mac OS; **Figure 1a**) or PageMill.exe icon (Windows; **Figure 1b**).

or

Choose Start > Programs > Adobe > PageMill 3.0 > Adobe PageMill 3.0 (Windows only).

or

Double-click a PageMill document icon (Mac OS only; **Figure 2**).

or

1. Drag the icon for an HTML document onto the Adobe PageMill® 3.0 (Mac OS; **Figure 1a**) or PageMill.exe (Windows; **Figure 1b**) icon.

2. When the PageMill icon becomes highlighted (**Figures 3a** and **3b**), release the mouse button to open the program and document.

✔ Tips

- If you launch or start PageMill by double-clicking its icon (Mac OS or Windows) or using the Start menu (Windows), an empty document window appears (**Figure 4**).

- If you launch PageMill by double-clicking a document icon (Mac OS only) or dragging an HTML document onto its icon (Mac OS or Windows), a document window containing that HTML document appears (**Figure 5**).

Adobe PageMill® 3.0   PageMill.exe

Figures 1a & 1b. The PageMill application or program icon on Mac OS (left) and Windows (right).

personal.html

Figure 2. A PageMill document icon.

Figures 3a & 3b. Dragging an HTML document icon onto the PageMill program icon on Mac OS (left) or Windows (right).

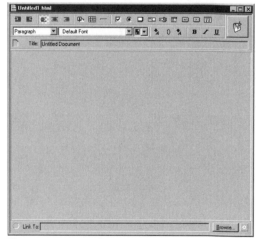

Figure 4. An empty document window.

LAUNCHING OR STARTING PAGEMILL

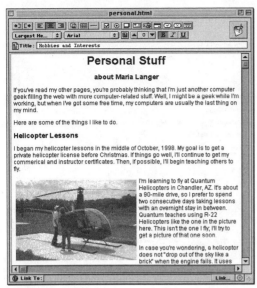

Figure 5. An HTML document opened in PageMill's Edit mode.

To quit or exit PageMill

◆ On Mac OS, choose File > Quit (**Figure 6a**) or press ⌃⌘Q.

◆ On Windows, choose File > Exit (**Figure 6b**), press Alt F4, or click the program window's close button.

✔ Tips

■ Closing all document windows is not the same as quitting the program. PageMill continues to run and take up RAM until you use its Quit or Exit command.

■ If you quit or exit PageMill without saving changes to an open document, PageMill warns you and gives you an opportunity to save the file. I tell you about saving files later in this chapter.

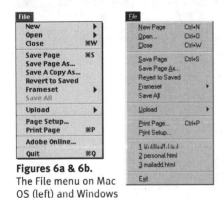

Figures 6a & 6b. The File menu on Mac OS (left) and Windows (right).

PageMill's Modes

PageMill offers two basic modes for working with the Web documents you create:

◆ **Edit mode** (**Figure 5**) lets you create and edit Web pages. You'll work in Edit mode throughout this book.

◆ **Preview mode** (**Figure 7**) lets you see what your Web pages will look like on the World Wide Web and test any links you may have included on them. I tell you about previewing and testing pages in **Chapter 9**.

✔ Tips

■ By default, when you open an existing PageMill document, it opens in Edit mode. You can use the General Preferences dialog box to change the default mode to Preview mode. I explain how to set preferences in **Chapter 11**.

■ In addition to the two basic modes, PageMill also offers a Source mode (**Figure 8**), which enables you to view and edit the HTML code underlying a Web page. I tell you more about Source mode in **Chapter 9**.

■ At first glance, Edit and Preview modes appear very similar. You can tell the difference between them by the toolbar that appears in Edit mode (**Figure 5**) and by the appearance of the Mode button (**Figures 9a** through **9d**).

■ The Windows version of PageMill offers an Explorer Preview mode. I explain how to use it in **Chapter 9**.

To toggle between Edit & Preview modes

Click the Mode button in the upper-right corner of the document window (**Figures 9a** through **9d**). The mode and button icon change.

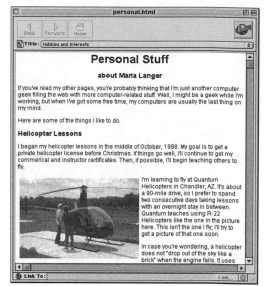

Figure 7. The document from **Figure 5** in Preview mode.

Figure 8. The document from **Figures 5** and **7** in Source mode.

Figures 9a, 9b, 9c, & 9d. From right to left, these mode button examples illustrate Edit mode (both Mac OS and Windows), Preview mode (Mac OS), PageMill Preview mode (Windows), and Explorer Preview mode (Windows).

The Toolbar

In Edit mode, a toolbar at the top of the window (**Figure 10**) offers easy access to a variety of options and commands. I discuss the toolbar's buttons throughout this book.

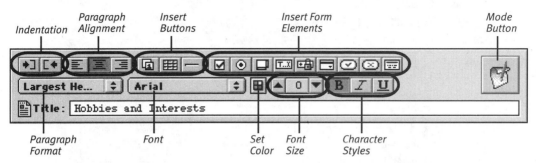

Figure 10. The toolbar in Edit mode.

Figure 11.
Point to a button to learn what it does.

Figure 12. The toolbar displays navigation buttons in Preview mode.

✔ Tips

- You can toggle the display of the toolbar by choosing View > Toolbar.

- The buttons that appear on the toolbar vary depending on what is selected in the document window.

- To learn what a toolbar button does, point to it with your mouse. The button name or description appears in a little box beneath the button (**Figure 11**).

- In Preview mode, the toolbar changes to offer several navigation buttons (**Figure 12**).

- **Appendix B** provides a reference guide for all of PageMill's toolbars.

PageMill's Menus

Most of PageMill's commands are accessible through its menus. **Figures 13** and **14** illustrate two of PageMill's menus.

◆ A menu command that appears in gray cannot currently be selected.

◆ A menu command followed by an ellipsis (...) displays a dialog box.

◆ A menu command followed by a triangle has a submenu. The submenu displays additional commands when the main command is highlighted.

◆ A menu command followed by a modifier key and a letter, number, or symbol can be chosen with a shortcut key. **Table 1** lists the Mac OS and Windows modifier keys.

◆ A menu command preceded by a check mark has been "turned on." You can toggle the on/off setting for an item by chosing it from the menu.

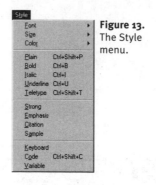

Figure 13. The Style menu.

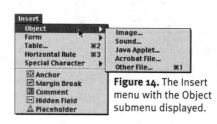

Figure 14. The Insert menu with the Object submenu displayed.

To use a menu

1. Click on the name of the menu from which you want to choose a command. The menu appears.

2. If necessary, click on the name of the submenu from which you want to choose a command to display the submenu.

3. Click on the command that you want.

✔ Tips

■ These instructions assume that Mac OS users are using Mac OS version 8.0 or later, which includes the sticky menus feature. If an earlier version of Mac OS is installed, you must click and drag to pull down a menu and select a command.

■ Throughout this book, I use the following notation to indicate menu commands: *Menu Name > Submenu Name* (if necessary) > *Command Name*. For example, to instruct you to choose Acrobat PDF from the Object submenu under the Insert menu (**Figure 14**), I'd say "choose Insert > Object > Acrobat File."

■ Windows users can also use mouseless menus. Press (Alt), then use the letter and arrow keys to display and select menus and commands. Press (Enter) to activate a selected command.

Figure 15. The contextual menu that appears when you Control-click an image on Mac OS...

Figure 16. ...and the contextual menu that appears when you right-click selected text on Windows.

Key Name	Mac OS Key	Windows Key
Command	⌃ ⌘ or ⌃	n/a
Control	Control	Ctrl
Shift	Shift	Shift
Option	Option	n/a
Alt	n/a	Alt

Table 1. Modifier keys used in PageMill for shortcut keystrokes.

To use a contextual menu

1. Point to the item on which you want to use a menu command.

2. Then:

   ◆ On Mac OS, hold down Control while clicking on the item to display a contextual menu (**Figure 15**).

   ◆ On Windows, right-click on the item to display a contextual menu (**Figure 16**).

3. Click or drag to choose the command you want.

To use a shortcut key

1. Hold down the modifier key(s) (normally ⌃ ⌘ or ⌃ ⌘ Shift on Mac OS and Ctrl or Ctrl Shift on Windows).

2. Press the letter, number, or symbol key for the shortcut.

For example, as the Insert menu on a Mac OS system indicates (**Figure 14**), the shortcut key for the Horizontal Rule command is Command-3. To use this shortcut, hold down the ⌃ ⌘ key and press 3.

✔ Tips

■ If a menu command is not available, its shortcut key won't work either.

■ Shortcut keys for menu commands and toolbar buttons are discussed with their corresponding commands or buttons throughout this book.

■ **Appendix A** includes a complete listing of PageMill's shortcut keys.

USING CONTEXTUAL MENUS & SHORTCUT KEYS

The Pasteboard

The Pasteboard (**Figures 17a** and **17b**) is a place within PageMill where you can store frequently used Web page elements like text and graphics.

For example, say you include your company logo on every Web page you create. If you store it on the Pasteboard, it will be within mouse pointer reach each time you create a new page.

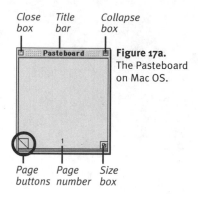

Close box   Title bar   Collapse box

Figure 17a.
The Pasteboard on Mac OS.

Page buttons   Page number   Size box

✔ Tips

■ You can store more than one item on each Pasteboard page.

■ The Pasteboard is a lot like any other Mac OS or Windows window. You can move it by dragging its title bar and resize it by dragging its size box.

■ I provide details about using the Pasteboard in **Chapters 2** and **4**.

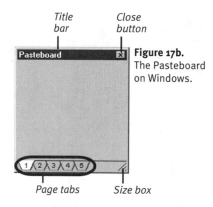

Title bar   Close button

Figure 17b.
The Pasteboard on Windows.

Page tabs   Size box

To show the Pasteboard

◆ On Mac OS, choose Window > Show Pasteboard (**Figure 18**) or press Option ⌘ B.

◆ On Windows, choose View > Show Pasteboard (**Figure 19**).

To "turn" Pasteboard pages

◆ On Mac OS, click one of the page button triangles (**Figure 17a**). Click the top triangle to switch to the next page; click the bottom triangle to switch the previous page.

◆ On Windows, click one of the page number tabs (**Figure 17b**).

To hide the Pasteboard

◆ On Mac OS, choose Window > Hide Pasteboard, press Option ⌘ B, or click the Pasteboard's close box.

◆ On Windows, choose View > Hide Pasteboard or click the Pasteboard's close button.

Figure 18. Commands to display or hide the Inspector, Color Panel, Pasteboard, and Java Console appear on the Window menu on a Mac OS system...

Figure 19. ...and on the View menu of a Windows system.

Frame *Form*
tab *tab*
Page *Object*
tab *tab*

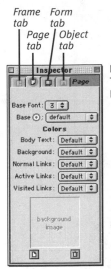

Figure 20.
The Inspector's
Page panel.

The Inspector

The Inspector (**Figure 20**) is a floating palette you can use to set attributes for Web page elements. Click a tab near the top of the Inspector to view the corresponding panel:

■ Use the **Frame** panel to set attributes for frames.

■ Use the **Page** panel (**Figure 20**) to set attributes for an entire page.

■ Use the **Form** panel to set attributes for CGI scripts used with forms.

■ Use the **Object** panel to set attributes for selected objects, including images, form elements, and table cells.

✔ Tips

■ The Inspector will only offer options when a page is in Edit mode. When no page is open or when the open page is in Preview mode, the Inspector window is empty.

■ I explain how to use the Inspector's options throughout this book.

■ To move the Inspector, drag it by its title bar.

To show the Inspector

◆ On Mac OS, choose Window > Show Inspector or press ⌊Option⌋⌊⌃⌋⌊⌘⌋⌊I⌋.

◆ On Windows, choose View > Show Inspector (**Figure 19**) or press ⌊F8⌋.

To hide the Inspector

◆ On Mac OS, choose Window > Hide Inspector (**Figure 18**), press ⌊Option⌋⌊⌃⌋⌊⌘⌋⌊I⌋, or click the Inspector's close box.

◆ On Windows, choose View > Hide Inspector, press ⌊F8⌋, or click the Inspector's close button.

The Color Panel

The Color Panel is a floating palette of 16 (**Figures 21a** and **21b**) or 256 (**Figures 22a** and **22b**) color swatches you can use to change text, link, and background colors.

✔ Tips

- All colors on the Color Panel are *web-safe*— they will not change when viewed on the Web.

- To learn the hexadecimal code for a color on the 216-color palette, point to it. A yellow box with the color's number appears (**Figure 23**).

- To change a color on the 16-color palette, Control-click (Mac OS) or right-click (Windows) it and choose Set Custom Color from the contextual menu that appears (**Figure 24**). Then use the standard color picker (Mac OS) or Color (Windows) dialog box that appears to select a new color. To reset the colors choose Set Default Colors from the contextual menu.

To show the Color Panel

- On Mac OS, choose Window > Show Color Panel (**Figure 18**) or press Option ⌃ ⌘ C.

- On Windows, choose View > Show Color Panel (**Figure 19**) or press F5.

To expand or collapse the Color Panel

Click the triangle at the bottom of the color panel (**Figures 21a**, **21b**, **22a**, and **22b**).

To hide the Color Panel

- On Mac OS, choose Window > Hide Color Panel, press Option ⌃ ⌘ C, or click the Inspector's close box.

- On Windows, choose View > Hide Inspector, press F5, or click the Inspector's close button.

Figures 21a & 21b. The 16-color Color Panel on Mac OS (left) and Windows (right).

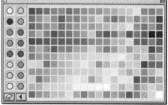

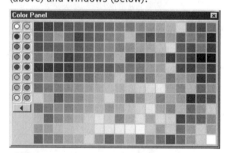

Figures 22a & 22b. The Color Panel expanded to show all 216 Web-safe colors on Mac OS (above) and Windows (below).

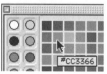

Figure 23. Pointing to a color displays its hexadecimal value.

#CC3366

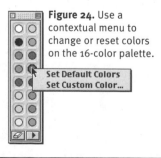

Figure 24. Use a contextual menu to change or reset colors on the 16-color palette.

Set Default Colors
Set Custom Color...

Comment   Margin   Hidden
  Anchor   Break   Field

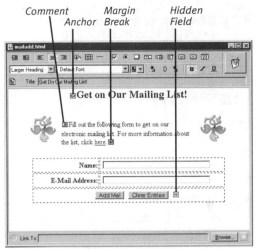

Figure 25. Here's a Web page with all four kinds of invisibles inserted.

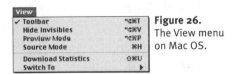

Figure 26.
The View menu
on Mac OS.

Figure 27. The Web page from **Figure 25** with invisibles hidden.

Invisibles

PageMill offers commands to insert four different sets of HTML codes that may affect the appearance of the Web page but do not appear on the page when viewed. PageMill refers to these codes as *invisibles*:

◆ **Anchors** let you create links to specific positions within a page. I tell you about anchors and links in **Chapter 6**.

◆ **Margin breaks** insert blank space between a positioned object and the margin at the bottom of the object. I tell you about positioned objects in **Chapter 4**.

◆ **Comments** let you insert notations within a Web page that do not appear anywhere on the page. I tell you about inserting comments in **Chapter 9**.

◆ **Hidden fields** are special form fields for passing default information to CGIs used to process forms. I tell you about forms and CGIs in **Chapter 8**.

Figure 25 shows an example of a Web page in Edit mode with all four kinds of invisibles inserted.

✔ Tip

■ By default, invisibles are displayed in Edit mode.

To hide invisibles

Choose View > Hide Invisibles (**Figures 19** and **26**) or press Option ⌂ ⌘ V (Mac OS only).

Figure 27 shows the same page as **Figure 25**, but with the invisibles hidden.

To show invisibles

Choose View > Show Invisibles or press Option ⌂ ⌘ V (Mac OS only).

INVISIBLES

Pages & Page Files

Each document you create with PageMill is a *page*. Don't let this familiar term fool you—a Web page can be as long or short as you like.

To create a new page

◆ On Mac OS, choose File > New > New Page (**Figure 28**) or press ⌃ ⌘ N.

◆ On Windows, choose File > New Page (**Figure 6b**) or press Ctrl N.

An empty document window appears (**Figure 4**).

✔ Tip

■ The file name extension of a new file can be either *.html* or *.htm*, depending on preference settings. I explain how to set preferences in **Chapter 11**.

To open an existing page

1. Use the Open command:

   ◆ On Mac OS, choose File > Open > Open (**Figure 29**) or press ⌃ ⌘ O.

   ◆ On Windows, choose File > Open (**Figure 6b**) or press Ctrl O.

2. In the Open dialog box that appears (**Figures 30a** and **30b**), locate and select the Web page document you want to open.

3. Click Open.

or

On Mac OS, in the Finder, double-click the icon for the PageMill document you want to open.

or

Drag the Web page document icon onto the PageMill program icon (**Figures 3a** and **3b**).

✔ Tip

■ You can use the Show (Mac OS; **Figure 31a**) or Files of type (Windows; **Figure 31b**) menu in the Open dialog box to display only certain types of files.

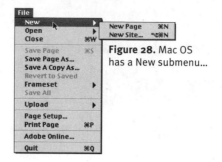

Figure 28. Mac OS has a New submenu...

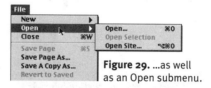

Figure 29. ...as well as an Open submenu.

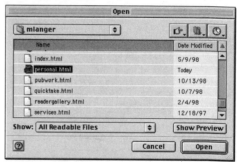

Figures 30a & 30b. The Open dialog box on Mac OS (above) and Windows (below).

Figures 31a & 31b. Use the Show menu (Mac OS; left) or the Files of type menu (Windows; right) to specify the kinds of files to display in the Open dialog box.

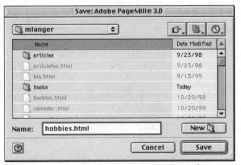

Figures 32a & 32b. The Save As dialog box on Mac OS (above) and Windows (below).

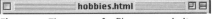

Figure 33. The name of a file appears in its title bar.

To save a page

1. Choose File > Save Page (**Figures 6a** and **6b**) or press ⌃ ⌘ S (Mac OS) or Ctrl S (Windows).

   If the file has already been saved at least once, changes you made to the file are saved. You're finished.

   or

   If this is the first time you are saving the file, the Save As dialog box appears (**Figures 32a** and **32b**). Follow the steps below.

2. Use the Save As dialog box to open the disk location in which you want to save the file.

3. Enter a name for the file in the Name (Mac OS) or File name (Windows) box.

4. Click Save.

   The file is saved. The name you entered appears in the document window's title bar (**Figure 33**).

✔ Tips

- Until you save a file, any change to it exists only in your computer's random access memory (RAM). If your computer loses power or crashes, all work done since the last time you saved is lost. This is why it's important to save frequently while you work.

- The first time you save a file, the Save Page and Save Page As commands do the same thing—open the Save As dialog box.

- Be sure to follow any file naming guidelines required by your server. If you're not sure what they are, ask the Webmaster or System Administrator.

- When you use the Save Page As command, the Save As dialog box appears, enabling you to save the file with a different name or in a different location. If you change the name or location of the file, subsequently using the Save Page command to save changes to the page will save changes to the new version, not the original.

SAVING PAGES

The Page Title

The page *title* is the name of the page as it appears on the World Wide Web. When you specify a page title, it appears in the title bar of Web browser windows (**Figure 34**).

Figure 34. A page's title appears in the title bar of a Web browser.

✔ Tips

- The page title is not the same as the page's file name. The file name, which you specify when you save a file, is subject to the file naming restrictions of your Web server. The page title, however, can be almost anything you like.

- PageMill assigns a default page title of *Untitled Document* to every page you create.

- A page title is used as entry text when someone "bookmarks" your page while viewing it with a Web browser. By making the title descriptive, you make the bookmark name descriptive, too.

Title: Untitled Document

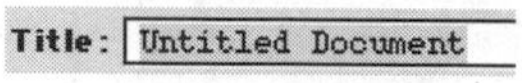

Figure 35. Select the existing title...

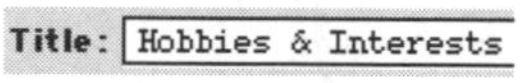

Title: Hobbies & Interests

Figure 36. ...then type in a new title and press Enter.

To edit or remove a page title

1. Select the contents of the Title box near the top of the document window (**Figure 35**).

2. To edit the title, type in the desired text and press Enter. The text you entered appears in the Title box (**Figure 36**).

    or

    To remove the title, select the title, press Delete (Mac OS) or Backspace (Windows) to delete it, and press Enter. The title is removed.

EDITING OR REMOVING PAGE TITLES

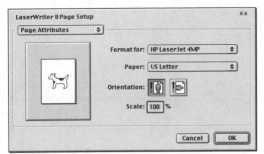

Figure 37a. The Page Setup dialog box for a laser printer on Mac OS.

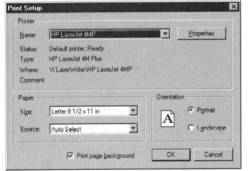

Figure 37b. The Page Setup dialog box for a laser printer on Windows.

Printing

Although Web pages are normally viewed on screen and are seldom printed, you can use the Page Setup (Mac OS) or Print Setup (Windows) and Print Page commands to prepare pages for printing and print them.

✔ Tip

- The options offered in the Page Setup (**Figure 37a**) or Print Setup (**Figure 37b**) and Print (**Figures 38a** and **38b**) dialog boxes depend on your printer and its printer driver. Consult the documentation that came with your printer or computer for more information about printer options and setting up a printer.

To specify Page Setup or Print Setup options

1. Choose File > Page Setup (Mac OS; **Figure 6a**) or File > Print Setup (Windows; **Figure 6b**).

2. In the Page Setup (Mac OS; **Figure 37a**) or Print Setup (Windows; **Figure 37b**) dialog box that appears, change settings for paper size, orientation, and other options as desired.

3. On Windows, to print the page's background (which I tell you about in **Chapter 3**), be sure to turn on the Print page background check box. (This is done in the Print dialog box on Mac OS systems; consult the next page for details.)

4. Click OK to save your settings.

To print a page

1. Choose File > Print Page (**Figures 6a** and **6b**) or press ⌃⌘P (Mac OS) or Ctrl P (Windows).

2. In the Print dialog box that appears (**Figures 38a** and **38b**), set the number of copies, page range, and paper source.

3. On Mac OS, to print the page's background (which I tell you about in **Chapter 3**), be sure to turn on the Print Page Background check box. Depending on your printer, you may have to choose Adobe PageMill® 3.0 from a pop-up menu at the top of the dialog box (**Figure 39**) to switch to PageMill-specific printing options (**Figure 40**). (This is done in the Print Setup dialog box on Windows systems; consult the previous page for details.)

4. Click Print (Mac OS) or OK (Windows) to print.

✔ Tip

■ PageMill, like Web browser software, automatically paginates documents when it prints them. You cannot override its page breaks. It will not, however, break a page in the middle of a graphic object.

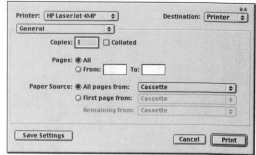

Figure 38a. The General options in the Print dialog box for a laser printer on Mac OS.

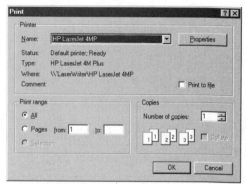

Figure 38b. The Print dialog box for a laser printer on Windows.

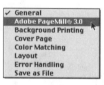

Figure 39. On Mac OS, you may have to choose Adobe PageMill® 3.0 to...

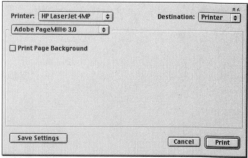

Figure 40. ...turn on page background printing in the PageMill-specific options of the Print dialog box.

Figure 41.
The Window menu
on Windows.

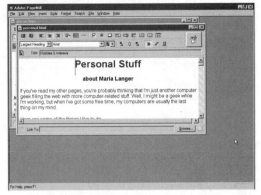

Figure 42. Stacked or cascaded windows.

Figure 43. Horizontally tiled windows.

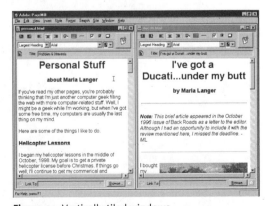

Figure 44. Vertically tiled windows.

Document Windows

Like most other Mac OS and Windows programs, PageMill enables you to have more than one document window open at a time.

✔ Tip

- PageMill's windows work just like the document windows in any other Mac OS or Windows program. Use standard techniques to move, resize, collapse (Mac OS) or minimize (Windows), and expand (Mac OS) or maximize (Windows) them.

To switch document windows

Click any exposed portion of the window with which you want to work.

or

Choose the name of the window with which you want to work from the list at the bottom of the Window menu (**Figures 18** and **41**).

The window you clicked or chose comes to the front and becomes the active window.

To arrange document windows

- ◆ To stack or cascade windows, choose Window > Stack (**Figure 18**) or Window > Cascade (**Figure 41**). The windows are neatly stacked, with the active window on top (**Figure 42**).

- ◆ To tile windows, choose Window > Tile Horizontally or Window > Tile Vertically (**Figures 18** and **41**). The windows are resized and tiled across the entire screen, either Horizontally (**Figure 43**) or vertically (**Figure 44**), with the active window on top.

To close a document window

1. If necessary, switch to the window you want to close.

2. Choose File > Close (**Figures 6a** and **6b**), press ⌃ ⌘ W (Mac OS) or Ctrl W (Windows), or click the window's close box (Mac OS) or close button (Windows).

3. If you have made changes to the contents of the window since the last time you saved it, a dialog box like the one in **Figure 45a** or **45b** appears.

   ◆ Click Save to save the changes. If you have never saved the file, a Save As dialog box (**Figure 32a** and **32b**) appears so you can choose a disk location, enter a name, and save the file.

   ◆ Click Don't Save (Mac OS) or No (Windows) to close the window without saving changes.

   ◆ Click Cancel to dismiss the dialog box without closing the window or saving its contents.

To close all document windows

Choose Window > Close All (**Figures 18** and **41**).

A dialog box like the one in **Figure 45a** or **45b** appears for every window whose contents you have changed since you last saved. Follow the instructions in step 3 above to dismiss this dialog box each time it appears.

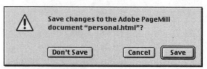

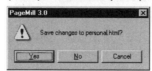

Figures 45a & 45b. When you close a window that contains unsaved changes dialog boxes like these appear on Mac OS (above) and Windows (below).

TEXT ENTRY & EDITING BASICS

Entering & Editing Text with PageMill

One of the best features of PageMill is its word processor-like interface. As you work with PageMill, you'll use the same techniques you use with your word processor. Here are some examples:

- ◆ Enter text by typing at an insertion point.
- ◆ Edit text by selecting and typing to replace, or pressing Delete or Backspace to delete.
- ◆ Use the Cut, Copy, and Paste commands or drag-and-drop editing to duplicate or move text.
- ◆ Use the Undo command to reverse your last action.

In addition to these standard techniques, PageMill offers additional features and techniques that make it easy to enter and edit text in documents, including:

- ◆ The Pasteboard to store items you use repeatedly.
- ◆ The Revert to Saved command to throw away all changes to an open document.

Best of all, at any time during the Web page creation process, you can click the Mode button to see how your page will look and work on the World Wide Web.

Figures 1a, 1b, & 1c. In Preview mode, the Mode button looks like the button on the left on Mac OS or one of the other two buttons on Windows.

✔ Tip

- ■ To enter or edit the contents of a PageMill document, you must be in Edit mode. To go to Edit mode, click the Mode button which, in Preview mode, looks like the button in **Figure 1a** on Mac OS and either **Figure 1b** or **1c** on Windows.

Entering Text

In most cases, text will form the basis of your Web page. Entering text in a PageMill document is as easy as entering it in any word processing document.

To enter text by typing

1. Position the blinking insertion point where you want the text to appear (**Figure 2**) by clicking or using the arrow keys on your keyboard.

2. Type the text you want to enter.

    The text you type appears at the insertion point (**Figure 3**).

✔ Tips

- Text automatically wraps when it reaches the right side of the window (**Figure 3**).

- Word wrap is determined by the width of the window. It cannot be controlled through the use of margins—HTML does not support margins. To set the width of a column of text, you must enter the text in the cell of an HTML table. I explain how to set up and use tables in **Chapter 5**.

- When you press Return (Mac OS) or Enter (Windows) a new paragraph is created with an empty line between it and the previous paragraph (**Figure 3**).

- To start a new line without starting a new paragraph, choose Insert > Special Character > Line Break (**Figures 4a** and **4b**) or press Shift Return (Mac OS) or Shift Enter (Windows).

- To insert a space character that does not break between two words, choose Insert > Special Character > Nonbreaking Space (**Figures 4a** and **4b**) or press ⌃ ⌘ Spacebar (Mac OS) or Shift Enter (Windows).

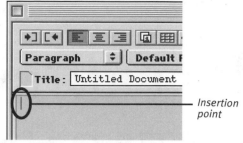

Insertion point

Figure 2. The blinking insertion point indicates where the text you type will appear.

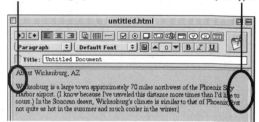

PageMill puts a blank line between paragraphs.

Text automatically wraps to the next line as you type.

Figure 3. The PageMill document window works very much like a word processing document window.

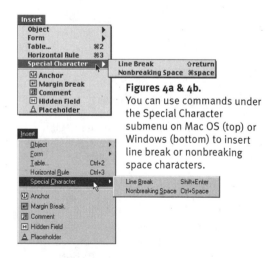

Figures 4a & 4b. You can use commands under the Special Character submenu on Mac OS (top) or Windows (bottom) to insert line break or nonbreaking space characters.

ENTERING TEXT

Insertion point

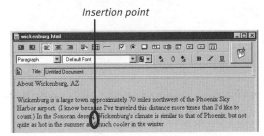

Figure 5. To insert text, begin by positioning the insertion point...

Inserted text

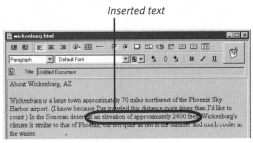

Figure 6. ...then type. The text you type is inserted and the text to the right of it moves to the right or down to make room for it.

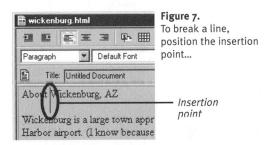

Figure 7.
To break a line, position the insertion point...

Insertion point

Figure 8.
...then insert the line break character.

Editing Text

Once text has been entered, it's easy to edit. As you might imagine, standard word processing techniques apply.

To insert text

1. Position the blinking insertion point where you want the text to appear (**Figure 5**). You can do this by clicking or using the arrow keys.

2. Type the text you want to insert.

Because PageMill uses an insertion cursor, text you type is inserted at the blinking insertion point (**Figure 6**). Text to the right of or below the insertion point is pushed aside or down to make room for the new text.

To insert a paragraph or line break

1. Position the insertion point before the character you want to appear on the next line (**Figure 7**).

2. Insert the break:
    ◆ On Mac OS, press [Return] to insert a paragraph break or [Shift][Return] to insert a line break.
    ◆ On Windows, press [Enter] to insert a paragraph break or [Shift][Enter] to insert a line break (**Figure 8**).

✔ Tip

■ Pressing [Shift][Return] or [Shift][Enter] ends the line without beginning a new paragraph (**Figure 8**). Pressing [Return] or [Enter] ends the line and begins a new paragraph (**Figure 3**).

EDITING TEXT

To delete text

1. Position the blinking insertion point to the right of the character(s) you want to delete.

2. Press `Delete` (Mac OS) or `Backspace` (Windows) to delete the character to the left of the insertion point. To delete multiple characters, just keep pressing `Delete` or `Backspace` until they're all gone.

or

1. Position the blinking insertion point to the left of the character(s) you want to delete.

2. Press `Del` (Mac OS) or `Delete` (Windows) to delete the character to the right of the insertion point. To delete multiple characters, just keep pressing `Del` or `Delete` until they're all gone.

or

1. Select the text you want to delete. (I tell you how to select text on the next page.)

2. Press `Delete`, `Backspace`, or `Del`.

   or

   Choose Edit > Clear (**Figures 9a** and **9b**).

To remove a paragraph or line break

1. Position the insertion point at the beginning of the second line. This is immediately after the paragraph or line break (**Figure 8**) you want to remove.

2. Press `Delete` (Mac OS) or `Backspace` (Windows) to delete the invisible paragraph or line break character at the end of the previous line.

Figures 9a & 9b. The Edit menu on Mac OS (left) and Windows (right) offers a number of commands for editing text.

I-beam pointer

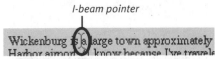

Figure 10. Position the I-beam pointer at the beginning of the text you want to select...

Drag to select

Figure 11. ...then drag to select the text.

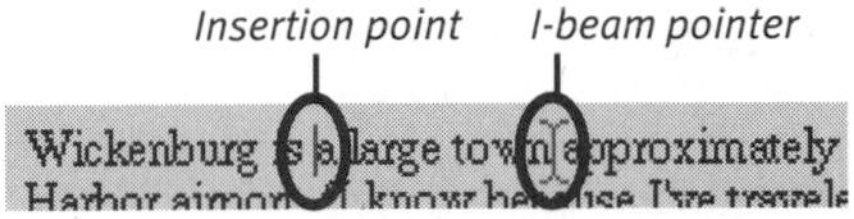

Insertion point   I-beam pointer

Figure 12. Hold down (Shift) and click to select all text between the blinking insertion point and the mouse pointer.

Mouse pointer

Figure 13. Position the mouse pointer on a word...

Figure 14. Then double-click to select the word.

To select text characters

1. Position the mouse pointer, which must look like an I-beam pointer (**Figure 10**), at the beginning of the text you want to select.

2. Press the mouse button down and drag to the end of the text you want to select (**Figure 11**). As you drag, text is selected.

or

1. Click at the beginning of the text you want to select to position the insertion point there (**Figure 12**).

2. Hold down (Shift) and click at the end of the text you want to select (**Figure 11**). The text between the first and second click is selected.

✔ Tip

■ If the mouse pointer looks like an arrow pointer when you drag to select text using the first technique above, you probably already have text selected and will move it when you drag. Click once on any other text in the document window to clear the selection and try again.

To select a word

1. Position the mouse pointer, which must look like an I-beam pointer (**Figure 13**), in the middle of a word you want to select.

2. Double-click. The entire word is selected and the mouse pointer turns into an arrow pointer (**Figure 14**).

To select all document contents

Choose Edit > Select All (**Figures 9a** and **9b**) or press ⌘ A (Mac OS) or Ctrl A (Windows).

SELECTING TEXT

To replace text

1. Select the text you want to replace (**Figure 11**).

2. Type the replacement text.

The text you type replaces whatever text was selected when you began typing (**Figure 15**).

✔ Tips

■ Pressing Delete, Backspace, or Del or choosing Edit > Clear (**Figures 9a** and **9b**) while text is selected deletes the text and replaces it with nothing.

■ You can also replace text by using the Paste command when text is selected. I tell you about the Paste command on the next few pages.

■ If you accidentally replace text instead of inserting it, immediately use the Undo command, which I tell you about later in this chapter, to get back the original text.

To deselect text

Click once on any other text in the document window. The selection clears.

✔ Tip

■ It's vital that no text is selected when you type if you want to insert (not replace) text. Make sure you know exactly where the insertion point is before typing. If text is selected, there won't be an insertion point. Remember, when text is selected, anything you type will overwrite the selected text.

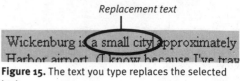

Replacement text

Figure 15. The text you type replaces the selected text.

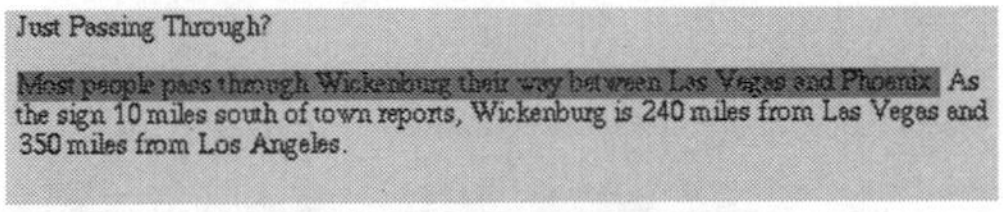

Just Passing Through?

Most people pass through Wickenburg their way between Las Vegas and Phoenix. As the sign 10 miles south of town reports, Wickenburg is 240 miles from Las Vegas and 350 miles from Los Angeles.

Figure 16. Select the text you want to copy.

Insertion point

About
Wickenburg, AZ

Wickenburg is a small city approximately 70 miles northwest of the Phoenix Sky Harbor airport. (I know because I've traveled this distance more times than I'd like to count.) In the Sonoran desert at an elevation of approximately 2400 feet, Wickenburg's climate is similar to that of Phoenix, but not quite as hot in the summer and much cooler in the winter.

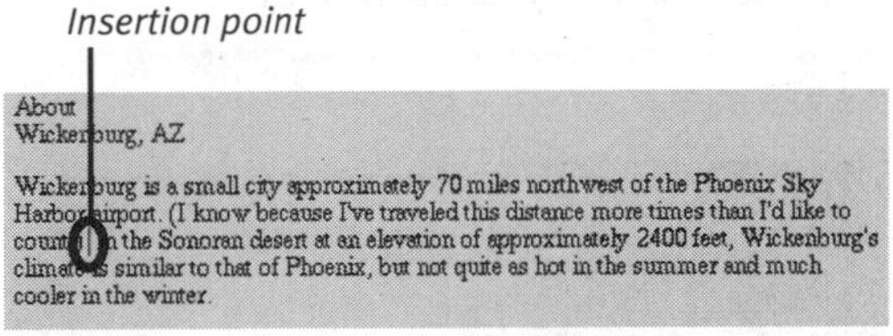

Figure 17. Position the insertion point where you want the copied text to appear.

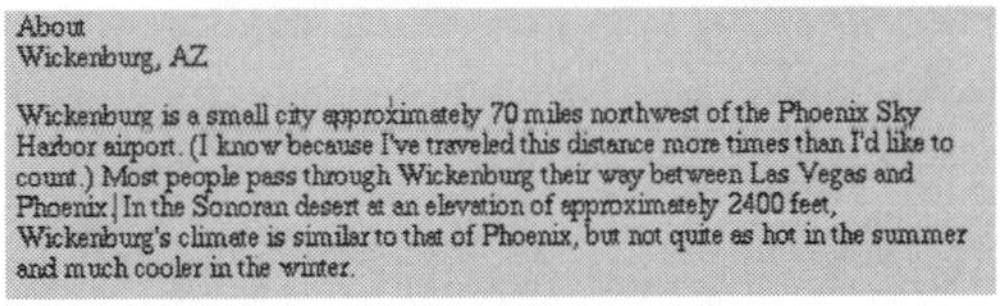

About
Wickenburg, AZ

Wickenburg is a small city approximately 70 miles northwest of the Phoenix Sky Harbor airport. (I know because I've traveled this distance more times than I'd like to count.) Most people pass through Wickenburg their way between Las Vegas and Phoenix. In the Sonoran desert at an elevation of approximately 2400 feet, Wickenburg's climate is similar to that of Phoenix, but not quite as hot in the summer and much cooler in the winter.

Figure 18. When you use the Paste command, the copied text appears at the insertion point.

Copying & Moving Text

PageMill offers a variety of ways to copy and move text:

◆ The Copy and Paste commands let you copy text from one place and paste it in another.

◆ The Cut and Paste commands let you cut text from one place and paste it in another, thus moving the original text.

◆ Drag and drop text editing lets you move or copy selected text by simply dragging it.

◆ The Pasteboard lets you store text that you can drag into a document window.

To copy text with Copy & Paste

1. Select the text you want to copy (**Figure 16**).

2. Choose Edit > Copy (**Figures 9a** and **9b**) or press ⌘ C (Mac OS) or Ctrl C (Windows).

   The text is copied. It remains selected in the document.

3. Position the insertion point where you want the copied text to be inserted (**Figure 17**).

4. Choose Edit > Paste (**Figures 9a** and **9b**) or press ⌘ V (Mac OS) or Ctrl V (Windows).

   A copy of the text is pasted into the document at the insertion point (**Figure 18**).

USING THE COPY & PASTE COMMANDS

To move text with Cut & Paste

1. Select the text you want to move (**Figure 19**).

2. Choose Edit > Cut (**Figures 9a** and **9b**) or press ⌃ ⌘ X (Mac OS) or Ctrl X (Windows).

   The text is removed from the document (**Figure 20**).

3. Position the insertion point where you want the cut text to be moved (**Figure 21**).

4. Choose Edit > Paste (**Figures 9a** and **9b**) or press ⌃ ⌘ V (Mac OS) or Ctrl V (Windows).

   A copy of the cut text is pasted into the document at the insertion point (**Figure 22**).

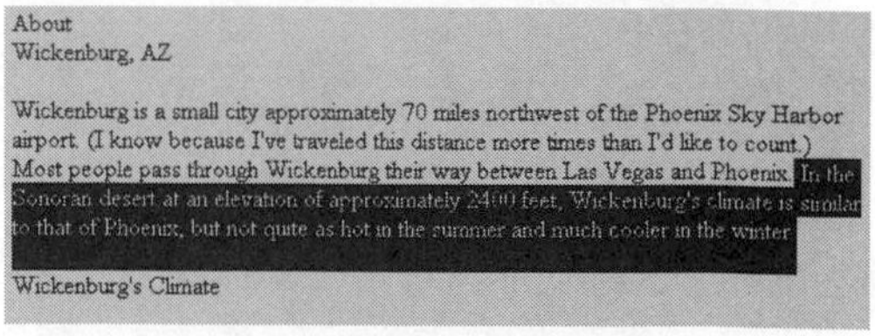

✔ Copy, Cut, & Paste Tips

- When you use the Copy or Cut command, the selection is placed on the *Clipboard*, a temporary holding place for information. The selection stays there until you use the Copy or Cut command again or shut off your computer.

- You can use the Paste command to paste the contents of the Clipboard again and again in the same document or in other documents.

- You can use the Paste command to put a copy of the Clipboard contents into another PageMill document (**Figures 16** through **18**) or any other document.

- You can also use Copy and Paste or Cut and Paste to take text from other documents and paste it into PageMill documents.

Figure 19. Select the text you want to cut.

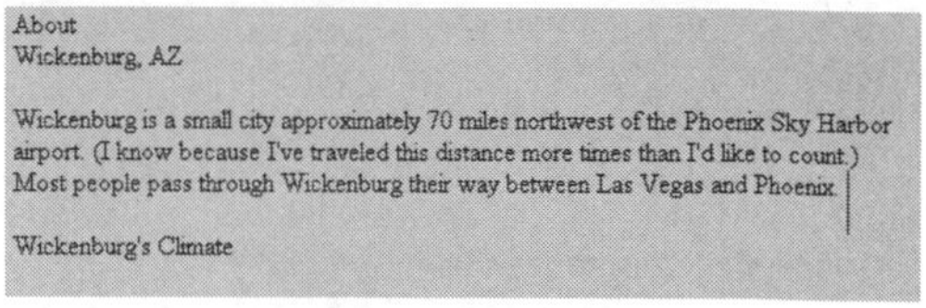

Figure 20. When you use the Cut command, the selected text is removed from the document.

Insertion point

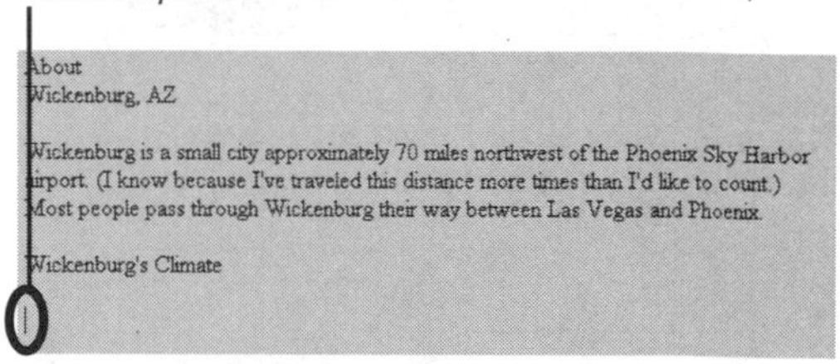

Figure 21. Position the insertion point where you want the text to appear.

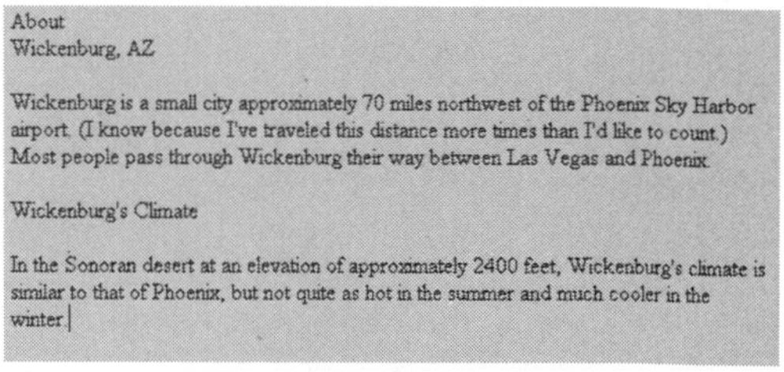

Figure 22. When you use the Paste command, the text appears at the insertion point.

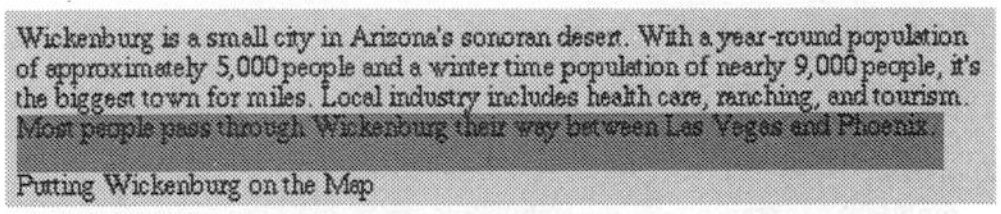

Figure 23. Select the text you want to move or copy.

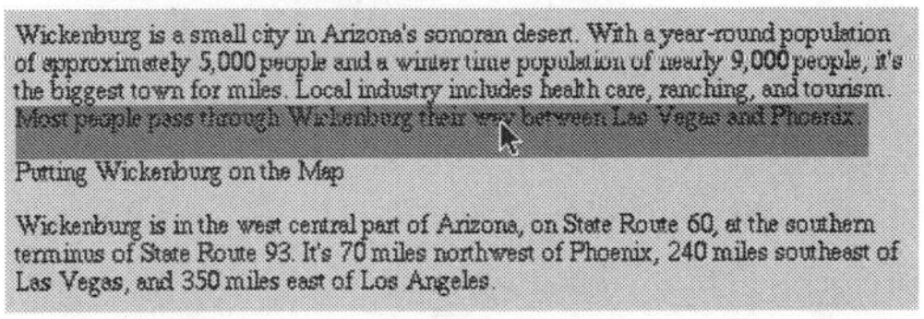

Figure 24. When you position the mouse pointer on selected text, it turns into an arrow pointer.

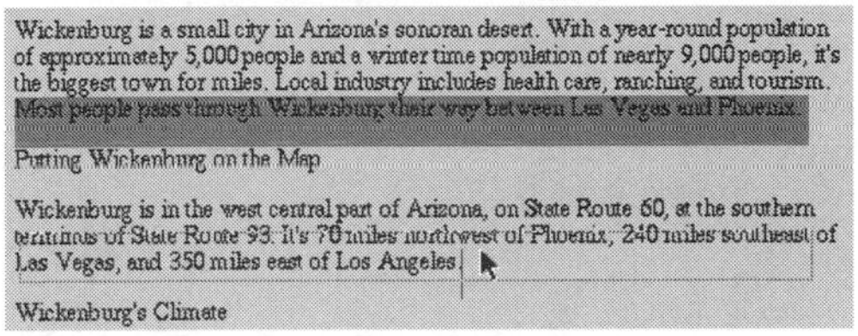

Figure 25. As you drag, an insertion point moves with the mouse pointer. On Mac OS, the outline of the selected text moves, too.

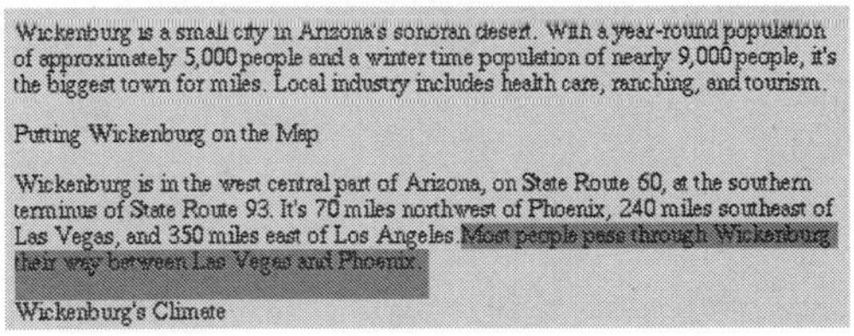

Figure 26. Release the mouse button to move the text.

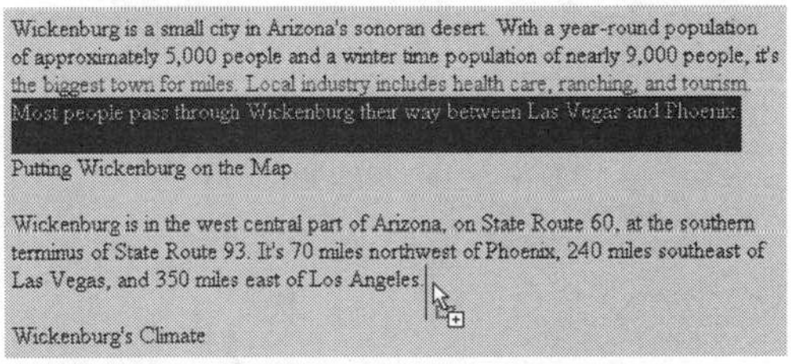

Figure 27. On Windows, when you drag to copy, a plug sign appears beside the mouse pointer.

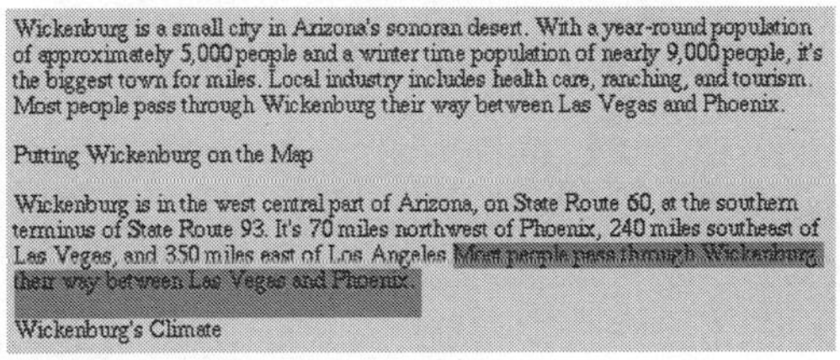

Figure 28. Release the mouse button to copy the text.

To move text with drag & drop

1. Select the text you want to move (**Figure 23**).

2. Position the mouse pointer within the selected text. It turns into an arrow pointer (**Figure 24**).

3. Press the mouse button down and drag. As you drag, a blinking insertion point indicates where the text will go when you let go of the mouse button. On Mac OS, a dotted line box the size and shape of the selection also moves. You can see all this in **Figure 25**.

4. When the blinking insertion point is in the proper position, release the mouse button. The selected text moves (**Figure 26**).

To copy text with drag & drop

1. Select the text you want to copy (**Figure 23**).

2. Position the mouse pointer within the selected text. It turns into an arrow pointer (**Figure 24**).

3. Hold down (Option) (Mac OS) or (Ctrl) (Windows) as you press the mouse button down and drag to the location to which you want to copy the selection. On Windows, a plus sign appears beside the mouse pointer to indicate that the selection is being copied (**Figure 27**).

4. When the blinking insertion point is in the proper position, release the mouse button. The selected text is copied (**Figure 28**).

✔ Tip

■ To copy a selection from one document to another with drag-and-drop editing, simply drag the text. There's no need to hold down the (Option) or (Ctrl) key.

MOVING & COPYING WITH DRAG & DROP

To copy text to the Pasteboard

1. If the Pasteboard is not showing, display it.

2. Select the text you want to put on the Pasteboard (**Figure 29**).

3. Use the drag and drop techniques discussed on the previous page to drag the text from the PageMill document window to the Pasteboard window (**Figure 30**).

4. Release the mouse button. A copy of the selected text is placed on the Pasteboard (**Figure 31**).

✔ Tips

■ Although the Pasteboard has only five pages, you can copy more than one item to each page (**Figure 32**).

■ You can add an item to the Pasteboard by dragging it from the window of any application that supports drag-and-drop editing.

■ I explain how to show and hide the Pasteboard in **Chapter 1**.

To use a Pasteboard item

1. Position the mouse pointer on the Pasteboard item you want to use (**Figure 32**).

2. To move the Pasteboard item, drag the item into position in a PageMill document.

   or

   To copy the Pasteboard item, hold down (Option) (Mac OS) or (Ctrl) (Windows) while dragging the item into position in a PageMill document.

✔ Tip

■ Dragging an item off the Pasteboard and into a PageMill window is the only way to remove it from the Pasteboard.

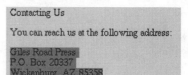

Figure 29. Select the text that you want to copy to the Pasteboard.

Figure 30. Drag the selection onto the Pasteboard.

Figure 31. When you release the mouse button, the selection is copied to the Pasteboard.

Figure 32. To use a Pasteboard item, "grab it" with the mouse pointer and drag it into a PageMill document.

Figures 33a, 33b, & 33c.
Two versions of the Undo
command on Mac OS (above)
and the Undo command on
Windows (left).

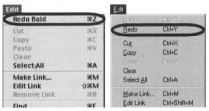

Figures 34a & 34b. The Redo command on
Mac OS (left) and Windows (right).

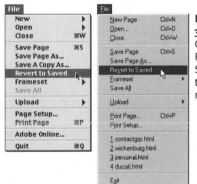

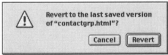

**Figures
35a & 35b.**
Choose
Revert to
Saved from
the File
menu.

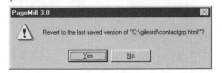

Figures 36a & 36b. The dialog box that appears
on Mac OS (above) and Windows (below) when
you use the Revert to Saved command.

Undoing Actions

PageMill offers two commands to help you
correct errors by undoing or reversing them:

◆ Undo reverses your last action.

◆ Revert to Saved throws away all changes
you made to a document since the last
time you saved it.

To undo the last action

Choose Edit > Undo (**Figures 33a**, **33b**, and
33c) or press ⌘Z (Mac OS) or Ctrl Z
(Windows).

The last action you performed is reversed.

✔ Tips

■ On Mac OS, the exact wording of this
command depends on the last action you
performed. **Figures 33a** and **33b** show two
examples.

■ If the Undo command is unavailable, it will
be gray.

■ If the last action you performed was to use
the Undo command, the Redo command
will be available (**Figures 34a** and **34b**).
Choosing this command or pressing
⌘Z again (Mac OS) or Ctrl Y (Windows) "undoes" the Undo command, thus
restoring the document to the way it was
before you chose Undo.

To revert to the saved page

1. Choose Revert to Saved from the File menu
(**Figures 35a** and **35b**).

2. A dialog box appears, asking you to confirm
that you want to revert to the last saved
version of the file (**Figures 36a** and **36b**).
Click Revert (Mac OS) or Yes (Windows).

All changes you made to the file since the last
time it was saved are reversed.

Finding & Replacing Text

PageMill's find and replace features make it easy to locate and/or change text, URLs, and objects throughout a Web page document. You use the Find dialog box (**Figures 37a** and **37b**) to specify your find and, if applicable, replacement text. Then use buttons within the Find dialog box or on the Edit menu (Mac OS; **Figure 9a**) or Search menu (Windows; **Figure 38**) to locate and/or replace text as specified.

✔ Tips

- When you use the find and replace features, the search begins at the insertion point and goes forward to the end of the document.

- Until you specify find and/or replacement text, the only find and replace command you can select from the Edit menu (Mac OS; **Figure 9a**) or Search menu (Windows; **Figure 38**) menu is Find; all others will be gray.

- I tell you about URLs in **Chapter 6** and about objects in **Chapter 4**.

- The find and replace features can also be used in Source mode. I tell you about working with HTML source code in **Chapter 9**.

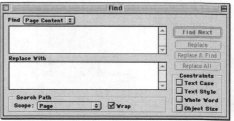

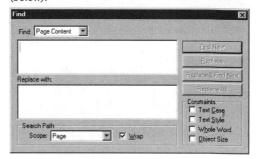

Figures 37a & 37b. The Find dialog box on Mac OS (above) is virtually identical to the one on Windows (below).

Figure 38. On Windows, you access find and replace feature commands from the Search menu.

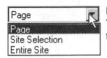

Figure 39. The Find menu within the Find dialog box.

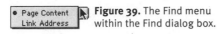

Figure 40. The Scope menu within the Find dialog box.

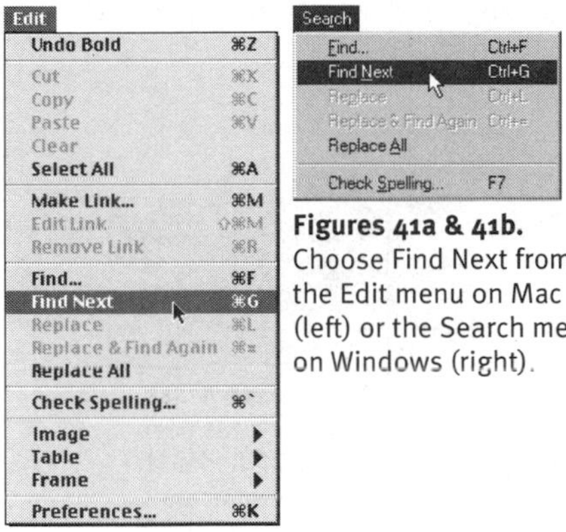

Figures 41a & 41b. Choose Find Next from the Edit menu on Mac OS (left) or the Search menu on Windows (right).

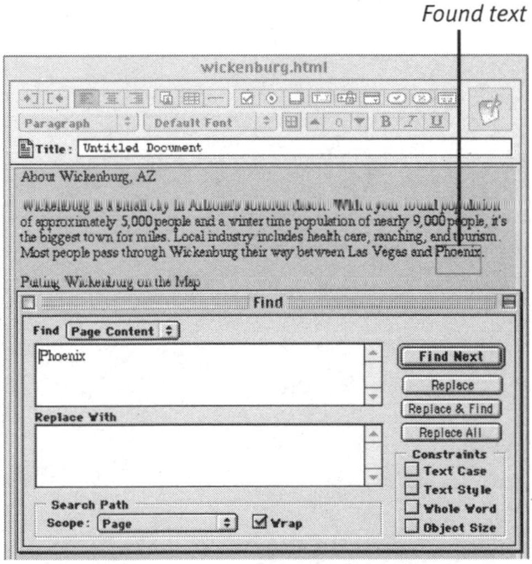

Found text

Figure 42. On Mac OS, a selection box appears around found text in the document window. **Figure 45** shows how found text appears on Windows.

To find text

1. Activate the window for the document you want to search.

2. Display the Find dialog box (**Figures 37a** and **37b**):
   - On Mac OS, choose Edit > Find (**Figure 9a**) or press ⌃ ⌘ F.
   - On Windows, choose Search > Find (**Figure 38**) or press Ctrl F.

3. Choose Page Content from the Find menu within the dialog box (**Figure 39**).

4. Enter the text you want to find in the Find box.

5. Turn on check boxes for find constraints as desired:
   - **Text Case** finds text only if its capitalization exactly matches the search text.
   - **Text Style** finds text only if its style matches the search text. You can use commands under the Style and Format menus to change the appearance of selected text in the Find dialog box.
   - **Whole Word** finds text only if it is not part of another word.
   - **Object Size** is for searching for objects. I tell you about objects in **Chapter 4**.

6. Choose Page from the Scope menu within the dialog box (**Figure 40**).

7. To search the entire document, no matter where the insertion point is, turn on the Wrap check box.

8. Initiate the search by clicking the Find Next button or:
   - On Mac OS, choose Edit > Find Next (**Figure 41a**) or press ⌃ ⌘ G.
   - On Windows, choose Search > Find Next (**Figure 41b**) or press Ctrl G.

   If the text exists in the document, it is highlighted (**Figures 42** and **45**).

Continued on next page...

FINDING TEXT

Continued from previous page.

9. To find the next occurrence of the text, repeat step 8.

10. When you're finished finding text, click the close box (Mac OS) or close button (Windows) in the Find dialog box to dismiss it.

✔ Tips

■ I tell you about text styles and commands under the Style and Format menus in **Chapter 3**.

■ I explain the options on the Scope menu in the Find dialog box in **Chapter 10**.

To replace text

1. Follow steps 1 through 7 on the previous page to specify criteria for the text you want to replace.

2. In the Replace with box, enter the replacement text (**Figure 43**).

3. Click the Find Next button or:

   ◆ On Mac OS, choose Edit > Find Next (**Figure 44a**) or press ⌃ ⌘ G.

   ◆ On Windows, choose Search > Find Next (**Figure 44b**) or press Ctrl G.

   The first occurrence of the Find text is located (**Figures 42** and **45**).

4. Click the Replace button or:

   ◆ On Mac OS, choose Edit > Replace (**Figure 44a**) or press ⌃ ⌘ L.

   ◆ On Windows, choose Search > Replace (**Figure 44b**) or press Ctrl L.

   Repeat step 3 and this part of step 4 until all desired occurrences are replaced.

   or

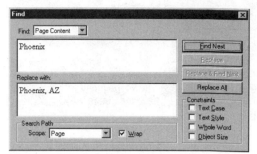

Figure 43. To replace text, enter the replacement text in the Replace with box.

Figures 44a & 44b. Once text has been found, all find and replace commands become available under the Edit menu on Mac OS (left) or the Search menu on Windows (above).

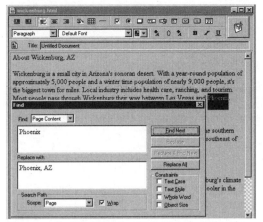

Figure 45. On Windows, found text is selected in the document window. **Figure 42** shows how found text appears on Mac OS.

Click the Replace & Find button or:

◆ On Mac OS, choose Edit > Replace & Find Again (**Figure 44a**) or press ⌃ ⌘ =.

◆ On Windows, choose Search > Replace & Find Again (**Figure 44b**) or press Ctrl =.

Repeat this part of step 4 until all desired occurrences are replaced.

5. When you're finished replacing text, click the close box (Mac OS) or close button (Windows) in the Find dialog box to dismiss it.

✔ Tips

■ To replace all occurrences of the text at once, follow steps 1 and 2 above, then click the Replace All button or choose Edit > Replace All (Mac OS; **Figure 44a**) or Search > Replace All (Windows; **Figure 44b**).

■ To delete text, enter the text you want to delete in the Find box and leave the Replace with box empty. When you replace some or all of the occurrences of the Find text with nothing, the Find text is deleted.

REPLACING TEXT

Checking Spelling

PageMill includes a spelling check feature that you can use to check your Web page documents for spelling, typographical, and possible capitalization errors before publishing them on the Web. This feature works with three dictionaries:

◆ The main dictionary contains thousands of words that PageMill refers to first when checking spelling.

◆ The Internet dictionary contains words commonly found on the Internet, like cyberspace, Netscape, WWW, and Yahoo. PageMill refers to this dictionary when it can't find a word in the main dictionary.

◆ The User Dictionary contains the words you add while performing a spelling check. This would include uncommon words like your name or company name. PageMill refers to this dictionary when it can't find a word in the main or Internet dictionaries.

✔ Tips

■ A spelling check always begins at the insertion point and moves forward through the document.

■ Never rely on a program's spelling check feature to find typographical errors! If a spelling error correctly spells another word—like *form* instead of *from*—the spelling checker will not flag it as an error. Remember, a spelling checker is no substitute for thorough proofreading.

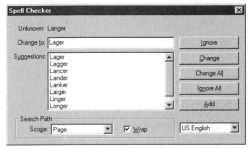

Figures 46a & 46b. The Spell Checker dialog box on Mac OS (above) and Windows (below).

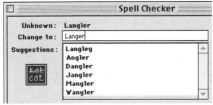

Figure 47. If the word is spelled incorrectly but the correct spelling is not in the Suggestions scrolling window, simply enter the correct spelling in the Change to box.

Figure 48.
When the spelling check is complete, the phrase *No more unknown words* appears.

✔ Tip

■ Do not click the Add button unless the unknown word is spelled correctly! If you add an incorrectly spelled word to the User Dictionary, PageMill will never identify it as unknown again!

To check spelling

1. Activate the window for the document you want to check.

   or

   Select the words you want to check within the document window.

2. Start the spelling check:

   ◆ On Mac OS, choose Edit > Check Spelling (**Figure 44a**) or press ⌘ ⌘ ` .

   ◆ On Windows, choose Search > Check Spelling (**Figure 44b**) or press F7 .

3. The spelling checker goes to work. When it finds an unknown word, it displays the Spell Checker dialog box (**Figures 46a** and **46b**). You have several options:

   ◆ To ignore the word, click the Ignore button (to ignore just one occurrence) or the Ignore All button (to ignore all occurrences).

   ◆ To change the word to one of the words in the Suggestions scrolling list, select the word you want to use and click the Change button (to change just one occurrence) or the Change All button (to change all occurrences).

   ◆ To change the word to a word that is not in the Suggestions scrolling window, click in the Change to box and enter the word you want to use (**Figure 47**). Then click the Change button (to change just one occurrence) or the Change All button (to change all occurrences).

   ◆ To add the word to the User Dictionary, click the Add button.

4. Repeat step 3 as necessary until the spelling check is complete.

5. When the spelling check is complete, the phrase *No more unknown words* appears above the Start button (**Figure 48**). Click the close box (Mac OS) or close button (Windows) to dismiss the Spell Checker dialog box.

To set spelling check options

1. Start a spelling check:

   ◆ On Mac OS, choose Edit > Check Spelling (**Figure 44a**) or press ⌃⌘⌐.

   ◆ On Windows, choose Search > Check Spelling (**Figure 44b**) or press F7.

2. In the Spell Checker dialog box that appears (**Figures 46a** and **46b**), set any of the following options as desired:

   ◆ To choose the language for the main dictionary to be used for the spelling check, choose an option from the menu in the lower-right corner of the Spell Checker dialog box (**Figures 49a** and **49b**).

   ◆ To prevent PageMill from continuing a spell check at the top of the page if it began somewhere other than the top of the page, turn off the Wrap check box.

3. Continue the spelling check as discussed on the previous page.

   or

   Click the close box (Mac OS) or close button (Windows) to dismiss the Spell Checker dialog box. Your settings will be saved for the next spelling check you perform.

✔ Tip

■ I tell you about the options on the Scope menu in the Spell Checker dialog box in **Chapter 10**.

Figure 49a & 49b.
The menu in the lower-right corner of the Spell Checker dialog box enables you to select a spelling check language. Here are the menus that appear for the English version of PageMill on Mac OS (top) and Windows (bottom).

SETTING SPELLING CHECK OPTIONS

FORMATTING TEXT 3

Formatting Text

PageMill enables you to apply two kinds of text formatting that are supported by HTML:

◆ **Character styles** affect the way individual text characters appear. Examples include bold, italic, font size, and font color.

◆ **Paragraph formats** affect the way entire paragraphs of text appear. Examples include headings, bulleted and numbered lists, and alignment.

No matter what kind of formatting you apply, PageMill takes care of inserting the proper HTML tags for you. You simply select the text you want to format and choose the character style or paragraph format you want. PageMill's WYSIWYG (what-you-see-is-what-you-get) formatting shows you what the formatted characters will look like when viewed with standard Web browsers.

✔ Tip

■ Text formatting makes pages visually interesting—without using graphics—and easier to read. But don't get carried away with formatting. Too much formatting can make a page downright ugly or difficult to read.

Physical vs. Logical Formatting

Although the formatting options offered by PageMill and HTML may seem similar to those offered by most word processors, there is a subtle difference worth mentioning. HTML distinguishes between two classifications of formatting:

◆ **Physical formatting** specifies how text should look, regardless of its use within the document. A physical character style such as bold, for example, will always look bold, no matter how it is used in the document or which Web browser is used to view it.

◆ **Logical formatting** specifies how text should look based on its use within a document. A logical character style such as strong, for example, may appear bold when viewed with some browsers and underlined when viewed with others. The point is, strong-formatted characters are formatted differently from unformatted characters, making them stand out.

The main problem with using logical styles is that you can't always predict how logically formatted characters will appear when viewed with various Web browsers—especially older Web browsers. For that reason, you may prefer to use physical formatting.

✔ Tip

■ Do you need to concern yourself with the difference between physical and logical formatting? Not really. As Web publishing and HTML evolve, Web browsers are becoming more and more standardized in the way they display logically formatted text. These days, logical formatting will appear the same to most of the people who visit your Web site.

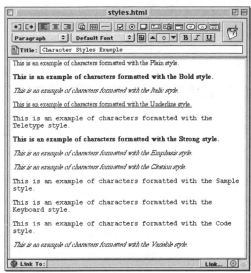

Figure 1. Examples of character styles applied to text.

Figures 2a & 2b.
The Style menu on Mac OS (left) and Windows (right).

Character Styles

PageMill directly supports the following character style options:

◆ Physical Styles:

❖ **Plain** is plain text, without formatting.

❖ **Bold** is bold text.

❖ **Italic** is italicized text.

❖ **Underline** is underlined text.

❖ **Teletype** is monospaced text.

❖ **Font** enables you to change the typeface, size, or color of text.

◆ Logical Styles:

❖ **Strong** is for strong emphasis.

❖ **Emphasis** is for emphasis.

❖ **Citation** is for titles of books and other references.

❖ **Sample** is for computer status messages.

❖ **Keyboard** is for user keyboard entry.

❖ **Code** is for computer programming code.

❖ **Variable** is for variables which must be replaced by the user.

Figure 1 shows examples of text with various character styles applied. You can apply a character style using commands under the Style menu (**Figures 2a** and **2b**), toolbar buttons, and shortcut keys.

✔ Tips

■ The appearance of logical styles may vary from one Web browser to another.

■ In some instances, two or more logical styles—such as Sample, Keyboard, and Code (**Figure 1**)—may look the same.

■ You can apply more than one style to text. Simply apply each style, one at a time, as discussed on the next few pages.

■ You can combine physical and logical styles if desired. For example, you can apply Bold and Emphasis styles to get bold, italic text.

■ You can apply character styles to text already formatted with paragraph formatting. I tell you about paragraph formatting later in this chapter.

■ Character styles do not change the way PageMill or Web browsers treat multiple spaces, tabs, or returns in a page document. These characters are stripped out. In order to include additional spaces or empty lines, use Preformatted paragraph formatting, which I discuss later in this chapter.

To apply a character style

1. Select the text you want to format (**Figure 3**).

2. Choose a style command from the Style menu (**Figures 2a** and **2b**).

   or

   Click a style button on the toolbar (**Table 1**).

   or

   Press a style shortcut key (**Table 1**).

   The selected text changes to the style you specified (**Figure 4**).

✔ Tip

- When you apply a character style you, in effect, "turn it on" for selected text. You can see which styles are applied to text by displaying the Style menu while the text is selected; check marks appear beside applied styles (**Figure 5**). (This technique does not work when different styles are applied to characters within a selection.)

To remove a character style

1. Select the text from which you want to remove the style.

2. Choose the name of the style you want to remove from the Style menu.

   or

   Click the toolbar button for the style you want to remove.

   or

   Press the shortcut key for the style you want to remove.

To remove all styles

1. Select the text from which you want to remove all styles.

2. Choose Plain from the Style menu or press Shift ⌃ ⌘ P (Mac OS) or Ctrl Shift P (Windows).

To demonstrate character format, we need some text to apply the formatting change to. Here's some Sample Text. Let's see how many changes we can apply to is and how it looks when we're finished.

Figure 3. Select the text you want to format.

Character Style	Toolbar Button	Mac OS Keystroke	Windows Keystroke
Plain		Shift ⌃ ⌘ P	Ctrl Shift P
Bold	**B**	⌃ ⌘ B	Shift B
Italic	*I*	⌃ ⌘ I	Shift I
Underline	U	⌃ ⌘ U	Shift U
Teletype		Shift ⌃ ⌘ T	Shift T
Code		Shift ⌃ ⌘ C	Ctrl Shift C

Table 1. Toolbar buttons and keystrokes to apply character styles.

To demonstrate character format, we need some text to apply the formatting change to. Here's some **Sample Text**. Let's see how many changes we can apply to is and how it looks when we're finished.

Figure 4. The formatting option you chose is applied to the selected text.

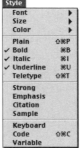

Figure 5. When you apply a style, you "turn it on." Check marks appear on the Style menu beside applied styles for selected text.

✔ Tip

- If these techniques do not remove a physical style, some kind of paragraph formatting is probably applied to the text. You must remove the paragraph formatting to change the appearance of the text. I tell you about paragraph formatting later in this chapter.

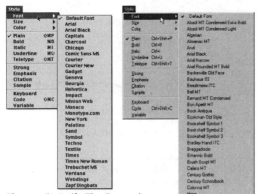

Figures 6a & 6b. The Font submenu on Mac OS (left) and Windows (right).

Figure 7a & 7b. The Font menu on the toolbar on Mac OS (left) and Windows (above).

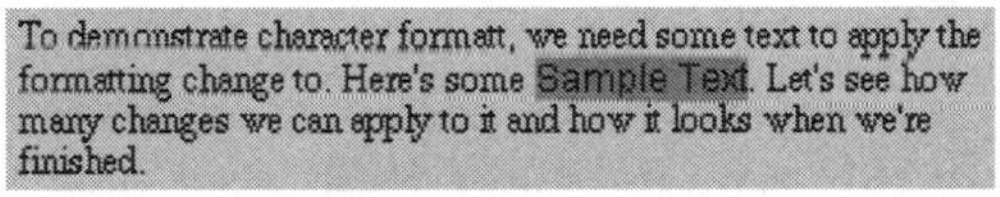

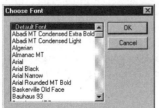

Figure 8. Here's the sample text with Arial font applied.

Figure 9. The Choose Font dialog box on Windows.

To change the typeface of characters

1. Select the text you want to format (**Figure 3**).

2. Choose a typeface from the Font submenu under the Style menu (**Figures 6a** and **6b**).

    or

    Choose a typeface from the Font menu on the toolbar (**Figures 7a** and **7b**).

    The typeface you selected is applied to the selected text (**Figure 8**).

✔ Tips

- The Font submenu (**Figures 6a** and **6b**) displays only the fonts that are properly installed on your computer system. The fonts on your computer will probably differ from the ones shown here.

- On Windows, only the first twenty-five or so installed fonts appear on the Font submenu. To use a font that does not appear, choose Style > Font > More to display the Choose Font dialog box (**Figure 9**). Select the font you want to apply and click OK.

- If the typeface you apply to characters is not installed on the computer of someone viewing your Web page on the Internet, the characters will appear in the default font (normally Times or New Times Roman). To prevent this from happening, only apply commonly used typefaces, such as the ones installed with your computer's operating system.

To restore the typeface of characters

1. Select the text you want to restore to the default font.

2. Choose Style > Font > Default Font (**Figures 6a** and **6b**).

    or

    Choose Default Font from the Font menu on the toolbar (**Figures 7a** and **7b**).

CHANGING CHARACTER TYPEFACE

To change the size of characters

1. Select the text you want to format (**Figure 3**).

2. Choose a command from the Size submenu under the Style menu (**Figures 10a** and **10b**):

   ◆ To set a specific relative increase or decrease, choose the desired + or - value from the Size submenu under the Style menu.

   ◆ To make text larger, choose Style > Size > Increase Font Size.

   ◆ To make text smaller, choose Style > Size > Decrease Font Size.

   or

   Click a Relative Font Size button on the toolbar (**Table 2**).

   or

   Choose a specific relative increase or decrease value from the Relative Font Size menu on the toolbar (**Figures 11a** and **11b**).

   or

   Press a font size shortcut key (**Table 2**).

   The size you selected is applied to the selected text (**Figure 12**).

✔ Tips

   ■ You increase or decrease the size of text characters relative to the size of the default font.

   ■ The default font size is determined by font preferences set within the Web browser used to view the page and the Base Font settings specified for the page. I tell you about setting the Base Font size later in this chapter.

   ■ Another way to change the size of text is to use heading formats. I tell you about headings later in this chapter.

Figures 10a & 10b. The Size submenu under the Style menu on Mac OS (left) and Windows (right).

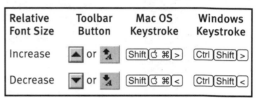

Relative Font Size	Toolbar Button	Mac OS Keystroke	Windows Keystroke
Increase	▲ or	Shift ⌃ ⌘ >	Ctrl Shift >
Decrease	▼ or	Shift ⌃ ⌘ <	Ctrl Shift <

Table 2. Toolbar buttons and keystrokes to change the relative font size of selected characters.

Figures 11a & 11b. The Relative Font Size menu on the toolbar on Mac OS (left) and Windows (right).

To demonstrate character format, we need some text to apply the formatting change to. Here's some **Sample Text**. Let's see how many changes we can apply to it and how it looks when we're finished.

Figure 12. The sample text with the font size increased two levels.

To restore character size

1. Select the text you want to restore to the default size.

2. Choose Style > Size > 0 (**Figures 10a** and **10b**).

   or

   Choose 0 from the Relative Font Size menu on the toolbar (**Figures 11a** and **11b**).

CHANGING CHARACTER SIZE

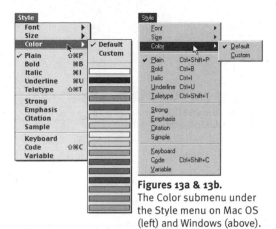

Figures 13a & 13b.
The Color submenu under the Style menu on Mac OS (left) and Windows (above).

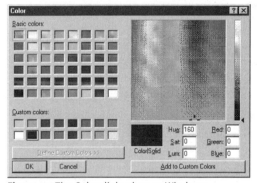

Figure 14. The Color dialog box on Windows.

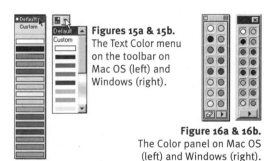

Figures 15a & 15b.
The Text Color menu on the toolbar on Mac OS (left) and Windows (right).

Figure 16a & 16b.
The Color panel on Mac OS (left) and Windows (right).

To demonstrate character formatt, we need some text to apply the formatting change to. Here's some Sample Text. Let's see how many changes we can apply to it and how it looks when we're finished.

Figure 17. The sample text turned yellow.

To change the color of characters

1. Select the text you want to recolor (**Figure 3**).
2. Choose an option from the Color submenu:
   - On Mac OS, choose a color from the Color submenu under the Style menu (**Figure 13a**).
   - On Windows, choose Style > Color > Custom (**Figure 13b**) to display the Color dialog box (**Figure 14**). Select a color and click OK.

   or

   Click the Text Color button on the toolbar and choose a color from the menu that appears (**Figures 15a** and **15b**).

   or

   Display the Color panel (**Figures 16a** and **16b**) and click one of its color swatches.

   The color you selected is applied to the selected text (**Figure 17**).

✔ Tips

- The default font color is determined by color preferences set in the Web browser used to view the page and color settings for the page. I explain how to change page colors later in this chapter.

- On Mac OS, if you choose Custom from the Color submenu (**Figure 13a**) or Text Color menu on the toolbar (**Figure 15a**), you can use a color picker to select a custom color.

- I tell you how to display the Color panel in **Chapter 1**.

To restore character color

1. Select the text you want to restore to the default color.
2. Choose Style > Color > Default (**Figures 13a** and **13b**).

   or

   Choose Default from the Text Color menu on the toolbar (**Figures 15a** and **15b**).

CHANGING CHARACTER COLOR

Paragraph Formats

Paragraph formats are used to format entire paragraphs of information. PageMill supports the following HTML paragraph formatting options:

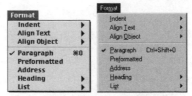

- **Indentation** options specify the amount of space between the sides of the window and the text.

- **Text Alignment** options specify the way text is positioned between the left and right sides of the window.

- **Heading** formats specify the size of headings.

- **List** formats specify the way lists of information appear.

- **Preformatted** format enables you to create tables of information without using HTML cell tables.

- **Address** format applies special formatting to addresses.

Figures 18a & 18b. The Format menu on Mac OS (left) and Windows (right).

You can apply paragraph formatting using commands under the Format menu (**Figures 18a** and **18b**), toolbar buttons, and shortcut keys.

✔ Tips

- In PageMill (as in most other programs), a paragraph is defined by return characters. Each time you press [Return] (Mac OS) or [Enter] (Windows), you end the current paragraph and begin a new one.

- When applying paragraph formatting to only one paragraph, simply position the insertion point within the paragraph, and then choose a formatting option. Formatting is applied to the entire paragraph even though nothing is technically "selected."

PARAGRAPH FORMATS

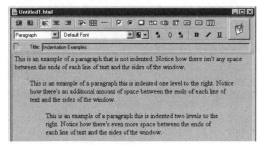

Figure 19. Examples of indented text.

Figure 20. Select the text you want to indent.

Figures 21a & 21b. The Indent submenu on the Format menu on Mac OS (left) and Windows (right).

Indentation Option	Toolbar Button	Mac OS Keystroke	Windows Keystroke
Indent Right	→] or ⊒	⌘]	Ctrl]
Indent Left	[← or ⊑	⌘[	Ctrl[

Table 3. Toolbar buttons and keystrokes to set paragraph indentation.

Figure 22. Using the Indent Right command adds space between the text and the edge of the window.

Indentation

PageMill's indentation options specify the amount of space between the left and right sides of the browser window and the text.

◆ **Indent Left** removes space between the text and the sides of the window.

◆ **Indent Right** adds space between the text and the sides of the window.

Figure 19 shows examples of indented text.

✔ Tips

■ By default, text is not indented.

■ You can indent text more than one level. Each time you use the Indent Right command, you increase the amount of indentation.

■ You can use indentation in combination with any other character or paragraph formatting option.

To set paragraph indentation

1. Select all or part of the paragraph(s) for which you want to change indentation (**Figure 20**).

2. Choose the indentation option you want from the Indent submenu under the Format menu (**Figures 21a** and **21b**).

   or

   Press an indentation shortcut key (**Table 3**).

   or

   Click an indentation button on the toolbar (**Table 3**).

   The selected paragraph(s) change accordingly (**Figure 22**).

SETTING INDENTATION

Alignment

PageMill's alignment options specify the way text is positioned between the left and right sides of the browser window. PageMill offers three options:

◆ **Left Align Text** aligns text with the left side of the window.

◆ **Center Align Text** centers text between the left and right sides of the window.

◆ **Right Align Text** aligns text with the right side of the window.

Figure 23 shows an example of each alignment option.

✔ Tips

■ By default, text is left aligned.

■ You can use indentation in combination with any other character or paragraph formatting option.

To set paragraph alignment

1. Select all or part of the paragraph(s) for which you want to change alignment (**Figure 24**).

2. Choose the alignment option you want from the Align Text submenu under the Format menu (**Figures 25a** and **25b**).

   or

   Click an alignment button on the toolbar:

    Left Align Text

   ⬛ Center Align Text

   ⬛ Right Align Text

   The selected paragraph(s) change accordingly (**Figure 26**).

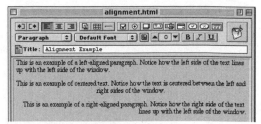

Figure 23. Examples of text alignment.

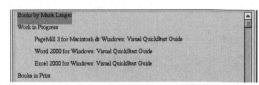

Figure 24. Select the text you want to align.

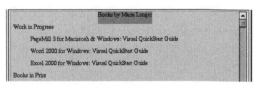

Figures 25a & 25b. The Align Text submenu on the Format menu on Mac OS (left) and Windows (right).

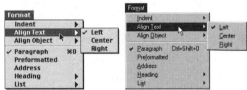

Figure 26. Using the Center command centers the selected text.

SETTING ALIGNMENT

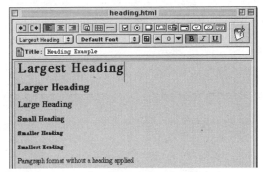

Figure 27. Examples of the six heading formats.

Figures 28a & 28b. The Heading submenu under the Format menu on Mac OS (left) and Windows (right).

Heading Format	Mac OS Keystroke	Windows Keystroke
Smallest	Option ⌃ ⌘ 6	Ctrl Shift 6
Smaller	Option ⌃ ⌘ 5	Ctrl Shift 5
Small	Option ⌃ ⌘ 4	Ctrl Shift 4
Large	Option ⌃ ⌘ 3	Ctrl Shift 3
Larger	Option ⌃ ⌘ 2	Ctrl Shift 2
Largest	Option ⌃ ⌘ 1	Ctrl Shift 1

Table 4. Keystrokes to apply heading formats.

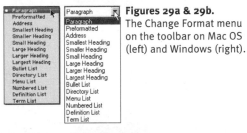

Figures 29a & 29b.
The Change Format menu on the toolbar on Mac OS (left) and Windows (right).

Figure 30. The selected text from **Figure 26** with the Larger heading format applied.

Headings

PageMill's heading options let you choose from among six heading levels, each of which applies a different text size:

◆ **Large**, **Larger**, and **Largest** set headings larger than the default text size.

◆ **Small** sets headings the same size as the default text size.

◆ **Smaller** and **Smallest** set headings smaller than the default text size.

Paragraphs formatted as headings also have bold style applied. **Figure 27** illustrates each heading option.

✔ Tips

■ By default, no heading is applied.

■ You cannot remove the bold style from a heading.

■ You can apply heading formats in combination with paragraph alignment and indentation options.

■ You can see which heading format is applied to a paragraph by clicking in the paragraph and looking at the Change Format menu on the toolbar (**Figure 27**).

To apply a heading format

1. Select all or part of the paragraph(s) you want to format as a heading (**Figure 26**).

2. Choose the heading option you want from the Heading submenu under the Format menu (**Figures 28a** and **28b**).

   or

   Press a heading shortcut key (**Table 4**).

   or

   Choose a heading option from the Change Format menu on the toolbar (**Figures 29a** and **29b**).

   The selected paragraph(s) change accordingly (**Figure 30**).

APPLYING HEADING FORMATS

✔ Tip

■ The shortcut keys for the heading formats
(**Table 4**) correspond to the HTML tags for
headings. For example, the HTML tag for
the Largest heading format is <H1>; the
shortcut key for the same heading format
in PageMill is Option ⌥ ⌘ 1 (Mac OS)
Ctrl Shift 1 (Windows). This makes it easy
for PageMill users with HTML knowledge
to remember the shortcut keys.

To remove a heading format

1. Select the paragraph(s) with the heading
   format applied.

2. Choose Format > Paragraph (**Figures 18a**
   and **18b**).

   or

   Press ⌥ ⌘ 0 (Mac OS) or Ctrl Shift 0
   (Windows).

   or

   Choose Paragraph from the Change Format
   menu on the toolbar (**Figures 29a** and **29b**).

   The heading format is removed.

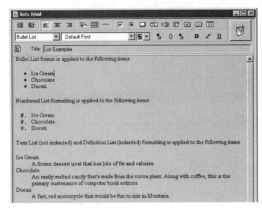

Figure 31. Examples of various list formats.

List Formats

PageMill's six list format options let you create a variety of nicely formatted lists:

◆ **Bullet List**, **Directory List**, and **Menu List** create bulleted lists. Bullets are inserted automatically.

◆ **Numbered List** creates a numbered list. The numbers are inserted automatically.

◆ **Definition List** indents the paragraph. It is designed to be used with **Term List**.

◆ **Term List**, when used with Definition List, lets you create glossary-style lists.

Figure 31 illustrates the list formats. (Directory List and Menu List formats, which are not illustrated, are identical in appearance to Bullet List format.)

✔ Tips

■ By default, no list formatting is applied.

■ Consecutive paragraphs with the same list formatting applied do not have additional space between them. You can see this in **Figure 31**; each list item is a separate paragraph.

■ When you create a numbered list, PageMill displays pound signs (#) where the numbers should go (**Figure 31**). Don't worry—when your page is viewed with a Web browser, the numbers will appear.

■ You can apply list formats in combination with paragraph alignment and indentation options.

■ You can see which list format is applied to a paragraph by clicking in the paragraph and looking at the Change Format menu on the toolbar (**Figure 31**).

■ If you indent part of a bulleted list, the indented part appears as a nested list (**Figure 35**).

To create a list

1. Select all or part of the paragraphs you want to include in your list (**Figure 32**).

2. Choose the list option you want from the List submenu under the Format menu (**Figures 33a** and **33b**).

    or

    Choose the list option you want from the Change Format menu on the toolbar (**Figures 29a** and **29b**).

    The selected paragraphs change to become part of a list (**Figure 34**).

To create a nested list

1. Follow the steps above to create a list.

2. Select the list items you want to indent more.

3. Choose Format > Indent > Indent Right (**Figures 21a** and **21b**).

    or

    Press ⌃ ⌘ [] (Mac OS) or Ctrl [] (Windows).

    or

    Click the Indent Right button on the toolbar.

The items are indented and the bullet or numbering scheme changes (**Figure 35**).

✔ Tip

■ To remove a nested list, select the nested items and choose Format > Indent > Indent Left (**Figures 21a** and **21b**), press ⌃ ⌘ [] (Mac OS) or Ctrl [] (Windows), or click the Indent Left button on the toolbar.

Figure 32. Select the paragraphs you want to include in the list.

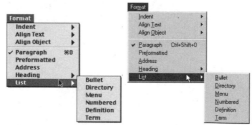

Figures 33a & 33b. The List submenu on the Format menu on Mac OS (left) and Windows (right).

Figure 34. Bullet List format applied to selected paragraphs.

Figure 35. You create a nested list by indenting items in the list.

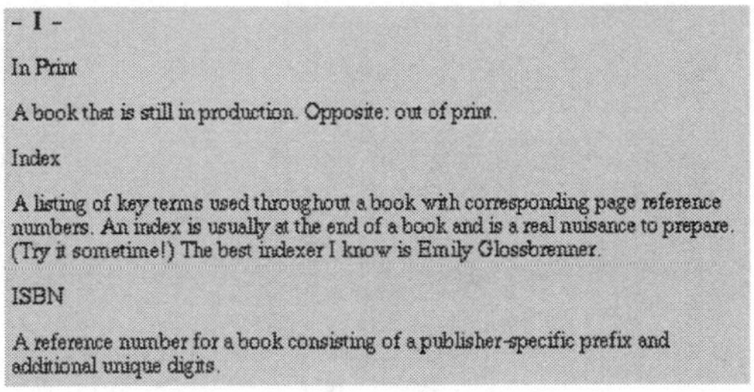

Figure 36. Begin by entering the terms and definitions you want to include in the list.

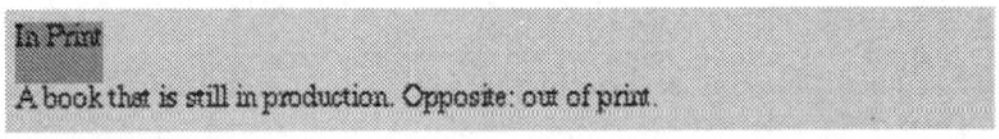

Figure 37. Select a term in the list and apply Term List formatting to it.

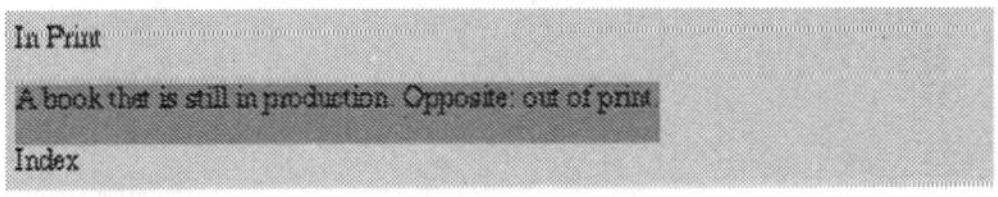

Figure 38. Select a definition in the list...

Figure 39. ...and apply Definition List formatting to it.

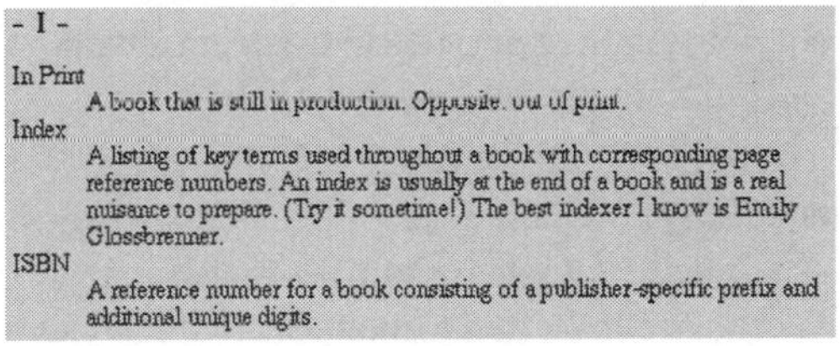

Figure 40. A completed term and definition list.

To create a term & definition list

1. Enter the text for the list by alternating between terms and definitions (**Figure 36**).

2. Select a term in the list (**Figure 37**).

3. Choose Format > List > Term (**Figures 33a and 33b**) or choose Term List from the Change Format menu on the toolbar (**Figures 29a** or **29b**).

4. Select the definition immediately following the term you just formatted (**Figure 38**).

5. Choose Format > List > Definition (**Figures 33a** and **33b**) or choose Definition List from the Change Format menu on the toolbar (**Figures 29a** or **29b**).

   The definition indents and moves up under the term (**Figure 39**).

6. Repeat steps 2 through 5 for each term and definition in the list.

When you're finished, your list might look something like the one in **Figure 40**.

To remove list formats

1. Select the paragraph(s) from which you want to remove the list formats.

2. Choose Format > Paragraph (**Figures 18a and 18b**).

   or

   Press (⌘ 0) (Mac OS) or (Ctrl)(Shift)(0) (Windows).

   or

   Choose Paragraph from the Change Format menu on the toolbar (**Figures 29a and 29b**).

   The list format is removed.

Preformatted Paragraphs

The characters you'd normally use to format documents in your favorite word processor or page layout application aren't always interpreted properly by Web browsers. Here are some examples:

◆ Multiple consecutive space characters are usually treated as a single space.

◆ Multiple consecutive return or line break characters are usually treated as a single return or line break character.

◆ Tab characters are often ignored or treated as a single space.

As you might imagine, this makes it a bit tougher to create spreadsheet-like tables in your Web page documents.

That's where the Preformatted format comes in. By combining the ability to include multiple consecutive spaces and return characters with a *monospaced* (or fixed-width) font like Courier, you can create simple tables—without creating HTML tables—and be confident that they'll look the same when viewed on any browser.

Figure 41 shows an example of a table created with the Preformatted format.

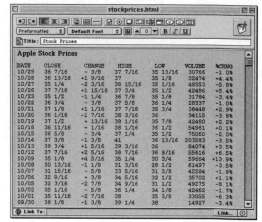

Figure 41. The Preformatted format is great for creating simple spreadsheet-like tables.

✔ Tips

■ PageMill does not allow you to enter multiple consecutive space characters in a paragraph unless that paragraph has the Preformatted format applied.

■ You can enter multiple consecutive *nonbreaking space* characters regardless of how a paragraph is formatted. To type a nonbreaking space, press [Option][Spacebar] (Mac OS) or [Ctrl][Spacebar] (Windows). Since these characters are interpreted differently by different Web browsers, you should not use them as an alternative to regular spaces in Preformatted format paragraphs.

■ You can drag or paste in text containing multiple consecutive spaces that was created in another application.

■ Using a monospaced character style like Code or Sample is not the same as using the Preformatted format. Character styles will not retain the extra spaces. I tell you about styles earlier in this chapter.

■ Another way to create a table is with HTML tables. I tell you how to use PageMill's table feature in **Chapter 5**.

```
Apple Stock Prices

DATE  CLOSE    CHANGE  HIGH    LOW    VOLUME  %CHNG

10/29  36 7/16    - 3/8   37 7/16  35 13/16  30766  -1.0%

10/28  36 13/16  +1 9/16  37       35 1/8   32474  +4.4%

10/27  35 1/4    -2 3/16  38 15/16 35 1/16  48053  -5.8%

10/26  37 7/16   +1 15/16 37 3/4   35 1/2   42486  +5.4%

10/23  35 1/2    -1 1/4   36 7/8   35 1/8   31784  -3.4%

10/22  36 3/4     - 3/8   37 5/8   36 1/4   28337  -1.0%

10/21  37 1/8    +1 1/16  37 7/16  35 3/4   38448  +2.9%

10/20  36 1/16   -1 7/16  38 3/16  36       34115  -3.8%

10/19  37 1/2    + 13/16  38 1/16  35 7/8   42480  +2.2%

10/16  36 11/16  + 1/16   38 1/16  36 1/2   54961  +0.1%

10/15  36 5/8     - 3/4   37 1/4   35 1/2   75060  -2.0%
```

Figure 42. Here's an example of tabular text prepared in another program and pasted into a PageMill document.

```
Apple Stock Prices

DATE  CLOSE    CHANGE  HIGH    LOW    VOLUME  %CHNG

10/29  36 7/16    - 3/8   37 7/16  35 13/16  30766  -1.0%

10/28  36 13/16  +1 9/16  37       35 1/8   32474  +4.4%

10/27  35 1/4    -2 3/16  38 15/16 35 1/16  48053  -5.8%

10/26  37 7/16   +1 15/16 37 3/4   35 1/2   42486  +5.4%

10/23  35 1/2    -1 1/4   36 7/8   35 1/8   31784  -3.4%

10/22  36 3/4     - 3/8   37 5/8   36 1/4   28337  -1.0%

10/21  37 1/8    +1 1/16  37 7/16  35 3/4   38448  +2.9%

10/20  36 1/16   -1 7/16  38 3/16  36       34115  -3.8%

10/19  37 1/2    + 13/16  38 1/16  35 7/8   42480  +2.2%

10/16  36 11/16  + 1/16   38 1/16  36 1/2   54961  +0.1%

10/15  36 5/8     - 3/4   37 1/4   35 1/2   75060  -2.0%
```

Figure 43. Select the text you want to format.

```
Apple Stock Prices
DATE   CLOSE    CHANGE   HIGH     LOW     VOLUME  %CHNG
10/29  36 7/16   - 3/8   37 7/16  35 13/16  30766  -1.0%
10/28  36 13/16  +1 9/16  37       35 1/8   32474  +4.4%
10/27  35 1/4    -2 3/16  38 15/16 35 1/16  48053  -5.8%
10/26  37 7/16   +1 15/16 37 3/4   35 1/2   42486  +5.4%
10/23  35 1/2    -1 1/4   36 7/8   35 1/8   31784  -3.4%
10/22  36 3/4     - 3/8   37 5/8   36 1/4   28337  -1.0%
10/21  37 1/8    +1 1/16  37 7/16  35 3/4   38448  +2.9%
10/20  36 1/16   -1 7/16  38 3/16  36       34115  -3.8%
10/19  37 1/2    + 13/16  38 1/16  35 7/8   42480  +2.2%
10/16  36 11/16  + 1/16   38 1/16  36 1/2   54961  +0.1%
10/15  36 5/8     - 3/4   37 1/4   35 1/2   75060  -2.0%
```

Figure 44. Applying the Preformatted format lines up table columns using the spaces in the text.

To apply the Preformatted format to existing text

1. Type, drag in, or paste in text you want to format with the Preformatted format (**Figure 42**).

2. Select all or part of the paragraph(s) you want to format (**Figure 43**).

3. Choose Format > Preformatted (**Figures 18a** and **18b**).

    or

    Choose Preformatted from the Change Format menu on the toolbar (**Figures 29a** and **29b**).

    The selected paragraph(s) change accordingly (**Figure 44**).

✔ Tips

- ■ I explain how to enter text by pasting or dragging it into a PageMill document in **Chapter 2**.

- ■ Text you drag or paste in can contain multiple consecutive spaces.

- ■ Once you apply the Preformatted format to text, you can adjust the spacing between words with space characters as necessary.

USING THE PREFORMATTED FORMAT

To use the Preformatted format as you enter text

1. Position the insertion point on an empty line where you want the preformatted text to begin (**Figure 45**).

2. Choose Format > Preformatted (**Figures 18a** and **18b**).

   or

   Choose Preformatted from the Change Format menu on the toolbar (**Figures 29a** and **29b**).

   This "turns on" preformatted formatting.

3. Type the text you want preformatted. It is entered in monospaced type (**Figure 46**).

4. Press Return (Mac OS) or Enter (Windows) after the last line of preformatted text.

5. Choose Format > Paragraph (**Figures 18a** and **18b**).

   or

   Press ⌘ ⌘ 0 (Mac OS) or Ctrl Shift 0 (Windows).

   or

   Choose Paragraph from the Change Format menu on the toolbar (**Figures 29a** and **29b**).

   This "turns off" preformatted formatting.

To remove the Preformatted format

1. Select the paragraph(s) from which you want to remove the Preformatted format.

2. Choose Format > Paragraph (**Figures 18a** and **18b**).

   or

   Press ⌘ ⌘ 0 (Mac OS) or Ctrl Shift 0 (Windows).

   or

   Choose Paragraph from the Change Format menu on the toolbar (**Figures 29a** and **29b**).

   The Preformatted format is removed.

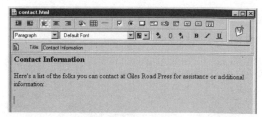

Figure 45. Position the insertion point on an empty line where you want to begin typing preformatted text.

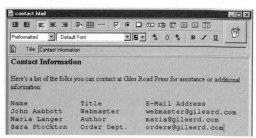

Figure 46. The text you type appears in the Preformatted format.

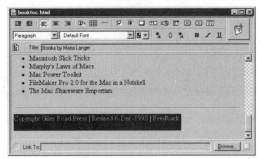

Figure 47. Select the text to which you want to apply the Address format.

Figure 48. As you can see here, the Address format applies an italic style to text when viewed in PageMill and many Web browsers.

Address Format

Often, one of the last lines in a Web page is the page author's name, e-mail address, page revision date, and/or copyright notice. Traditionally, the Address format is used to format this kind of information.

To apply the Address format

1. Select all or part of the paragraph(s) to which you want to apply the Address format (**Figure 47**).

3. Choose Format > Address (**Figures 18a** and **18b**).

   or

   Choose Address from the Change Format menu on the toolbar (**Figures 29a** and **29b**).

   The selected paragraph(s) change accordingly. As you can see in **Figure 48**, Address format includes italic style.

✔ Tip

■ You cannot remove italic style from the Address format. I tell you about character styles earlier in this chapter.

To remove the Address format

1. Select the paragraph(s) from which you want to remove the Address format.

2. Choose Format > Paragraph (**Figures 18a** and **18b**).

   or

   Press ⌘0 (Mac OS) or Ctrl Shift 0 (Windows).

   or

   Choose Paragraph from the Change Format menu on the toolbar (**Figures 29a** and **29b**).

   The Address format is removed.

APPLYING & REMOVING ADDRESS FORMAT

Page Attributes

In addition to formatting text characters or paragraphs, PageMill also enables you to set *page attributes*—formatting options that affect the entire page.

 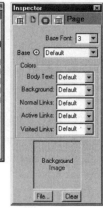

Figures 49a & 49b. The Inspector's Page panel on Mac OS (left) and Windows (right).

- ◆ **Base Font** determines the default font size for the page. The default size is 3. (This is not a point size, but a value that represents the default font size of all Web browsers.)

- ◆ **Colors** determines the default color of page elements:

  - ❖ **Body Text** is the color of text on the page that is not a link. The default color is black.

  - ❖ **Background** is the color of the page background. The default color is gray.

  - ❖ **Normal Links** is the color of links that have not been visited. The default color is blue.

  - ❖ **Active Links** is the color of links as they are clicked. The default color is red.

  - ❖ **Visited Links** sets the color of links that have been visited. The default color is purple.

- ◆ **Background image** puts a texture or image behind page text. By default, there is no background image.

These settings are made in the Page panel of the Inspector (**Figures 49a** and **49b**).

✔ Tips

- ■ If a page has both a background color and background image, only the background image will be displayed.

- ■ You can set the default color and background for all new pages in the Page options of the Preferences dialog box. This makes it easy to give your pages a consistent look and feel. I explain how to set preferences in **Chapter 11**.

Figures 50a & 50b.
The Base Font menu
on Mac OS (left) and Windows (right).

About the Base Font Size

By default, every page you create has a base font size of 3. This is not a point size, but a value that represents the default font size of all Web browsers. When you change the base font size, you change the default font size for all text on the page except text formatted with a heading format.

Figures 51 & 52. Two examples of base font size. The illustration above shows a base font size of 3. The illustration below shows the same text with a base font size of 4. Note how the heading is not affected.

About the Base Font Size

By default, every page you create has a base font size of 3. This is not a point size, but a value that represents the default font size of all Web browsers. When you change the base font size, you change the default font size for all text on the page except text formatted with a heading format.

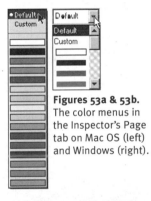

Figures 53a & 53b.
The color menus in
the Inspector's Page
tab on Mac OS (left)
and Windows (right).

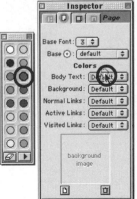

Figure 54.
Drag a color swatch
from the Color panel
onto the menu for
the element you
want to change.

To set the base font size

1. Display the Inspector's Page panel (**Figures 49a** and **49b**).

2. Choose a relative font size from the Base Font menu (**Figures 50a and 50b**). Select a lower number to make the font size smaller and a higher number to make the font size larger.

The size of any text that is not formatted with a heading format changes to reflect the size you selected. **Figures 51** and **52** illustrate a change in the default base font size.

✔ Tip

- Windows Web browsers tend to display text larger than Mac OS Web browsers. If you're creating a Web page on Windows and reduce the base font size, preview the page with a Mac OS browser to ensure that all text is large enough to read.

To set colors

1. Display the Inspector's Page panel (**Figures 49a** and **49b**).

2. Choose a color from the menu for the element you want to change (**Figures 53a** and **53b**).

   or

   Display the Color panel (**Figures 16a** and **16b**) and drag one of its color swatches to the menu for the element you want to change (**Figure 54**).

3. Repeat step 2 for each element you want to change.

To restore default colors

1. Display the Inspector's Page panel (**Figures 49a** and **49b**).

2. Choose Default from the menu for the element you want to restore (**Figures 53a** and **53b**).

To add a background image

1. Display the Inspector's Page panel (**Figures 49a** and **49b**).

2. Click the tiny page icon (Mac OS) or File button (Windows) beneath the background image well in the Inspector.

3. Use the Insert (Mac OS) or Open (Windows) dialog box that appears (**Figures 55a** and **55b**) to locate and open the image you want to use as a background.

The image fills the background image well in the Inspector and becomes a repeating pattern in the background of the page (**Figure 56**).

✔ Tips

■ You can also add a background image by dragging an image from the PageMill window or another document window into the background image well in the Inspector (**Figures 49a** and **49b**) or onto the page icon beside the Title at the top of the page.

■ For best results, use small background images. They take less time to load so your pages display more quickly.

■ To speed up page loading, use a limited number of background images on the Web pages at your site. Since Web browsers cache recently downloaded page and image files, they won't need to download the same files repeatedly during the session.

■ Be sure a background image contrasts with the page text. If the colors are too similar or the background image is too "busy," page text will be illegible.

■ I tell you more about working with images in **Chapter 4**.

To remove a background image

Click the trash icon (Mac OS) or Clear button (Windows) beneath the background image well in the Inspector (**Figures 49a** and **49b**).

The image and background disappear.

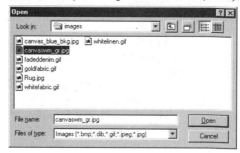

Figures 55a & 55b. The Insert dialog box on Mac OS (above) and Open dialog box on Windows (below).

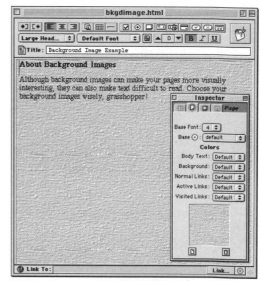

Figure 56. An example of text against a background image.

ADDING IMAGES & MULTIMEDIA OBJECTS 4

Figures 1 & 2. Graphics are heavily used in both the Apple (above) and Microsoft (below) home pages.

Images & Multimedia Objects

One of the best features of the World Wide Web is its ability to support graphic images, animations, movies, sounds, and Java applets. These multimedia elements or objects can be viewed by Web browsers on all major computer platforms. When used properly, they can help communicate information and make your Web pages stand out from the rest.

Figures 1 and **2** show examples of Web pages that include multimedia objects.

✔ Tips

- When using multimedia objects in your Web pages, be sure to keep file size in mind. Many Web "surfers" access the Internet via 28.8k and 33.6k bps modems. Large graphics, movies, and sounds are time-consuming to download through modem connections. If your pages contain many large multimedia elements, you'll discourage visits from modem users—and even many impatient users with direct connections.

- Multimedia elements can be used as simple page enhancements as well as links to other pages and form submission buttons. I tell you about links in **Chapter 6** and about forms in **Chapter 8**.

Multimedia File Formats

PageMill supports the following types of multimedia:

◆ **Images** in GIF, Interlaced GIF, JPEG, ProJPEG (Progressive JPEG), and Adobe Acrobat Portable Document File (PDF) formats.

◆ **Animations and movies** in Animated GIF, QuickTime, Microsoft Video, MPEG. and Shockwave formats.

◆ **Sounds** in AU, Audio Interchange File Format (AIFF), MIDI, Real Audio, and Windows Sound (WAV) formats.

◆ **Applets and controls** in Java and ActiveX formats.

✔ Tips

■ GIF and JPEG are the standard image formats for the World Wide Web. GIF is an 8-bit (256 colors) format good for simple graphic images. JPEG is a 24-bit (16 million colors) format good for high quality graphics and photographic images.

■ PageMill can also import PICT (Mac OS) and BMP (Windows) files, which it automatically converts to GIF file format.

■ Animated GIF files contain multiple GIF images that, when displayed in sequence, make an animation. They offer a great way to include animation in your Web pages without inserting movie files, which tend to be large.

■ If you do not use the correct file extension when including multimedia objects in your Web pages, the objects will not display properly when viewed with a Web browser. A file extension is a series of characters at the end of a file name that is used by browsers and some operating systems to identify file format. **Table 1** lists the file formats PageMill supports and their extensions.

FORMAT NAME	EXTENSION	PLUG-IN REQUIRED?
GIF	.gif	N
Interlaced GIF	.gif	N
JPEG	.jpeg or .jpg	N
ProJPEG	.jpeg or .jpg	N
Acrobat PDF	.pdf	Y
Animated GIF	.gif	N
QuickTime	.mov	Y
Microsoft Video	.avi	Y
MPEG	.mpg or .mpeg	Y
Shockwave	.dcr	Y
AU	.au	N
AIFF	.aiff or .aif	Y
MIDI	.mid or .rmi	Y
Real Audio	.ra	Y
Windows Sound	.wav	Y
Java	.class	*
ActiveX	.ocx	**

* Older Web browsers do not support Java applets. To use Java in PageMill on Mac OS, you must have Mac OS 8 or later installed.

** Older Web browsers do not support ActiveX. You can only preview ActiveX controls from within PageMill on the Windows version in Internet Explorer Preview mode.

Table 1. Image and multimedia object formats with corresponding file name extensions.

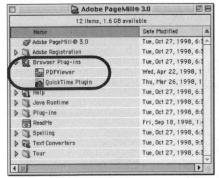

Figures 3a & 3b. Use the Finder on Mac OS (above) and Windows Explorer on Windows (below) to copy browser plug-in files to the Browser Plug-ins folder.

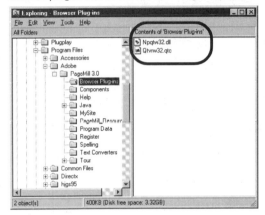

Browser Plug-ins

To include certain types of multimedia objects in your PageMill documents—and view them with Web browser software—you must have the appropriate browser plug-in file installed.

✔ Tips

- **Table 1** indicates which file formats require a plug-in to view.

- PageMill is compatible only with plug-ins that work with Netscape Navigator 2.0. A good place to find Navigator plug-ins is the Netscape Navigator Plug-Ins Page, *http://www.netscape.com/plugins/*

- Think twice about including multimedia objects that require obscure plug-ins to view. Doing so may prevent many of your page's visitors from getting the full impact of your page.

To install browser plug-ins

1. If PageMill is running, choose File > Quit (Mac OS) or File > Exit (Windows).

2. Copy the plug-in to PageMill's Browser Plug-ins folder:

   ◆ On Mac OS, use the Finder to copy the plug-in file to the Browser Plug-ins folder in the Adobe PageMill® 3.0 folder (**Figure 3a**).

   ◆ On Windows, use Windows Explorer to copy the plug-in file to the Browser Plug-ins folder in the PageMill 3.0 folder (**Figure 3b**).

3. Restart PageMill.

✔ Tip

- You should also make sure the plug-in file is properly installed for the browsers you use to access the Web and test the pages you create with PageMill. Consult the documentation that came with your browser for details.

Inserting Objects

PageMill offers several ways to insert object files into PageMill documents:

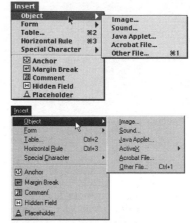

- Use one of the commands on the Object submenu under the Insert menu (**Figures 4a** and **4b**) or click the Insert Object button on the toolbar. These methods will work with any type of object you want to insert in a PageMill document.

- Use the Copy (or Cut) and Paste commands. This method is handy when inserting objects from other windows.

- Use drag-and-drop editing to drag an object from another document window or the Pasteboard. This method is also handy when inserting objects from other windows. In order for this method to work, however, the application in which the object resides must support drag-and-drop editing.

Figures 4a & 4b. The Object submenu under the Insert menu on Mac OS (top) and Windows (bottom).

✔ Tips

- Not all methods work with all types of multimedia objects. When in doubt, use the commands under the Object submenu (**Figures 4a** and **4b**) since they recognize all types of objects.

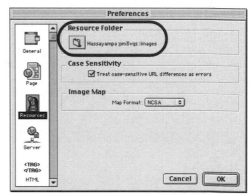

- When you insert an object into a PageMill document, PageMill automatically writes HTML code to indicate the image size. This can speed up the loading of the page when viewed with a Web browser.

Figures 5a & 5b. The Resources Preferences on Mac OS (above) and Windows (below). The Resource Folder determines where images and multimedia objects are stored.

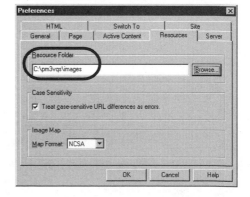

- Before adding object files to your Web pages, you should properly set Resources Preferences (**Figures 5a** and **5b**). Neglecting this simple step can cause errors in the pathnames to object files written in the PageMill Web page document. I tell you about preferences in **Chapter 11**.

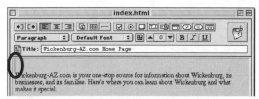

Figure 6. Position the insertion point where you want the object to appear.

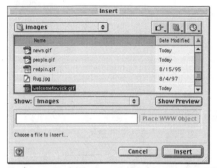

Figures 7a & 7b. The Insert dialog box on Mac OS (above) and Insert Object dialog box on Windows (below).

Figure 8. An inserted image.

Figures 9a & 9b. The Show menu on Mac OS (left) and the Files of type menu on Windows (right).

To insert an object

1. Position the insertion point where you want the object to appear (**Figure 6**).

2. Choose the appropriate option from the Object submenu under the Insert menu (**Figures 4a** and **4b**).

   or

   Click the Insert Object button on the button bar.

   or

   Press ⌘1 (Mac OS) or Ctrl 1 (Windows).

3. Use the Insert (Mac OS; **Figure 7a**) or Insert Object (Windows; **Figure 7b**) dialog box that appears to locate and select the file containing the object you want to insert.

4. Click the Insert (Mac OS) or Place (Windows) button.

The object in the file you selected appears in the PageMill window (**Figure 8**).

✔ Tips

- To specify which types of files should appear in the Insert (Mac OS; **Figure 7a**) or Insert Object (Windows; **Figure 7b**) dialog box, choose a specific file type from the Show (Mac OS; **Figure 9a**) or Files of type (Windows; **Figure 9b**) menu.

- If the file you insert is a PICT or BMP file, PageMill automatically converts it to GIF format and saves it in the Resource Folder set in the Preferences dialog box (**Figures 5a** and **5b**). Converted files have the name *Imagen.gif*, where *n* is a number.

INSERTING OBJECTS

To insert an object that resides on another Web server

1. Position the insertion point where you want the object to appear (**Figure 6**).

2. Choose the appropriate option from the Object submenu under the Insert menu (**Figures 4a** and **4b**).

   or

   Click the Insert Object button on the button bar.

   or

   Press ⌃ ⌘ 1 (Mac OS) or Ctrl 1 (Windows).

3. In the box at the bottom of the Insert (Mac OS; **Figure 7a**) or Insert Object (Windows; **Figure 7b**) dialog box that appears, enter the complete URL for the object you want to insert (**Figures 10a** and **10b**). On Windows, a check mark automatically appears in the Remote URL check box.

4. Click the Place WWW Object button (Mac OS) or Place button (Windows).

A placeholder for the object appears in the document window (**Figure 11**). If the URL was entered correctly, the actual object will appear when viewed with a Web browser.

✔ Tips

- By using a reference to an object on a remote server, it's possible to include objects in your Web pages without maintaining them on your own server. This can save disk space—especially when the objects are large.

- I tell you more about URLs in **Chapter 6**.

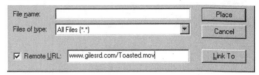

Figures 10a & 10b. Enter the URL for the object you want to insert at the bottom of the Insert dialog box on Mac OS (above) or Insert Object dialog box on Windows (below).

Figure 11. A placeholder for the object appears on the page.

Figure 12.
An image selected in a Photoshop LE window.

Figure 13.
Choosing Copy from the Edit menu in Photoshop LE.

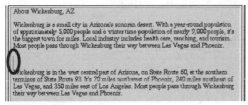

Figure 14. Position the insertion point where you want the copied object to appear.

Figure 15.
Choose Paste from PageMill's Edit menu.

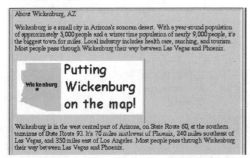

Figure 16. The copied graphic is inserted in the PageMill document.

To insert an object with the Copy & Paste commands

1. Open the document containing the object you want to use.

2. Select the object you want to copy (**Figure 12**).

3. Choose Edit > Copy (**Figure 13**) or press ⌘C (Mac OS) or Ctrl C (Windows) to copy the object.

4. Open or activate the PageMill document in which you want to insert the object.

5. Position the insertion point where you want the copied object to appear (**Figure 14**).

6. Choose Edit > Paste (**Figure 15**) or press ⌘V (Mac OS) or Ctrl V (Windows) to paste a copy of the object into the PageMill document (**Figure 16**).

✔ Tips

- You can use this method to copy and paste objects between PageMill windows or, as the figures on this page illustrate, between PageMill and another program's windows.

- To select an object in another program's window, consult the documentation that came with that program. I explain how to select objects in a PageMill window later in this chapter.

To insert an object by dragging

1. Open the document containing the object you want to use.

2. Open the PageMill document in which you plan to use the object.

3. Arrange the windows so you can see their contents (**Figure 17**).

4. Activate the window containing the object you want to use.

5. Select the object you want to copy (**Figure 18**).

6. Position the mouse pointer within the selected image. (If the image has selection handles, don't position the mouse pointer on any of them.)

7. Press the mouse button down and drag the object from its window to the PageMill document window. As you drag, an insertion point indicates where the object will go when you release the mouse button. On Mac OS, the outline of the object also appears in the PageMill window; on Windows, a plus sign appears beside the mouse pointer (**Figure 19**).

8. When the insertion point is in the proper position, release the mouse button. The object is copied from its source window to the PageMill document window (**Figure 20**).

✔ Tips

- For this to work, the application in which the object resides must support drag-and-drop editing.

- You can use this method to drag and drop objects between PageMill windows or, as the figures on this page illustrate, between PageMill and another program's windows.

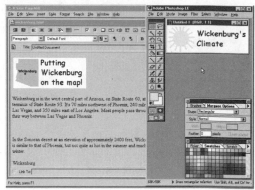

Figure 17. Arrange the windows so you can see their contents.

Figure 18. A selected Photoshop LE image.

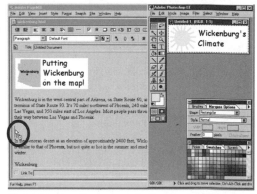

Figure 19. Drag the image into the PageMill document window.

Figure 20. When you release the mouse button, the image appears in the PageMill document.

INSERTING OBJECTS BY DRAGGING

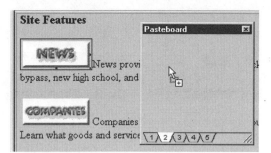

Figure 21. Drag an object in a PageMill window onto the Pasteboard.

Figure 22.
The object appears on the Pasteboard.

Figure 23.
Each Pasteboard page can hold more than just one item.

To copy an object to the Pasteboard

1. If necessary, display the Pasteboard and switch to the page where you want to copy the object.

2. Use the drag-and-drop techniques discussed on the previous page to drag an object from a PageMill document window to the Pasteboard window. As you drag, on Mac OS the outline of the object will move with the mouse pointer; on Windows, a plug sign appears beside the mouse pointer (**Figure 21**).

A copy of the object is placed on the Pasteboard (**Figure 22**).

✔ Tips

■ Although the Pasteboard has only five pages, you can copy more than one item to each page (**Figure 23**). You can resize the Pasteboard to make it bigger, too.

■ I tell you more about working with the Pasteboard in **Chapters 1** and **2**.

To insert an object from the Pasteboard

1. Position the mouse pointer on the Pasteboard item you want to use (**Figure 23**).

2. Use the drag-and-drop techniques discussed on the previous page:

   ◆ To move the item off the Pasteboard and into the document window, simply drag it.

   ◆ To copy the item from the Pasteboard to the document window, hold down Option (Mac OS) or Ctrl (Windows) while dragging it.

✔ Tip

■ Dragging an item off the Pasteboard is the only way to remove it from the Pasteboard.

The Missing-Image Icon

If PageMill cannot locate the file for an object on a page, it displays a missing-image icon (**Figure 24**). This can occur if you rename, move, or delete an image referred to by a PageMill document.

✔ Tips

■ One way to avoid seeing missing-image icons is to make sure all objects you insert in a PageMill document are within the Resources folder you specified in the Preferences dialog box (**Figures 5a** and **5b**). I tell you about setting preferences in **Chapter 11**.

■ If you insert an object that resides on another server (as discussed earlier in this chapter), an icon will appear instead of the object when the page is viewed within PageMill (**Figure 11**). If the object does not appear when you test the page, you'll need to resolve the missing object problem before you can publish the page. I tell you about testing in **Chapter 9**.

To find a missing object

1. Double-click the missing-image icon.

2. Use the Insert (Mac OS; **Figure 7a**) or Insert Object (Windows; **Figure 7b**) dialog box that appears to locate and select the object that's missing.

3. Click the Open (Mac OS) or Place (Windows) button to reinsert the image in the document.

To delete a missing-image icon

1. Click the missing-image icon once to select the image placeholder.

2. Press `Del`, `Delete` (Mac OS only) or `Backspace` (Windows only) to remove the icon and its placeholder.

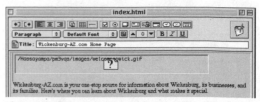

Figure 24. The missing-image icon appears when an image cannot be found.

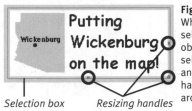

Selection box   Resizing handles

Figure 25. When you select an object, a selection box and resizing handles appear around it.

Selecting Objects

To modify, copy, move, or delete an object in a PageMill document, you must begin by selecting it.

To select an object

Click once on the object you want to select.

A selection box appears around the object and three resizing handles appear (**Figure 25**).

✔ Tip

■   You can only select one object at a time.

To deselect an object

Click inside the document window anywhere other than on the selected object.

The selection box and handles disappear.

Copying, Moving, & Deleting Objects

Like text, once an object is in a PageMill document, it can be moved or copied a number of different ways:

◆ The Edit menu's Copy and Paste commands (**Figures 26a** and **26b**) let you copy an object from one place and paste it in another.

◆ The Edit menu's Cut and Paste commands (**Figures 26a** and **26b**) let you cut an object from one place and paste it in another, thus moving the original object.

◆ Drag-and-drop editing lets you move or copy a selected object simply by dragging it.

◆ The Pasteboard (**Figures 22** and **23**) lets you store objects that you can drag into a document window.

I discuss the first three techniques for text in **Chapter 2**. They work the same way for objects. I discuss using the Pasteboard for objects earlier in this chapter.

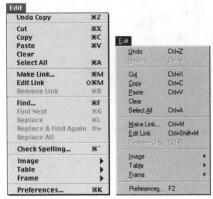

Figures 26a & 26b. The Edit menu on Mac OS (left) and Windows (right).

To delete an object

1. Select the object you want to delete.

2. Press ⌐Del⌐, ⌐Delete⌐ (Mac OS only) or ⌐Backspace⌐ (Windows only).

    or

    Choose Edit > Clear (**Figures 26a** and **26b**).

The object disappears.

✔ Tip

■ When you delete an object, its file remains on disk, even if it is an image file that was saved into the Resources folder by PageMill. I tell you about the Resources folder earlier in this chapter and in **Chapter 11**.

COPYING, MOVING, & DELETING OBJECTS

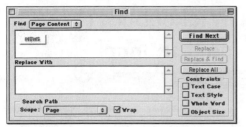

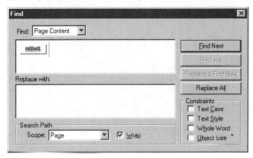

Figures 27a & 27b. The Find dialog box on Mac OS (above) and Windows (below).

Finding & Replacing Objects

PageMill's find and replace features can be used to locate and/or change objects throughout a document. You use the Find dialog box (**Figures 27a** and **27b**) to set your find and, if applicable, replacement objects. Then use buttons within the Find dialog box or on the Search menu to locate and/or replace objects as specified.

I discuss the find and replace features in detail in **Chapter 2**. They work the same way for objects, with the following exceptions:

◆ To enter a search object in the Find or Replace With boxes (**Figures 27a** and **27b**):

▲ Use the Edit menu's Copy and Paste commands (**Figures 26a** and **26b**) to copy the image and then paste it into the appropriate box.

▲ Drag the object from a document window into the appropriate box.

◆ To find only those objects that match the size of the object in the Find box, turn on the Object Size check box in the lower-right corner of the Find window (**Figures 27a** and **27b**).

✔ Tip

■ To delete an object throughout a document, leave the Replace With scrolling window empty. Then replace every occurrence of the object with nothing, thus deleting it.

Resizing Objects

Once an object has been inserted in a PageMill document, it can be resized as needed by either dragging its resizing handles or using the Inspector.

✔ Tips

- Although you can make an object larger or smaller, you may find that images lose their clarity when enlarged.

- Reducing the size of an object within PageMill does not reduce its file size.

To resize an object by dragging

1. Select the object you want to resize.

2. Position the mouse pointer over one of the object's resizing handles (**Figure 28**):

   ◆ To change the object's width, position the mouse pointer over the handle on the right side of the object.

   ◆ To change the object's height, position the mouse pointer over the handle on the bottom of the object.

   ◆ To change the object's width and height, position the mouse pointer over the handle in the bottom-right corner of the object.

3. Press the mouse button down and drag. As you drag, an outline indicates the size of the object when you release the mouse button (**Figure 29**).

4. Release the mouse button. The object resizes (**Figure 30**).

✔ Tip

- To change both the width and height of an object without changing its proportions, hold down (Shift) while dragging the bottom right resizing handle as instructed above. Release the mouse button first, then release (Shift).

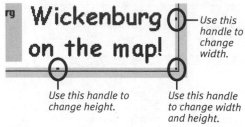

Figure 28. Choose a resizing handle based on the way you want to resize the object.

Use this handle to change width.

Use this handle to change height.

Use this handle to change width and height.

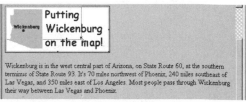

Figure 29. As you drag, an outline indicates the final size of the object.

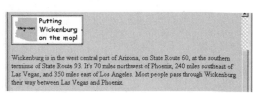

Figure 30. When you release the mouse button, the object resizes.

Figure 31.
The Object panel of the Inspector with an image selected.

Figures 32a & 32b.
This menu appears beside the Width and Height edit boxes on Mac OS (top) and Windows (bottom), enabling you to specify a measurement in pixels or as a percentage of the page width or height.

Figure 33.
This example shows how an object can be resized proportionally by turning on only the Scale to Width check box and entering a new value in the Width edit box.

To resize an object with the Inspector

1. Select the object you want to resize.
2. If necessary, display the Inspector and its Object panel (**Figure 31**).
3. To change the width or height to an exact pixel measurement or percentage of the window's size, make sure the Scale to Height and Scale to Width check boxes are turned off. Then choose Pixels or Percent from the Width and Height menus (**Figures 32a** and **32b**) and enter values in the Width and Height boxes.

   or

   To resize an object proportionally, turn on either the Scale to Height or Scale to Width check box. Then choose Pixels or Percent from the opposite menu (**Figures 32a** and **32b**) and enter a value in the box beside it (**Figure 33**).
4. Press ⌐Return⌐ (Mac OS) or ⌐Enter⌐ (Windows) to accept your settings.

✔ Tips

- To reset an object to its original size, turn on both the Scale to Height and Scale to Width check boxes in the Object panel of the Inspector (**Figure 31**).
- Make sure the Behavior radio button is set to Picture unless the object will be used as a button or an image map. I tell you about buttons in **Chapter 8** and about image maps in **Chapter 6**.

Object Alignment

Objects can be aligned two ways:

◆ Align an object vertically to adjust its position in relation to the top or baseline of the text around it. This is effective when the image is in the same line as text (**Figures 34**, **36**, and **37**).

◆ Align an object horizontally to adjust its position in relation to the edges of the Web page. This is effective when wrapping text around an object (**Figures 38** and **39**).

✔ Tips

■ By default, object alignment is set to bottom aligned (**Figure 34**).

■ You can also use text alignment to horizontally align an object in a paragraph by itself between the window's right and left sides. I cover text alignment in **Chapter 3**.

To align an object vertically

1. Select the object you want to align (**Figure 34**).

2. Choose a command from the Align Object submenu under the Format menu (**Figures 35a** and **35b**) or click a toolbar button:

   ◆ To align the top of the object with the top of the text (**Figure 36**), choose Format > Align Object > Top or click the Top Align Object button.

   ◆ To align the middle of the object with the middle of the text (**Figure 37**), choose Format > Align Object > Middle or click the Middle Align Object button.

   ◆ To align the bottom of the object with the bottom of the text (**Figure 34**), choose Format > Align Object > Bottom or click the Bottom Align Object button.

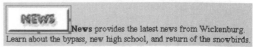

Figure 34. Begin by selecting the object you want to align. By default, objects are bottom aligned, as shown here.

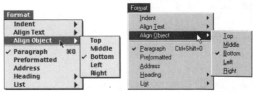

Figures 35a & 35b. The Align Object submenu under the Format menu on Mac OS (left) and Windows (right).

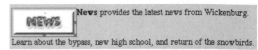

Figure 36. Top aligned aligns the top of the object with the top of the text.

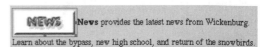

Figure 37. Middle aligned aligns the middle of the object with the middle of the text.

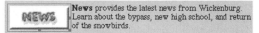

News provides the latest news from Wickenburg. Learn about the bypass, new high school, and return of the snowbirds.

Figure 38. Left aligned moves the object to the left and wraps text around it.

Nèws provides the latest news from Wickenburg. Learn about the bypass, new high school, and return of the snowbirds.

Figure 39. Right aligned moves the object to the right and wraps text around it.

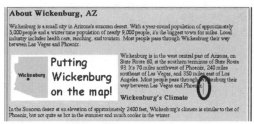

Figure 40. To stop word wrap, begin by positioning the insertion point where you want word wrap to end.

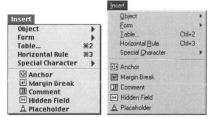

Figures 41a & 41b. The Insert menu on Mac OS (left) and Windows (right).

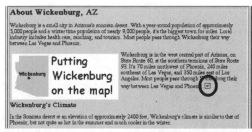

Figure 42. Word wrap ends at the margin break.

To align an object horizontally

1. Select the object you want to align (**Figure 34**).

2. Choose a command from the Align Object submenu under the Format menu (**Figures 35a and 35b**) or click a toolbar button:

   ◆ To shift the object to the left side of the window and wrap the text beside the object around the object's right side (**Figure 38**), choose Format > Align Object > Left or click the Left Align Object button.

   ◆ To shift the object to the right side of the window and wrap the text beside the object around the object's left side (**Figure 39**), choose Format > Align Object > Right or click the Right Align Object button.

To end word wrap around a horizontally aligned object

1. Position the insertion point where you want the word wrap to end (**Figure 40**).

2. Choose Insert > Margin Break (**Figures 41a and 41b**).

A margin break character is inserted and the word wrap ends (**Figure 42**).

✔ Tip

■ A margin break character can be deleted like any other character or object—by selecting it and pressing Del , Delete (Mac OS only), or Backspace (Windows only).

The Image Window

The Image window (**Figures 43a** and **43b**) gives you access to several image features:

◆ Make a certain color within the image transparent so the background shows through it.

◆ Create an image map so that clicking a "hot spot" in the image displays another page. I tell you more about image maps in **Chapter 6**.

◆ Save an image as an *interlaced GIF*, which loads into a Web browser quickly as a blurred image, then progressively clears. This is especially useful for large images that could take more than a few seconds to load.

To open the Image window

1. Select the image you want to open.

2. Choose Edit > Image > Open Image Window (**Figures 44a** and **44b**) or press ⌘ D (Mac OS) or Ctrl D (Windows).

or

1. Double-click the image you want to open.

2. Click the Open Image Window button on the toolbar.

or

Hold down ⌘ (Mac OS) or Ctrl (Windows) while double-clicking the image you want to open.

The image opens in the Image window (**Figures 43a** and **43b**).

✔ Tips

■ The image you want to open must be visible in a PageMill document window before you can open it in an Image window using one of the techniques here.

■ You can also open an image in the Image window by using the Open command and Open dialog box. I explain how to open documents in **Chapter 1**.

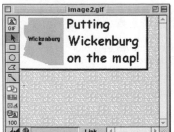

Figures 43a & 43b. The Image window on Mac OS (left) and Windows (below).

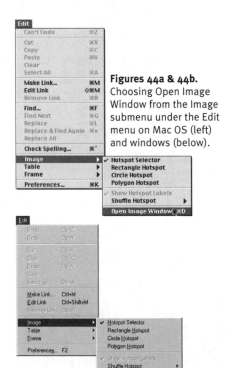

Figures 44a & 44b. Choosing Open Image Window from the Image submenu under the Edit menu on Mac OS (left) and windows (below).

OPENING THE IMAGE WINDOW

Figure 45. When you click the Make Transparent button, the mouse pointer turns into a Make Transparent tool.

Figure 46. When you click a color—in this case, the white background color—it becomes transparent.

Figures 47a & 47b. Choosing Save Image from the File menu on Mac OS (left) and Windows (right).

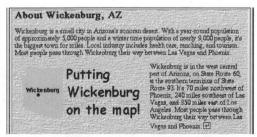

Figure 48. When the background for an image is made transparent as shown here, the page's background color or pattern shows through.

To make an image color transparent

1. In the Image window, click the Make Transparent button. The mouse pointer, when moved on top of the image, changes to a Make Transparent tool (**Figure 45**).

2. On the image, click any color you want to make transparent. The image changes so you can see the Image window background through the color you made transparent (**Figure 46**).

3. Choose File > Save Image (**Figures 47a** and **47b**) or press ⌘S (Mac OS) or Ctrl S (Windows).

✔ Tips

- The Make Transparent button is available only for GIF format images.

- PageMill can make only one color transparent at a time.

- When you make a color transparent, the transparency information is saved with the image file so it is transparent on every page in which it is used.

- To restore the transparent color, use the Make Transparent tool to click the transparent area. The color returns.

- Anti-aliased images do not work well with the transparency feature. For best results, turn the anti-alias feature in your graphic application off when creating or editing images for use on Web pages.

- Use the Make Transparent tool to make the background color of an image transparent. This greatly improves the appearance of an image with a large background (**Figure 48**).

- You can combine transparent image backgrounds with page backgrounds to give your pages professional polish (**Figure 48**). I tell you about page backgrounds in **Chapter 3**.

To create an interlaced GIF or progressive JPEG

1. In the Image window, click the Interlace button.

2. Choose File > Save Image (**Figures 47a** and **47b**) or press ⌥ ⌘ S (Mac OS) or Ctrl S (Windows).

✔ Tips

- The Interlace button appears for both GIF images (to create interlaced GIFs) and JPEG images (to create progressive JPEGs).

- You can tell whether the interlacing feature is turned on for an image by looking at the Interlace button in the Image window. On Mac OS, horizontal lines appear across the button's icon (**Figure 49a**) when the feature is enabled. On Windows, the button appears "pushed in" (**Figure 49b**) when the feature is enabled.

- To remove the interlacing feature, click the Interlace button again.

- Interlaced GIFs and progressive JPEGs are good for large images that could take more than a few seconds to load. The entire image loads as a blurred image that progressively clears until it is completely loaded.

To close the Image window

Choose File > Close or press ⌥ ⌘ W (Mac OS) or Ctrl W (Windows).

or

Click the Image window's close box (Mac OS) or close button (Windows).

✔ Tip

- If you don't save changes before closing the Image window, a dialog box like the one in **Figure 50a** or **50b** will appear. Click Save (Mac OS) or Yes (Windows) to save changes before closing the window.

Figures 49a & 49b.
The appearance of the Interlace button changes when it is enabled. Here's what it looks like on Mac OS (left) and Windows (right).

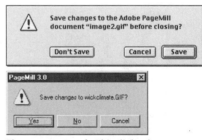

Figures 50a & 50b. This dialog box appears on Mac OS (top) and Windows (bottom) when you close the Image window without saving changes.

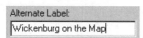

Figure 51. When you specify alternate text for an image,...

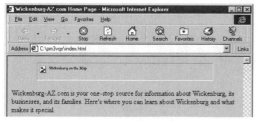

Figure 52. ...the text appears when the image is not displayed.

Figure 53. When you set the border thickness greater than 0 (zero),...

Figure 54. ...a border appears around the image.

Other Object Options

The Inspector enables you to change other options for objects:

◆ For images, specify alternate text (**Figure 52**) and border thickness (**Figure 54**).

◆ For Java applets, specify parameters and other settings.

To specify image alternate text

1. Select the image for which you want to specify alternate text.

2. If necessary, display the Inspector and its Object panel (**Figure 31**).

3. Click in the Alternate Label box to activate it and enter the text you want to appear (**Figure 51**).

4. Press (Return) (Mac OS) or (Enter) (Windows) to complete the entry.

✔ Tip

■ Some Web surfers turn off images to speed page loading. Alternate text can let these people know what they're missing.

To set image border thickness

1. Select the image for which you want to set the border thickness.

2. If necessary, display the Inspector and its Object panel (**Figure 31**).

3. Click in the Border box to activate it and enter a value, in pixels, for the thickness of the border (**Figure 53**).

4. Press (Return) (Mac OS) or (Enter) (Windows) to complete the entry.

✔ Tip

■ If you enter 0 in the Border box, no border appears—even if the image is used as a link. I tell you about links in **Chapter 6**.

SETTING OTHER IMAGE OPTIONS

To specify Java applet options

1. Select the placeholder for the Java applet for which you want to specify options (**Figure 55**).

2. If necessary, display the Inspector and its Object panel (**Figures 56a and 56b**).

3. For each parameter you want to set, enter a parameter name and corresponding value in the Name and Value boxes. Each time you add a name/value pair, a new line appears for another name/value pair. When you're finished entering parameter information, the Inspector might look something like **Figure 57**.

4. To pause operation of an applet, turn on the Suspend check box.

5. To restart an applet after making changes, click the Reload button.

6. Press ⟨Return⟩ (Mac OS) or ⟨Enter⟩ (Windows) to complete the entry.

✔ Tips

■ A Java applet is a small, cross-platform program that can be inserted in a Web page and run from within a Web browser.

■ To learn what parameters must be set for the applet you want to use, check the documentation that came with the applet.

■ You can also resize a Java applet by either dragging its resize handles or entering new measurements in the Inspector (**Figures 56a** and **56b**).

■ You can customize the way Java applets work within PageMill by setting options in the Preferences dialog box. I explain how in **Chapter 11**.

Figure 55.
A selected Java applet placeholder on Mac OS. On Windows, the placeholder looks like a plain white box.

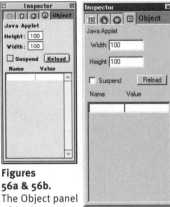

Figures 56a & 56b.
The Object panel of the Inspector with a Java applet selected on Mac OS (left) and Windows (right).

Figure 57.
After entering parameters in the Inspector, it might look something like this.

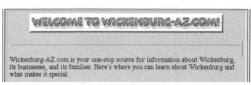

Figure 58. Position the insertion point where you want the horizontal rule to appear.

Figure 59. The horizontal rule appears at the insertion point.

Figure 60. When you select a horizontal rule, you'll see the same selection box and resizing handles that appear when you select any other object.

Horizontal Rules

A *horizontal rule* is a graphic element that is created with HTML tags. Its HTML code is interpreted by the Web browser and displayed as a horizontal line. No special graphic file is required.

✔ Tips

■ A horizontal rule is an excellent graphic tool because it loads just as quickly as text and does not require additional files to display.

■ You can use the text alignment buttons to left align, center align, or right align a horizontal rule.

To insert a horizontal rule

1. Position the insertion point where you want the horizontal rule to appear (**Figure 58**).

2. Choose Insert > Horizontal Rule (**Figures 41a** and **41b**) or press ⌘⌘3 (Mac OS) or Ctrl 3 (Windows).

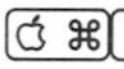

    or

    Click the Insert Horizontal Rule button on the toolbar.

The horizontal rule appears (**Figure 59**).

To remove a horizontal rule

1. Click the horizontal rule to select it. A selection box and resizing handles appear (**Figure 60**).

    or

    Position the insertion point immediately to the right of the horizontal rule (**Figure 59**).

2. Press Del , Delete (Mac OS Only), or Backspace (Windows only).

The horizontal rule disappears.

To resize a horizontal rule by dragging

1. Select the horizontal rule (**Figure 60**).
2. Drag a resizing handle to change the length (**Figure 61**) or thickness or both. When you release the mouse button, the size changes (**Figure 62**).

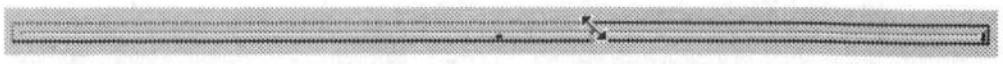

✔ Tip

■ You cannot make a horizontal rule's length exceed the page width by dragging a resizing handle.

To format a horizontal rule with the Inspector

1. Select the horizontal rule (**Figure 60**).
2. If necessary, display the Inspector and its Object panel (**Figures 63a and 63b**).
3. To change the width of the line, choose Pixels or Percent from the Width menu (**Figures 32a** and **32b**). Then enter a width value in the Width box.
4. Enter a thickness, in pixels, in the Size box.
5. Press ⸢Return⸣ (Mac OS) or ⸢Enter⸣ (Windows) to complete the entry.

Figure 64 shows an example of a 10-pixel thick, 60% wide horizontal rule.

✔ Tip

■ You can turn on the No Shade check box in the Inspector to remove the three-dimensional shadow effect from a horizontal rule. **Figure 65** shows the horizontal rule from **Figure 64** with the No Shade check box turned on.

Figure 61. Drag a resizing handle to change the size of a horizontal rule.

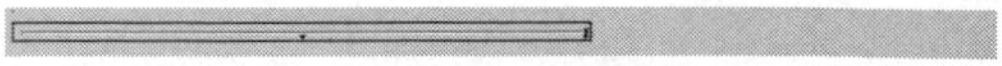

Figure 62. When you release the mouse button, the horizontal rule's size changes.

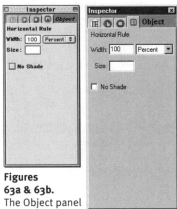

Figures 63a & 63b. The Object panel of the Inspector for a horizontal rule on Mac OS (left) and Windows (right).

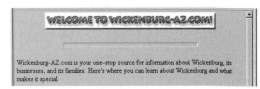

Figure 64. Here's a short, thick horizontal rule.

Figure 65. When you turn on the No Shade check box, the three-dimensional shadow effect is removed, leaving a gray (Windows) or black (Mac OS) line.

FORMATTING HORIZONTAL RULES

CREATING & EDITING TABLES

Figure 1.
A basic table like this one can present information in a spreadsheet-like format.

Figure 2.
Tables can also be used to recreate familiar objects, like this calendar.

Figure 3.
With a little imagination—and some borderless nested tables like these—you can lay out page components any way you like.

HTML Tables

HTML tables offer unsurpassed control over the positioning of text and objects on Web pages. You can create tables comprised of columns and rows and fill in the intersecting cells with text and graphic elements for a wide range of effects:

- Create simple tables to present data in a spreadsheet-like format (**Figure 1**).

- Create more complex tables to reproduce information in familiar formats (**Figure 2**).

- Use tables to lay out page components much as you would with a page layout application (**Figure 3**).

Creating tables—even complex nested tables—is easy with PageMill. This chapter will show you how.

✔ Tip

- Although today's graphic Web browsers recognize and properly interpret HTML codes for tables, some older browsers don't. In addition, no text browser displays table information properly. Keep this in mind when determining how to present information that may be viewed with a variety of browsers. You may prefer using Preformatted format, which I discuss in **Chapter 4**.

Creating Tables

PageMill offers three ways to create tables:

◆ Use the Insert Table button on the toolbar (**Figure 4**) to insert a table with the desired number of columns and rows.

◆ Use the Create Table (Mac OS; **Figure 5a**) or Insert Table (Windows; **Figure 5b**) dialog box to insert a table with the size and some of the formatting options desired.

◆ Paste in worksheet cells from a Microsoft Excel document (**Figure 9**) to insert a table with the number of columns and rows and all the table data desired (**Figure 12**).

✔ Tips

■ If you accidentally create a table with the wrong dimensions, use the Undo command to remove the table and then try again.

■ You can always add or remove columns or rows to a table after it has been created. I tell you how later in this chapter.

■ By default, all columns in a table are the same width. I tell you how to change column width later in this chapter.

■ You can insert a table within a table. Simply position the insertion point within a table cell before inserting a table.

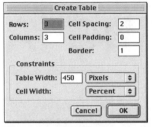

Figure 4.
As you drag away from the Insert Table button, a menu grows.

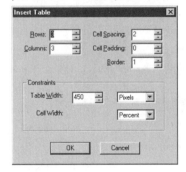

Figures 5a & 5b. When you create a table with the Create Table (Mac OS; above) or Insert Table (Windows; below) dialog box, you can set more than just the table's size.

CREATING TABLES

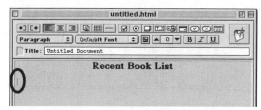

Figure 6. Begin by positioning the insertion point where you want the table to appear.

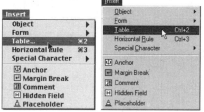

Figure 7. The table appears at the insertion point.

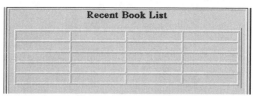

Figures 8a & 8b. Choosing Table from the Insert menu on Mac OS (left) and Windows (right).

To insert a table with the Insert Table button

1. Position the insertion point where you want the table to appear (**Figure 6**).

2. Position your mouse pointer on the Insert Table button, press the mouse button down, and drag down and to the right. A menu pops up and expands as you drag (**Figure 4**).

3. When the desired number of columns and rows is indicated by the Insert Table menu, release the mouse button.

The table appears (**Figure 7**).

To insert a table with the Create Table or Insert Table dialog box

1. Position the insertion point where you want the table to appear (**Figure 6**).

2. Choose Insert > Table (**Figures 8a** and **8b**) or press ⌘②(Mac OS) or Ctrl②(Windows).

   or

   Click the Insert Table button on the toolbar.

   The Create Table (Mac OS; **Figure 5a**) or Insert Table (Windows; **Figure 5b**) dialog box appears.

3. Enter the number of rows and columns desired in the Rows and Columns boxes.

4. If desired, enter values for table formatting options in the appropriate boxes.

5. Click OK.

The table appears (**Figure 7**).

✔ Tip

- I tell you about table formatting options like those in the Create Table (Mac OS; **Figure 5a**) or Insert Table (Windows; **Figure 5b**) dialog box later in this chapter.

INSERTING A TABLE

To insert Excel worksheet cells as a table

1. In an Excel worksheet document, select the cells you want to turn into a PageMill table (**Figure 9**).

2. Choose Edit > Copy (**Figure 10**) or press ⌃ ⌘ C (Mac OS) or Ctrl C (Windows).

3. Switch to or open the PageMill document in which you want to paste the Excel cells.

4. Position the insertion point where you want the table to appear.

5. Choose Edit > Paste (**Figure 11**) or press ⌃ ⌘ V (Mac OS) or Ctrl V (Windows).

The table appears (**Figure 12**).

✔ Tips

■ If you often use Excel to calculate or store information that may be used in Web pages, this is the easiest way to include that information in PageMill documents.

■ Some types of cell formatting are not carried forward from the Excel document to the PageMill document. Check the resulting PageMill table carefully to make sure number, date, and time formatting is correct.

■ You can also use drag-and-drop editing to drag selected worksheet cells from the Excel document window into the PageMill document window. I tell you more about both the Copy and Paste commands and drag-and-drop editing in **Chapter 2**.

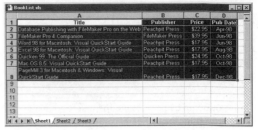

Figure 9. In an Excel worksheet, select the cells you want to use in a PageMill document.

Figure 10. Choose Copy from Excel's Edit menu to copy the selected cells.

Figure 11. Choose Paste from PageMill's Edit menu to paste the cells into the PageMill document.

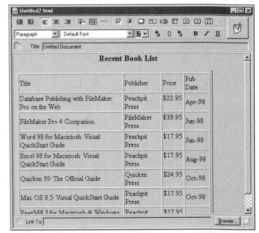

Figure 12. The Excel cells appear as a PageMill table at the insertion point.

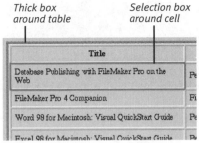

Figure 13. To select a single cell, click in the cell, then drag to the cell's border. Here's how it looks on Mac OS.

Thick box around table   Selection box around cells

Title	Publisher	P
Database Publishing with FileMaker Pro on the Web	Peachpit Press	$2:
FileMaker Pro 4 Companion	FileMaker Press	$3!
Word 98 for Macintosh: Visual QuickStart Guide	Peachpit Press	$1'
Excel 98 for Macintosh: Visual QuickStart Guide	Peachpit Press	$1'
Quicken 99: The Official Guide	Quicken Press	$2.

Figure 14. To select multiple cells, click in the first cell, then drag to the border of the last cell. Here's how it looks on Windows.

Selection box around entire table

Title	Publisher	Price	Pub Date
Database Publishing with FileMaker Pro on the Web	Peachpit Press	$22.99	04/98
FileMaker Pro 4 Companion	FileMaker Press	$39.95	09/98
Word 98 for Macintosh: Visual QuickStart Guide	Peachpit Press	$17.95	09/98
Excel 98 for Macintosh: Visual QuickStart Guide	Peachpit Press	$17.95	08/98
Quicken 99: The Official Guide	Quicken Press	$24.95	10/98
Mac OS 8.5: Visual QuickStart Guide	Peachpit Press	$17.95	10/98
PageMill 3 for Macintosh & Windows: Visual QuickStart Guide	Peachpit Press	$17.95	12/98

Figure 15. To select an entire table, click once in the table to display its thick border, then click on the thick border.

Selecting Cells & Tables

To make changes to the structure or formatting of a table or its cells, you must first select the table or cells you want to change.

To select a cell

1. Click once within the cell to position the insertion point inside it. A thick box appears around the entire table.

2. Press the mouse button down and drag to the border of the cell. A selection border appears around the cell (**Figure 13**).

✔ Tips

- When one or more cells is selected, clicking any other cell selects that cell.

- When selecting cells, be careful not to drag a selection. If you accidentally drag cells to a new position, use the Undo command to replace them.

To select multiple cells

1. Click once within the top left cell in the intended selection to position the insertion point inside it. A thick box appears around the entire table.

2. Press the mouse button down and drag to the border of the bottom right cell in the intended selection. A selection border appears around the cells (**Figure 14**).

To select an entire table

1. Click once anywhere within a table cell. A thick box appears around the entire table.

2. Click once on the thick box around the table. A thin selection box, complete with resizing handles, appears around the table (**Figure 15**).

To deselect a table or cell(s)

Click anywhere outside the table. The selection box disappears.

Entering Information into Cells

You can enter text or objects into table cells by typing, pasting, dragging, or placing it in.

✔ Tips

- Each table cell works like a tiny word processing document that expands vertically to accept what's entered into it.

- You can use standard text editing techniques to edit the contents of a cell. I tell you about editing text in **Chapter 2**.

- By default, each table cell contains a non-breaking space character. Deleting this character in an empty cell changes the appearance of the cell (**Figures 16** and **17**).

To type text into a cell

1. Click inside the cell to position the insertion point there (**Figure 18**).

2. Type the text you want to appear in the cell (**Figure 19**).

✔ Tips

- A cell's width may change depending on the length of the text you type and the contents of other cells (**Figure 20**). I tell you how to change column width manually later in this chapter.

- To begin a new line within a cell, press [Shift][Return] (Mac OS) or [Shift][Enter] (Windows). To begin a new paragraph within a cell, press [Return] (Mac OS) or [Enter] (Windows).

- Press [Tab] or [Shift][Tab] to select the contents of the next or previous cell in the table. Or hold down [Control] (Mac OS) or [Ctrl][Alt] (Windows) and press [←], [→], [↑], or [↓] to select an adjacent cell in a specific direction. This makes it possible to fill in table cells without using the mouse to click in each cell.

Figure 16. By default, each table cell has a single space character in it. This gives the appearance of empty cells.

Figure 17. As you can see by looking at the first cell in this table, removing all of a cell's contents changes the appearance of the cell.

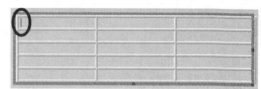

Figure 18. To type information into a cell, begin by positioning the insertion point inside it.

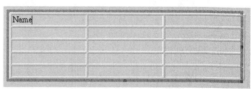

Figure 19. Then type in the information you want to appear.

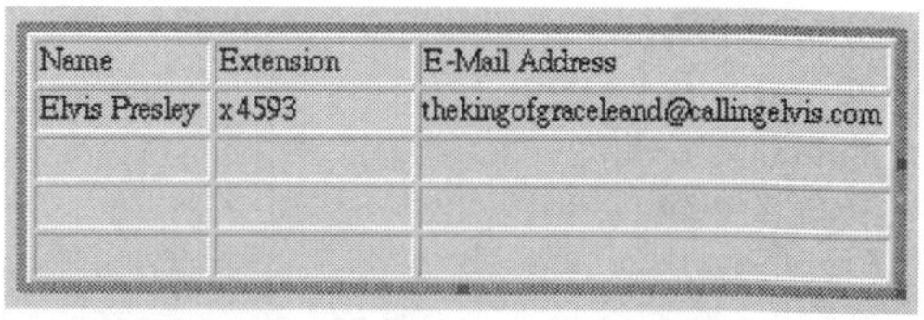

Name	Extension	E-Mail Address
Elvis Presley	x4593	thekingofgraceland@callingelvis.com

Figure 20. If the information you enter is lengthy, the width of columns in your table may change.

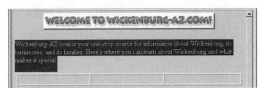

Figure 21. To paste information into a cell, begin by selecting what you want to paste in.

Figure 22. After copying or cutting the selection, position the insertion point in the cell in which you want to paste it.

Figure 23. When you use the Paste command, the text appears in the cell.

Figure 24. You can also drag selected objects or text into table cells.

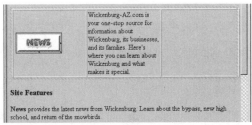

Figure 25. When you release the mouse button, the object or text appears in the cell.

To paste information into a cell

1. Select the information you want to paste into the cell (**Figure 21**).

2. Choose Edit > Copy or press ⌃ ⌘ C (Mac OS) or Ctrl C (Windows) to copy the selection.

   or

   Choose Edit > Cut or press ⌃ ⌘ X (Mac OS) or Ctrl X (Windows) to cut the selection from the document.

3. Click in the cell in which you want to paste the information to position the insertion point there (**Figure 22**).

4. Choose Edit > Paste or press ⌃ ⌘ V (Mac OS) or Ctrl V (Windows) to paste sin the copied selection (**Figure 23**).

To drag information into a cell

1. Select the information you want to drag into the cell.

2. Position your mouse pointer on the selection, press the mouse button down, and drag toward the destination cell.

3. When the insertion point appears inside the destination cell (**Figure 24**), release the mouse button. The selection appears in the cell (**Figure 25**).

✔ Tip

■ Both of the techniques on this page work with text, objects, or form elements. I tell you more about images and multimedia objects in **Chapter 4** and about form elements in **Chapter 8**.

PASTING & DRAGGING INFORMATION INTO CELLS

Modifying Table Structure

You can modify a table's structure a number of ways:

◆ Insert or delete columns or rows.

◆ Join or split cells.

◆ Place a table within a table cell to create a nested table.

◆ Delete a table.

✔ Tip

■ You can modify a table's structure before or after you have entered information into its cells.

To insert a column

1. Select the column or a cell in the column to the left of where you want the new column to go (**Figure 26**).

2. Click the Insert Column button on the toolbar.

   or

   Choose Edit > Table > Insert Column (**Figures 27a** and **27b**).

A new column appears to the right of the selected column or cell (**Figure 28**).

✔ Tips

■ If you select more than one column in step 1 above, inserting a column will insert the same number of columns you selected.

■ When you insert a column, other columns may resize and shift to the left to make room for it, depending on how table and cell size options are set. I tell you how to change table and column width later in this chapter.

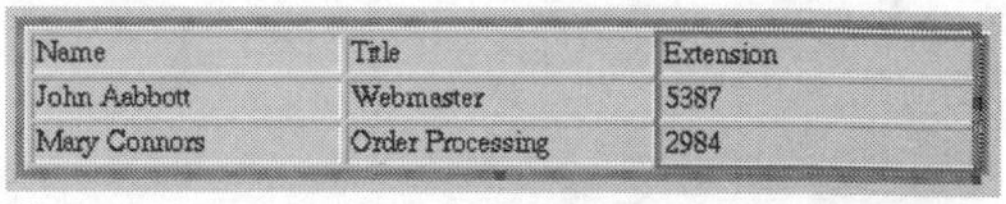

Figure 26. To insert a column, begin by selecting the column or a cell in the column to the left of where you want the new column to go. In this example, the last column is selected.

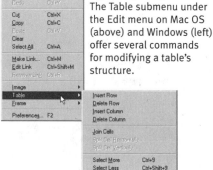

Figures 27a & 27b. The Table submenu under the Edit menu on Mac OS (above) and Windows (left) offer several commands for modifying a table's structure.

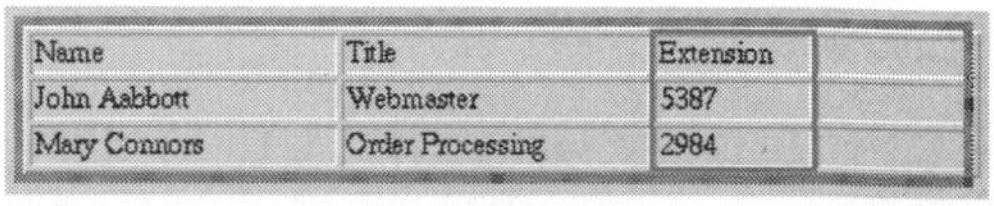

Figure 28. The new column appears to the right of the selected column.

Name	Title	Extension
John Aabbott	Webmaster	5428
Mary Connors	Order Processing	4253

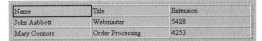

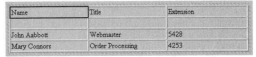

Figure 29. To insert a row, begin by selecting the row or a cell in the row above where you want the new row to go. In this example, a cell in the first row is selected.

Name	Title	Extension
John Aabbott	Webmaster	5428
Mary Connors	Order Processing	4253

Figure 30. The new row is inserted below the selected row or cell.

To insert a row

1. Select the row or a cell in the row above where you want the new row to go (**Figure 29**).
2. Click the Insert Row button on the toolbar.

   or

   Choose Edit > Table > Insert Row (**Figures 27a** and **27b**).

A new row appears beneath the selected row or cell (**Figure 30**).

✔ Tips

- If you select more than one row in step 1 above, clicking the Insert Row button will insert the same number of rows you have selected.
- When you insert a row, the rows beneath it shift down and the table resizes to make room for it.

To delete columns or rows

1. Select the column or a cell in the column you want to delete.

   or

   Select a row or a cell in the row you want to delete.
2. Click the Delete Column or Delete Row button on the toolbar.

   or

   Choose Edit > Table > Delete Column or Edit > Table > Delete Row (**Figures 27a** and **27b**).

The selected column or row is deleted.

✔ Tips

- When you delete a column or row, the column or row's contents are also deleted.
- You cannot use this method to delete all the columns or rows in a table.

To join cells

1. Select two or more cells in the same column or row (**Figure 31**).

2. Click the Join Cells button on the toolbar.

   or

   Choose Edit > Table > Join Cells (**Figures 27a** and **27b**).

The cells are joined to form one large cell (**Figure 32**).

✔ Tip

- Text or objects in cells you join appear in the joined cell. Cell contents are not lost.

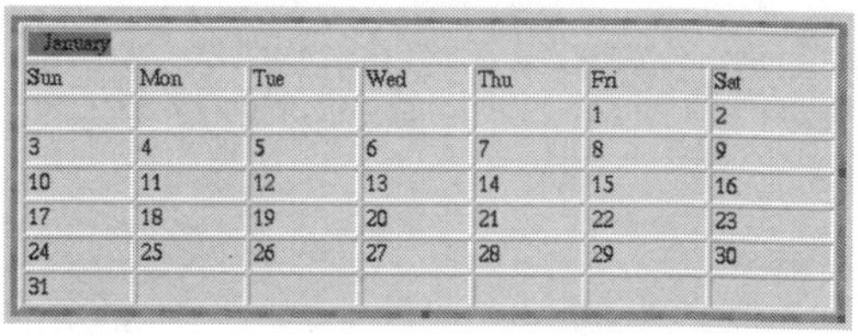

To split joined cells

1. Position the insertion point within the cell where you want the split to occur (**Figure 33**).

2. If the cells are in the same row, choose Edit > Table > Split Cell Vertically.

   or

   If the cells are in the same column, choose Edit > Table > Split Cell Horizontally.

The cell splits in the location you specified (**Figure 34**).

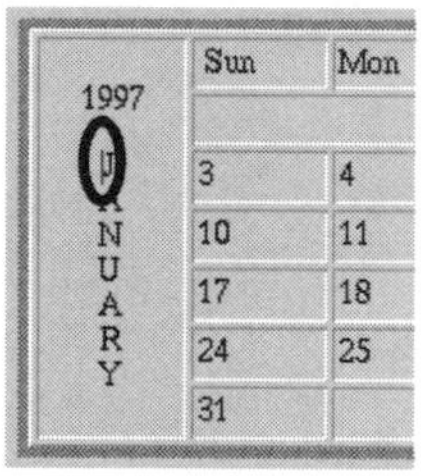

✔ Tips

- You can also split a cell by simply selecting the cell and clicking the Split Cell Vertically or Split Cell Horizontally button on the toolbar. If the cell contains text or objects, the split will occur after the cell's contents.

- You can only split cells that were previously joined. In a way, the Split Cells buttons are like "Unjoin Cells" buttons.

- The split cells feature can be tricky to use. If you split a joined cell and are disappointed by the results, use the Undo command to undo the split.

Figure 31. To join cells, begin by selecting the cells you want to join. In this example, all seven cells in the first row are selected.

Figure 32. The separate selected cells become one.

Figure 33. To split cells, begin by positioning the insertion point where you want the split to occur.

Figure 34. The cell splits at the insertion point.

JOINING & SPLITTING CELLS

Figure 35. Begin by positioning the insertion point where you want the nested table to appear.

Figure 36. The table is inserted within the cell you specified.

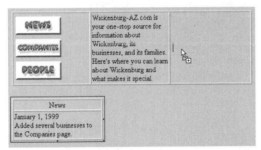

Figure 37. Another way to insert a table within a table is to simply drag it into a cell.

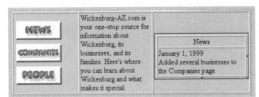

Figure 38. When you release the mouse button, the table moves into the cell. As you can see in this example, the table cell resized automatically to fit the table's width.

To create a nested table

1. Position the insertion point in the cell in which you want the nested table to appear (**Figure 35**).

2. Use one of the techniques discussed earlier in this chapter to insert a table with the number of columns and rows you want.

The table is inserted within the cell (**Figure 36**).

✔ Tips

- You can also insert a table within a table by dragging. Select the table you want to insert, then drag it into the cell in which you want it inserted (**Figure 37**). When you release the mouse button, the table moves (**Figure 38**).

- When you insert a table into a cell, one of two things will happen, depending on table width contraint settings (which I discuss on the next page):

  ▲ If the width of the table you insert is based on a percentage measurement, its width will change automatically to fit the cell's width.

  ▲ If the width of the table you insert is based on a pixel measurement, the cell's width will change automatically to accommodate the inserted table's width.

To delete a table

1. Select the entire table.

   or

   Position the insertion point immediately to the right of the table.

2. Press Del, Delete (Mac OS only), or Backspace (Windows only).

The table and all the information within it disappears.

Table Widths & Heights

When you create a table, certain default settings and behaviors are applied to the table, its columns, and its rows:

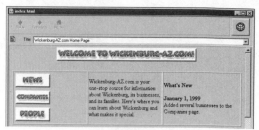

Figure 39. A table that's 100% of the window width stretches from one side of the window to the other...

◆ Table width is set to 450 pixels or the last table width setting used to create a table.

◆ Each column's width is set to an equal percentage of the entire table width.

◆ Table height is set to the amount of space needed to fit all rows.

◆ Row height is set to the amount of space needed to fit one line or the amount of space needed to fit the tallest cell's contents.

You can override table width and height settings by adjusting constraints:

Figure 40. ...even when the window is resized.

◆ Set table width and height as a percentage of the window size or as fixed measurements stated in pixels.

◆ Set column width as a percentage of the table width or as a fixed width stated in pixels.

◆ Set row height as a percentage of the table height or as a fixed height stated in pixels.

Figures 39 and **40** illustrate a table with both the table width and columns set as percentages. As you can see, when the window is wider, so is the table and its cells.

✔ Tips

■ You cannot make a table's height any shorter than it needs to be to properly display the contents of all rows.

■ As mentioned earlier in this chapter, column width can automatically adjust depending on cell contents. Width constraints you set will override any automatic adjustments.

■ You can specify table and column width constraints when you create a table by setting values in the Constraints area of the Create Table (Mac OS; **Figure 5a**) or Insert Table (Windows; **Figure 5b**) dialog box.

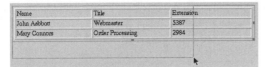

Figure 41. Drag a resizing handle...

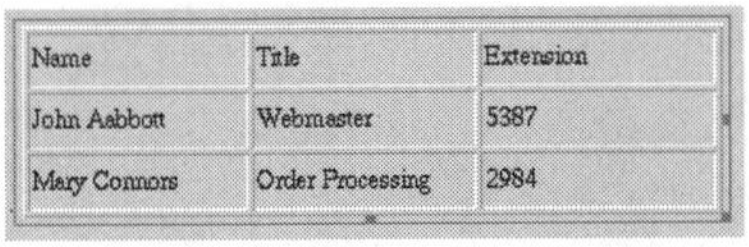

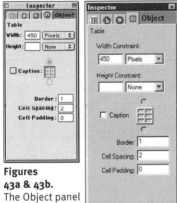

Figure 42. ...to change the dimensions of a table.

Figures 43a & 43b. The Object panel of the Inspector on Mac OS (left) and Windows (right) with a table selected.

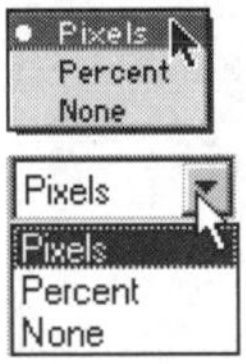

Figures 44a & 44b. Width and height unit menus in the Inspector on Mac OS (top) and Windows (bottom).

To change table width or height by dragging

1. Select the table.

2. Position the mouse pointer on a resizing handle, press the mouse button down, and drag as follows:

   ◆ Drag the right side resizing handle to the left or right to make the table narrower or wider.

   ◆ Drag the bottom resizing handle up or down to make the table shorter or longer.

   ◆ Drag the corner side resizing handle toward or away from the table to make it smaller or larger (**Figure 41**).

   As you drag, a dotted line border moves with the mouse pointer (**Figure 41**).

3. When the dotted border is in the desired position, release the mouse button. The table's width or height (or both) changes (**Figure 42**).

To change table width or height with the Inspector

1. Select the table.

2. If necessary, display the Inspector and click its Object tab to display Table options (**Figures 43a** and **43b**).

3. Choose an option from the Width (Mac OS) or Width Constraint (Windows) menu (**Figures 44a** and **44b**) and enter a value in the box beside it.

4. Choose an option from the Height (Mac OS) or Height Constraint (Windows) menu (**Figures 44a** and **44b**) and enter a value in the box beside it.

5. Press [Return] (Mac OS) or [Enter] (Windows) to save your settings.

To change column width or row height by dragging

1. Click inside the table. A thick border appears around it.

2. Position the mouse pointer over the border to the right of a column you want to resize or below a row you want to resize. The mouse pointer turns into a two-headed arrow (**Figure 45**).

3. Press the mouse button down and drag:

   ◆ Drag a column border to the left or right to make it narrower or wider (**Figure 46**).

   ◆ Drag a row border up or down to make to shorter or taller.

   As you drag, a double line border moves with the mouse pointer (**Figure 46**).

4. When the double line border is in the desired position, release the mouse button. The border shifts, resizing the column or row (**Figure 47**).

✔ Tip

■ You cannot drag the outside border of a table to change column width.

To change column width or row height with the Inspector

1. Select a cell in the column or row you want to resize.

2. If necessary, display the Inspector and click its Object tab to display Table Cell options (**Figures 48a** and **48b**).

3. Choose an option from the Width Constraint menu (**Figures 44a** and **44b**) and enter a value in the box beside it.

4. Choose an option from the Height Constraint menu (**Figures 44a** and **44b**) and enter a value in the box beside it.

5. Press [Return] (Mac OS) or [Enter] (Windows) to save your settings.

Figure 45. When you position the mouse pointer over a cell border, it turns into a double-headed arrow.

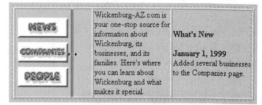

Figure 46. Drag the border...

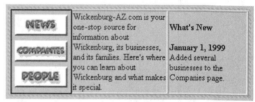

Figure 47. ...to resize the column or row.

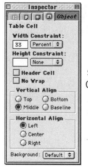
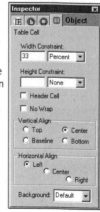

Figures 48a & 48b. The Object tab of the Inspector showing Table Cell options on Mac OS (left) and Windows (right).

✔ Tip

■ To allow column width and row height to change automatically based on table size and cell contents, choose None from the Width Constraint and Height Constraint menus (**Figures 44a** and **44b**).

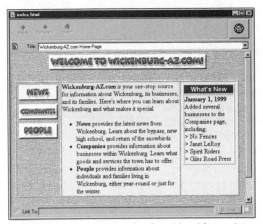

Figure 49. Here's an example of a table with a variety of text and cell formatting applied.

Formatting Cell Contents

You can format the contents of cells just as you format any other document contents. Simply select the text or object you want to format, then use menu commands, toolbar buttons, and shortcut keys:

◆ Apply character styles and paragraph formatting to text. I tell you how in **Chapter 3**.

◆ Change size and alignment for objects. I tell you how in **Chapter 4**.

In addition to these basic formatting techniques, you can also use the Inspector to apply special cell formatting to selected cells:

◆ Apply header cell formatting to make the cell's contents stand out.

◆ Use no wrap formatting to prevent automatic word wrap within a cell.

◆ Change the vertical alignment to shift a cell's contents up or down.

◆ Change the horizontal alignment to shift a cell's contents to the right or left.

◆ Change a cell's background color.

Figure 49 shows an example of a table with a variety of formatting options applied.

✔ Tip

■ To use the formatting techniques discussed in **Chapters 3** and **4**, you must select specific text or an object within a cell. This means you can only apply formatting to the contents of one cell at a time. When using the Inspector to format cells, however, you can select multiple cells and format multiple cells at once.

To apply header cell formatting

1. Select the cells to which you want to apply header cell formatting (**Figure 50**).
2. If necessary, display the Inspector and click its Object tab to display Table Cell options (**Figures 48a** and **48b**).
3. Turn on the Header Cell check box.

✔ Tip

- Header cell formatting makes cell contents bold and centers them within the cell boundaries (**Figure 51**).

To apply no wrap formatting

1. Select the cells to which you want to apply no wrap formatting (**Figure 52**).
2. If necessary, display the Inspector and click its Object tab to display Table Cell options (**Figures 48a** and **48b**).
3. Turn on the No Wrap check box.

✔ Tips

- No wrap cell formatting prevents automatic word wrap from occurring within a cell (**Figure 53**).
- If no wrap formatting is applied to a cell, the only way to break a line of text is to position the insertion point where you want the break to occur and insert a paragraph or line break. I explain how to insert paragraph and line breaks in **Chapter 2**.

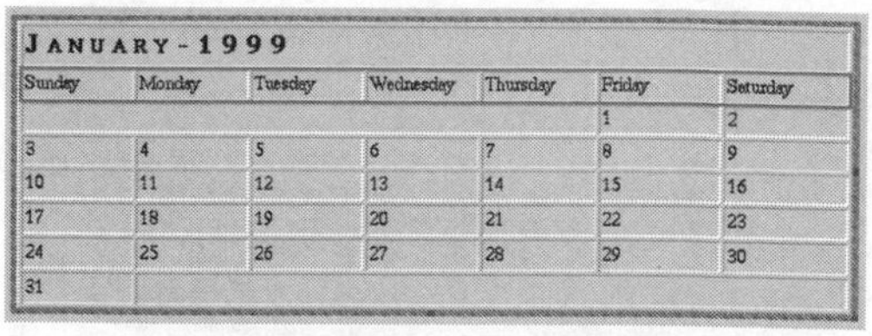

JANUARY - 1999

Sunday	Monday	Tuesday	Wednesday	Thursday	Friday	Saturday
					1	2
3	4	5	6	7	8	9
10	11	12	13	14	15	16
17	18	19	20	21	22	23
24	25	26	27	28	29	30
31						

Figure 50. Select the cells to which you want to apply header cell formatting. In this example, the cells containing the days of the week are selected.

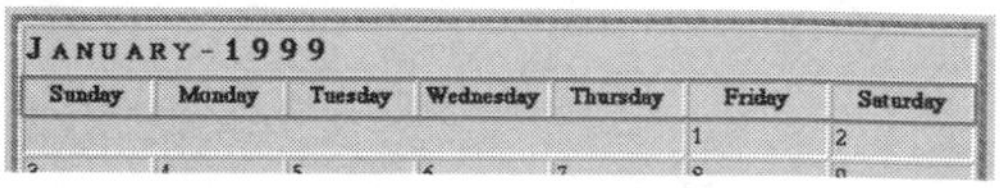

JANUARY - 1999

Sunday	Monday	Tuesday	Wednesday	Thursday	Friday	Saturday
					1	2

Figure 51. Header cell contents are bold and centered.

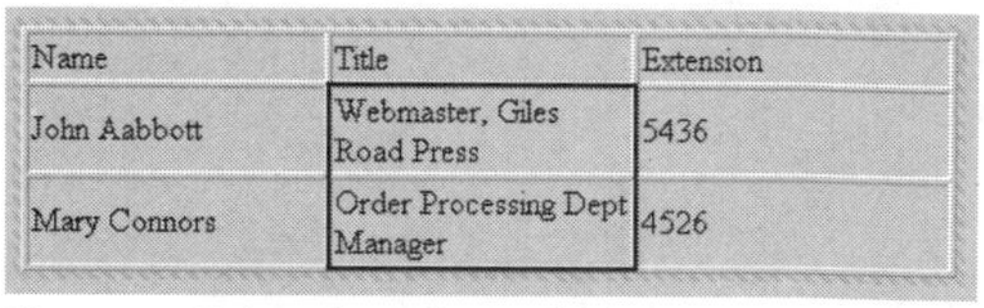

Name	Title	Extension
John Aabbott	Webmaster, Giles Road Press	5436
Mary Connors	Order Processing Dept Manager	4526

Figure 52. Select the cells to which you want to apply no wrap formatting. In this example the cells in the middle column are selected.

Name	Title	Extension
John Aabbott	Webmaster, Giles Road Press	5436
Mary Connors	Order Processing Dept Manager	4526

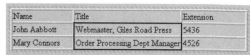

Figure 53. No wrap formatting prevents automatic word wrap. As this example shows, column width adjusts automatically to accommodate the text.

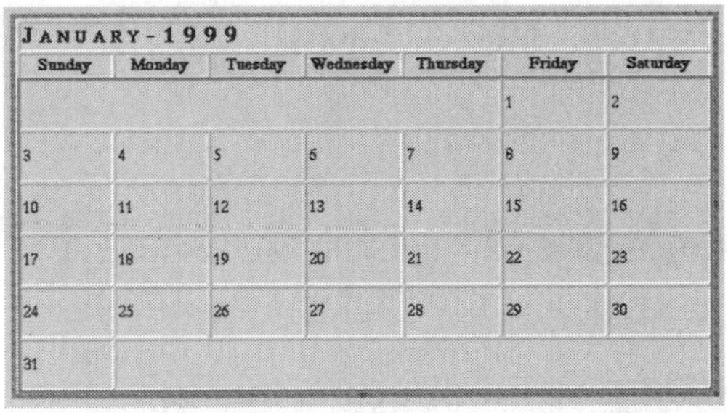

Figure 54. Select the cells you want to align. In this example, the cells containing the numbered days of the month are selected.

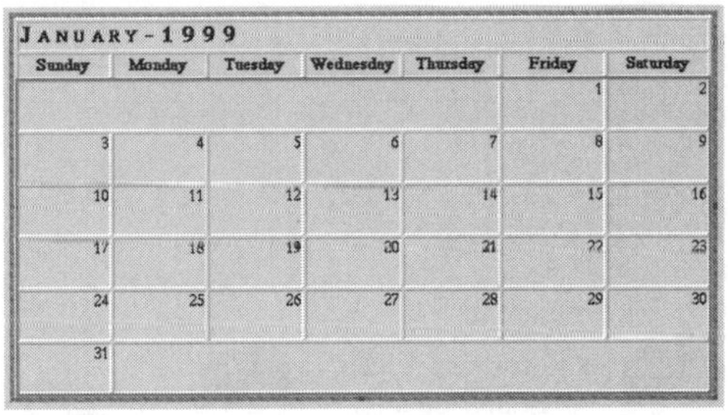

Figure 55. The selected cells here have Top vertical and Right horizontal alignment applied.

To change a cell's vertical & horizontal alignment

1. Select the cells for which you want to change the alignment (**Figure 54**).

2. If necessary, display the Inspector and click its Object tab to display Table Cell options (**Figures 48a** and **48b**).

3. To change vertical alignment, select one of the options in the Vertical Align area of the Inspector.

    or

    To change horizontal alignment, select one of the options in the Horizontal Align area of the Inspector.

Figure 55 shows an example of cells with Top vertical alignment and Right horizontal alignment applied.

✔ Tip

■ Horizontal cell alignment (discussed here) applies alignment to everything in the cell. Horizontal paragraph alignment (discussed in **Chapter 3**) only applies alignment to selected paragraphs. If a cell contains multiple paragraphs, you can use paragraph alignment to align individual paragraphs the way you want them.

CHANGING CELL ALIGNMENT

To change cell background color

1. Select the cells for which you want to change the background color (**Figure 56**).

2. If necessary, display the Inspector and click its Object tab to display Table Cell options (**Figures 48a** and **48b**).

3. Choose a color from the Inspector's Background menu (**Figures 57a** and **57b**).

   or

   Drag a color from the Color panel (**Figures 58a** and **58b**) to the Inspector's Background menu or the selected cells.

Figure 59 shows an example of cells with a different color background.

✔ Tip

- If you choose Custom from the Inspector's Background menu, you can use a standard color picker (Mac OS) or Color (Windows) dialog box to choose a color other than one of the colors on the menu. I tell you more about working with colors in **Chapter 3**.

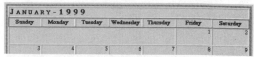

Figure 56. Select the cells for which you want to change the background color. In this example, the cells containing the days of the week are selected.

Figures 57a & 57b. The Background menu in the Object panel of the Inspector on Mac OS (left) and Windows (right).

Figures 58a & 58b. The Color panel on Mac OS (left) and Windows (right).

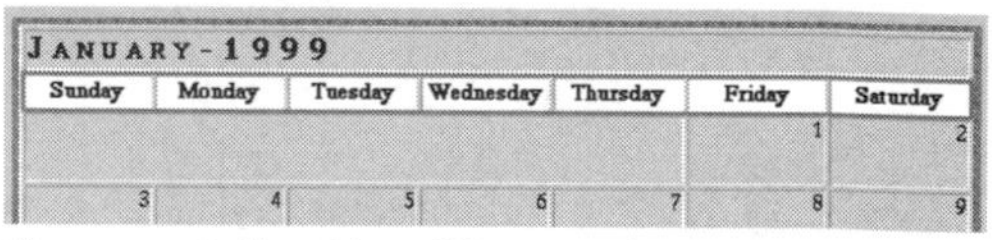

Figure 59. Cells with a different color background.

CHANGING CELL BACKGROUND COLOR

Cell padding
Cell spacing
Caption
Table border
Name
Title
Extension
John Aabbott
Webmaster, Giles Road Press
5436
Mary Connors
Order Processing Dept Manager
4526
Key Personnel

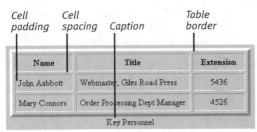

Figure 60. Table formatting options.

Name
Title
Extension
John Aabbott
Webmaster, Giles Road Press
5436
Mary Connors
Order Processing Dept Manager
4526

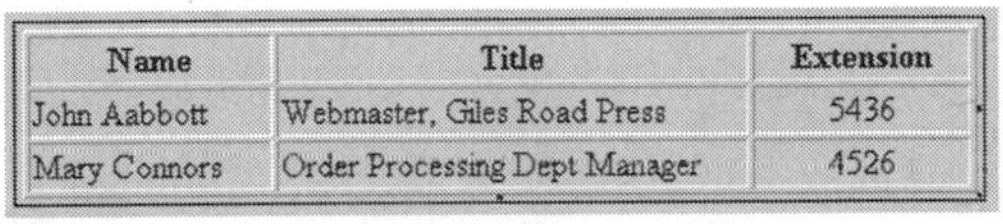

Figure 61. Select the table you want to format.

Caption

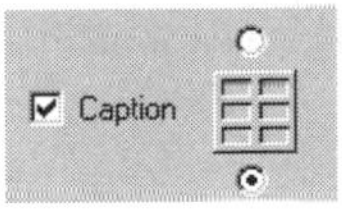

Figure 62. Turn on the Caption check box and select a position option.

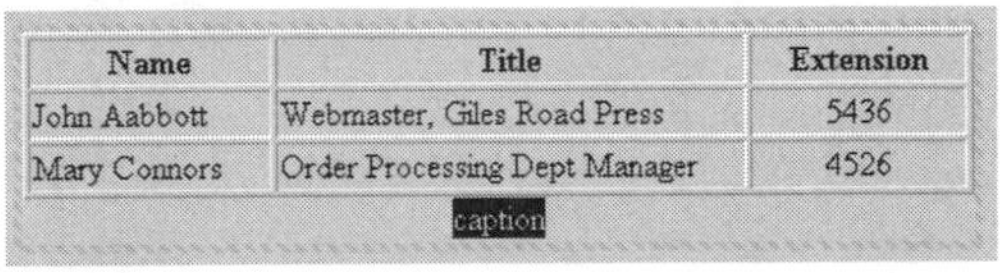

Name
Title
Extension
John Aabbott
Webmaster, Giles Road Press
5436
Mary Connors
Order Processing Dept Manager
4526
caption

Figure 63. Triple-click the default caption to select it.

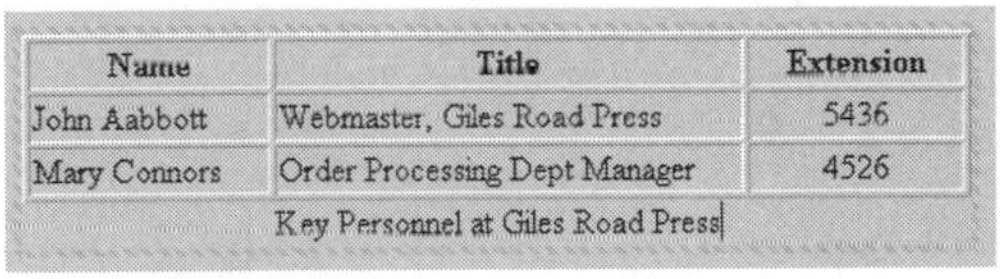

Name
Title
Extension
John Aabbott
Webmaster, Giles Road Press
5436
Mary Connors
Order Processing Dept Manager
4526
Key Personnel at Giles Road Press

Figure 64. Type in the text you want to appear as a caption.

Formatting Tables

The Inspector's Object panel offers options to format a selected table:

- Add a caption above or below the table.
- Set the table's *border*—the thickness of the line around the table.
- Set the table's *cell spacing*—the amount of space between table cells.
- Set the table's *cell padding*—the amount of space between a cell's border and contents.

Figure 60 illustrates the table formatting options you can change with the Inspector. In this example, the border, cell spacing, and cell padding options were all set to 5.

To add a caption

1. Select the table to which you want to add a caption (**Figure 61**).
2. If necessary, display the Inspector and click its Object tab to display Table options (**Figures 43a** and **43b**).
3. Turn on the Caption check box. Then select one of the Caption options to indicate whether the caption should be above or below the table (**Figure 62**).
4. Triple-click the word *caption* above or below the table to select it (**Figure 63**).
5. Type the text you want to appear in the caption (**Figure 64**).

✔ Tip

- To remove a caption, follow steps 1 and 2 above, then turn off the Caption check box.

To set table border, cell spacing, & cell padding

1. Select the table you want to format (**Figure 61**).

2. If necessary, display the Inspector and click its Object tab to display Table options (**Figures 43a** and **43b**).

3. To change the thickness of the border, enter a value in the Border box.

   or

   To change the amount of space between cells, enter a value in the Cell Spacing box.

   or

   To change the amount of space between a cell's border and contents, enter a value in the Cell Padding box.

Figures 60, **65**, and **66** show examples of the kinds of effects you can obtain with borders, spacing, and padding.

✔ Tips

- You can enter a value from 0 to 50 in the Border, Cell Spacing, and Cell Padding boxes. The default values are 1, 2, and 0 respectively.

- You can make any combination of changes to borders, spacing, and padding.

- A table's border has a three dimensional appearance. The higher you set the border value, the more three dimensional the table will look. **Figure 66** shows an exaggerated example with the border set to the maximum value of 50.

- To create a multicolumn effect like the table illustrated in **Figure 3**, set the table's border to 0.

Name	Title	Extension
John Aabbott	Webmaster, Giles Road Press	5436
Mary Connors	Order Processing Dept Manager	4526

Border: 5
Cell Spacing: 0
Cell Padding: 3

Figure 65. Here's one table formatting combination...

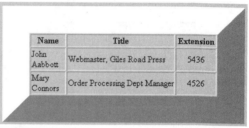

Name	Title	Extension
John Aabbott	Webmaster, Giles Road Press	5436
Mary Connors	Order Processing Dept Manager	4526

Border: 50
Cell Spacing: 2
Cell Padding: 0

Figure 66. ...and here's another.

SETTING BORDERS, SPACING, & PADDING

WORKING
WITH LINKS

Figure 1. This example shows several links from a "Home" page to other pages, an e-mail address, and an Adobe Acrobat PDF file on the same site.

Links

The real power of Web publishing lies in its ability to link your Web pages to each other and to other pages and references anywhere on the Internet (**Figure 1**). When properly set up, someone browsing your pages can click a hypertext or graphic link to display another page—even one that's on a server halfway across the world!

When working with links, there are two kinds of documents:

◆ The *source* document is the one containing the clickable link.

◆ The *destination* or *referenced* document is the one displayed when you click a link.

A link works by including the address or *URL (Uniform Resource Locator)* of the destination document within HTML codes that are associated with text or an image on the source page. While that may sound complex, with PageMill, it's easy since PageMill automatically prepares the HTML codes for you.

✔ Tips

■ You can often recognize linked text or a linked graphic on a Web page by the colored underline or border around it.

■ Although the default link color is blue, it can be changed. I tell you how in **Chapter 3**.

URLs

To create a link, you must provide a URL to the destination document. A URL is a document's address or location on the Internet. Just as every file on your hard disk has a pathname, every file on the Internet has a URL. But rather than all files being stored on a single hard disk, they're stored on hard disks all over the world.

There are two ways to include a URL in a Web page document:

◆ An *absolute* reference includes the entire pathname to the referenced location.

◆ A *relative* reference includes the pathname to the referenced location from the source document.

Figure 2 illustrates both the absolute and relative URLs for a destination page.

If a link's URL refers to a document that does not exist, anyone following that link will see an error message like the one in **Figure 3**. Links to locations that can't be found are often called broken links.

✔ Tips

■ I tell you more about URLs in the Introduction of this book.

■ You must use an absolute reference to create a link to a location outside your Web site.

■ Relative references to pages on your own Web site are less likely to "break" if you move your pages from one directory or server to another.

■ Although URLs most often refer to Web pages, they can also refer to other kinds of documents or Internet connections. **Table 1** provides a list of some of the URL types supported by PageMill. I tell you more about other types of links later in this chapter.

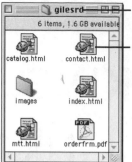

Root directory for domain gilesrd.com

Absolute reference: http://www.gilesrd.com/catalog.html

Relative reference from index.html: catalog.html

Figure 2. As this illustration shows, an absolute URL is the complete pathname to a destination file while a relative URL is the destination file's location from the source document. When referring to catalog.html from index.html, therefore, the relative reference includes only the file name.

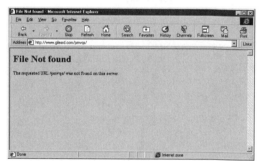

Figure 3. When you click a link to a URL that cannot be found, your browser displays an error message.

URL TYPE	DESCRIPTION
http://	Opens a Web page
file://	Opens a file
news:	Opens a Usenet newsgroup
mailto:	Sends an e-mail message
ftp://	Connects to an FTP server
gopher://	Connects to a Gopher server
telnet://	Connects to a server via Telnet

Table 1. Some of the URL types PageMill supports.

Figure 4.
The Page icon stores information about the location of a page.

Page icon

Figure 5.
If a document has not yet been saved, its Page icon area will be empty.

Empty Page icon

Figure 6. Position the insertion point where you want the anchor to appear.

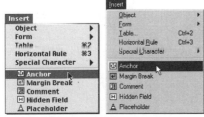

Figures 7a & 7b. Choosing Anchor from the Insert menu on Mac OS (left) and Windows (right).

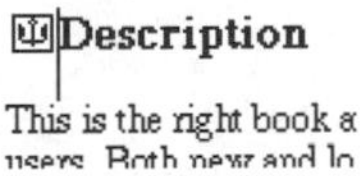

Description

This is the right book a users. Both new and lo

Figure 8. The anchor appears at the insertion point.

PageMill's Page Icons

PageMill stores information about a page location in the Page icon near the top-left corner of the window (**Figure 4**). One way to create a link is to drag the Page icon from one page to another.

✔ Tip

- If the page has not yet been saved, the Page icon area will be empty (**Figure 5**). You must save the page before you can drag its Page icon.

Anchors

An anchor is a marked or named position on a Web page. It works a lot like the bookmark feature in some word processors.

Normally, when you create a link to a page, clicking the link displays the top of the destination page. When you create a link to an anchor, however, clicking the link displays the anchor's location on the destination page.

✔ Tip

- Anchors are especially useful on long pages. Create a table of contents at the top of the page with links to anchors for topics throughout the page to provide access to topics without scrolling.

To create an anchor

1. Position the insertion point where you want the anchor to appear (**Figure 6**).

2. Choose Insert > Anchor (**Figures 7a** and **7b**).

The anchor appears at the insertion point (**Figure 8**).

✔ Tips

- If you can't see an anchor after inserting one, choose View > Show Invisibles.

- Anchors do not appear in Preview mode.

PAGE ICONS & ANCHORS

To move an anchor

Drag the anchor to a new position within the page. Any links that reference the anchor will automatically reference it in its new position.

To name an anchor

1. Select the anchor you want to name (**Figure 9**).

2. If necessary, display the Inspector and click its Object tab to display Anchor options (**Figures 10a** and **10b**).

3. In the Name box, type the name you want to use for the anchor (**Figure 11**).

4. Press Return (Mac OS) or Enter (Windows) to complete the entry.

✔ Tip

■ It is not necessary to name the anchors you create. You may find it helpful, however, if you plan to edit the HTML code PageMill creates. I tell you about editing HTML in **Chapter 9**.

To delete an anchor

1. Select the anchor you want to delete (**Figure 9**).

2. Press Del, Delete (Mac OS only), or Backspace (Windows only). The anchor disappears.

✔ Tip

■ If you delete an anchor that is referenced by a link, the link will no longer function.

Figure 9. Click an anchor to select it.

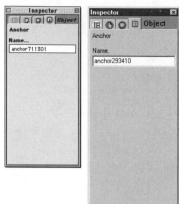
Figures 10a & 10b. The Inspector's Object tab displaying Anchor options on Mac OS (left) and Windows (right).

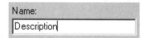
Figure 11. Enter a new name for the anchor in the Name box.

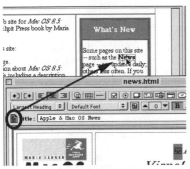

Figure 12. This example shows a Page icon being dragged onto selected text.

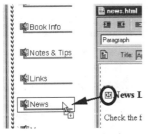

Figure 13. This example shows an anchor icon being dragged onto a selected image.

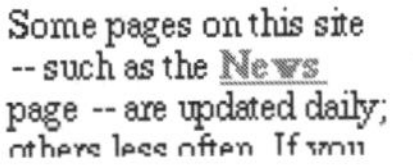

Some pages on this site
-- such as the News
page -- are updated daily;
others less often. If you

Figure 14. Here's the text link created in **Figure 12**...

Figure 15. ...and here's the image link created in **Figure 13**.

Adding Links

PageMill offers several methods for adding links to text and images:

◆ Use drag and drop to create links to pages you create.

◆ Use the Copy and Paste commands to copy links on one page to other pages.

◆ Type a URL into the Link Location bar.

◆ Use the Place command's Open dialog box to link to a local or remote URL.

To add a link by dragging

1. In the source document, select the text or image that you want to use as a link.

2. Drag the Page icon for the destination document onto the selection (**Figure 12**).

   or

   Drag the anchor for the destination location onto the selection (**Figure 13**).

   or

   Drag the icon for the destination document from a Finder window onto the selection in the PageMill window.

   or

   Drag a selected link from another PageMill window onto the selection.

   or

   Drag a selected link from the Pasteboard onto the selection.

When you release the mouse button, the selection gets a blue underline (if it's text; **Figure 14**) or a blue border (if it's an image; **Figure 15**) to indicate that it's a link.

✔ Tips

- If you drag a Page or anchor icon onto another page without dropping it on a selection, PageMill creates the link for you (**Figure 16**), using the page title or anchor name for the link text. (If the page does not have a title, PageMill uses the page's file name for the link text.) You can edit the link text just as you would any other text. I tell you about editing text and providing page titles in **Chapter 2**.

- When you select a link, the destination address appears in the Link To bar at the bottom of the page window (**Figure 17**). You can copy the link by dragging the URL icon to another location.

- Selected text on an inactive page appears with a selection border around it (**Figure 18**).

- To create a link to an anchor on the same page by dragging, hold down ⌘ (Mac OS) or Alt (Windows) while dragging the anchor into position. This creates a link to the anchor rather than moving the anchor.

- When you drag text or an image containing a link from the Pasteboard to a document window, the link is pasted into the document along with the text or image. I explain how to display and use the Pasteboard in **Chapters 1, 2, and 4**.

Pages on this site:
Apple & Mac OS News

Figure 16. Here's a link created by dropping a Page icon from a destination page onto an empty area of a source page.

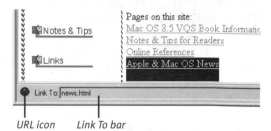

Figure 17. When a link is selected, its destination URL appears in the Link To bar at the bottom of the window.

URL icon   Link To bar

Figure 18. A selection on an inactive page appears with a border around it.

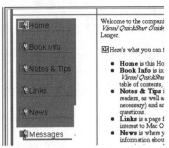

Figure 19. Select the link you want to copy. In this example, a number of graphic links are selected.

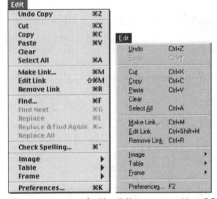

Figures 20a & 20b. The Edit menu on Mac OS (left) and Windows (right).

Figure 21. Position the insertion point where you want the copied links to appear.

Figure 22. The links appear at the insertion point.

To add a link with the Copy & Paste commands

1. Select the linked text or image (**Figure 19**) you want to copy.

2. Choose Edit > Copy (**Figures 20a and 20b**) or press ⌃⌘C (Mac OS) or Ctrl C (Windows).

3. Position the insertion point in the document where you want the link to appear (**Figure 21**).

4. Choose Edit > Paste (**Figures 20a and 20b**) or press ⌃⌘V (Mac OS) or Ctrl V (Windows).

The text or image, including its link, appears at the insertion point (**Figure 22**).

✔ Tips

- You can also use the Cut and Paste commands to move a link.

- Do not use the Copy and Paste commands to copy an anchor. Doing so will create a duplicate of the anchor, not a link.

- I tell you how to use Copy, Cut, and Paste for text in **Chapter 2** and for images in **Chapter 4**.

ADDING LINKS WITH COPY & PASTE

To add a link by typing in the Link To bar

1. In the source document, select the text or image that you want to use as a link (**Figure 23**).

2. Click in the Link To bar at the bottom-left side of the window.

   or

   Press the Enter key on the keypad.

   This activates the Link To bar (**Figure 24**).

3. Enter the URL for the destination (**Figure 25**) and press Return (Mac OS) or Enter (Windows).

The selected text or image turns into a link (**Figure 26**).

✔ Tips

- When typing a link, be sure to enter it correctly. If it has not been entered correctly, it will not work. I tell you how to test links in **Chapter 9**.

- You can also use the Copy and Paste commands to paste the URL for a page into the Link To bar.

- PageMill offers several shortcuts for typing common URL components into the Link To bar:

  ▲ To quickly enter the URL protocol, type its first letter and press Tab. To enter *http://*, for example, press H and then Tab.

  ▲ To quickly enter the document type, type its first letter and press Tab. To enter *www.* for example, press W and then press Tab.

  ▲ To quickly enter the domain, type its first letter and press Tab. To enter *com*, for example, press C and then Tab.

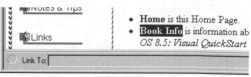

Figure 23. Select the text or image you want to use as a link.

Figure 24. When you click in the Link To bar, it becomes active and an insertion point appears within it.

Figure 25. Enter the URL for the destination. In this example, the URL is a relative reference to another page in the same directory on the Web server.

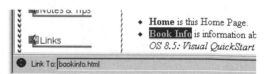

Figure 26. When you press Return (Mac OS) or Enter (Windows), the selected text or image becomes a link.

Figure 27.
Select the text or image you want to use as a link.

Figures 28a & 28b. The Link (Mac OS; above) and Browse (Windows; below) buttons are at the right end of the Link to bar.

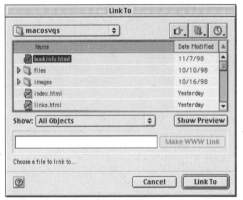

Figure 29a & 29b. The Link To (Mac OS; above) and Select File (Windows; below) dialog boxes.

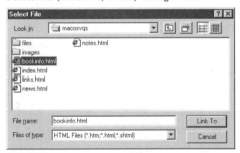

Figure 30. On Mac OS, you can enter the URL for a remote file in a box at the bottom of the Link To dialog box.

Figure 31.
The selected text or image becomes a link.

To add a link with the Make Link command

1. In the source document, select the text or image that you want to use as a link (**Figure 27**).

2. Choose Edit > Make Link (**Figures 20a** and **20b**) or press ⌃ ⌘ M (Mac OS) or Ctrl M (Windows).

   or

   Click the Link (Mac OS) or Browse (Windows) button at the right end of the Link To bar (**Figures 28a** and **28b**).

3. Use the Link To (Mac OS) or Select File (Windows) dialog box that appears to locate and select the file to which you want to link (**Figures 29a** and **29b**).

   or

   On Mac OS only, enter the complete URL for the file to which you want to link in the box at the bottom of the dialog box (**Figure 30**).

4. Click the Link To button (**Figures 29a** and **29b**).

   or

   For a remote link on Mac OS only, click the Make WW Link button (**Figure 30**).

   The selected text or image becomes a link (**Figure 31**).

✔ Tips

- In step 3, you can use the Show (Mac OS; **Figure 28a**) or Files of type (Windows; **Figure 28b**) menu to narrow down the list of files that appear in the Link To (Mac OS) or Select File (Windows) dialog box by type.

- If you use the Make Link command to add a link without first selecting text or an image, PageMill creates the entire link for you, using the page title or URL of the link as the linked text.

To edit a link

1. Select the text or image containing the link (**Figure 26** or **31**).

2. Activate the Link To bar using one of these methods:

    ◆ Click in the Link To bar.

    ◆ Press Enter on the numeric keypad.

    ◆ Choose Edit > Edit Link (**Figures 20a** and **20b**).

    ◆ Press Shift ⌘ M (Mac OS) or Ctrl Shift M (Windows).

3. Edit the contents of the Link To bar using standard editing techniques.

4. Press Return (Mac OS) or Enter (Windows) to complete the entry.

✔ Tips

■ To quickly select an entire text link, triple-click it.

■ You can also edit a link by linking something else to the linked text or image.

To remove a link

1. Select the text or image containing the link (**Figure 26** or **31**).

2. Choose Edit > Remove Link (Figures **20a** and **20b**) or press ⌘ R (Mac OS) or Ctrl R (Windows).

    or

    Delete the contents of the Link To bar, then press Return (Mac OS) or Enter (Windows) to complete the entry.

✔ Tips

■ Deleting text or an image containing a link also deletes the link.

■ Deleting a link does not delete the file that was linked.

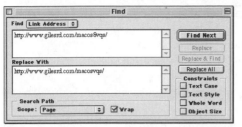

Figures 32a & 32b. Examples of the Find dialog box in action on Mac OS (above) and Windows (below).

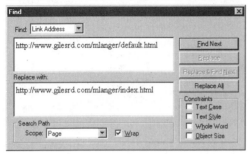

Figures 33a & 33b.
Use the Find menu at the top of the Find dialog box on Mac OS (left) and Windows (right) to indicate that you want to search for a Link Address rather than page content.

Finding & Replacing URLs

PageMill's find and replace features can be used to locate and/or change the URLs for links throughout a Web page document. You use the Find dialog box (**Figures 32a** and **32b**) to specify your find and, if applicable, replacement URL. Then use buttons within the Find dialog box or on the Edit (Mac OS) or Search (Windows) menu to locate and/or replace URLs as specified.

I discuss the find and replace features in detail in **Chapter 2**. They work the same way for URLs. Just remember to choose Link Address from the Find menu (**Figures 33a** and **33b**) at the top of the Find dialog box before beginning the search.

✔ Tips

- I provide step-by-step instructions for using the find and replace features in **Chapter 2**.

- To replace only part of a URL, make sure the Whole Word check box is turned off in the Find dialog box (**Figures 32a** and **32b**).

- To delete a URL throughout a document, leave the Replace With scrolling window empty. Then replace every occurrence of the URL with nothing, thus deleting it.

Other Links

When it comes to creating links, you're not limited to linking to the pages you create with PageMill. Using the Link To bar, you can also create links to:

◆ **Web pages on other sites.** These external links give the people who browse your pages access to more information than you offer.

◆ **E-mail addresses.** When a link to an e-mail address is clicked, an addressed e-mail form opens, making it convenient to send an e-mail message.

◆ **Files.** When a link to a file is clicked, the browser software downloads the file to the user's computer. This is a great way to distribute software and information for use offline.

◆ **FTP and Gopher servers.** These servers offer access to files and database information.

◆ **Newsgroups.** Providing easy access to specific Usenet newsgroups is a great way to add information to your site without adding files.

Table 2 provides examples of real URLs to a variety of destinations.

✔ Tips

■ No matter what kind of link you create, its URL must be entered correctly for it to work.

■ Links are often case-sensitive—especially links to files on UNIX servers. Be sure you enter URLs with correct capitalization or the link may not work.

■ Check all external links on a regular basis to make sure they're still valid. I tell you how to check external links in **Chapter 9**.

External Pages:
http://www.peachpit.com/
http://www.adobe.com/
http://www.gilesrd.com/
http://www.gilesrd.com/mlanger/

E-Mail Addresses:
mailto:ask@peachpit.com
mailto:maria@gilesrd.com

Files:
http://www.adobe.com/prodindex/acrobat/
    PDFS/AcrobatBrochure.pdf
ftp://ftp.apple.com/Quicktime/software/
    QuickTime/mac_pi.hqx
ftp://ftp.apple.com/Quicktime/software/
    QuickTime/QTPLUG32.EXE

FTP Servers:
ftp://ftp.apple.com/
ftp://ftp.microsoft.com/
ftp://ftp.adobe.com/

Newsgroups:
news:alt.comedy.standup
news:rec.pets.horses

Table 2. Here's a list of real URLs you can try on your Web pages. Remember, although this list was tested and known to be valid when this book went into production, the Internet is constantly changing—URLs that were valid today could become invalid tomorrow. If one of these links doesn't work when you try it, you may not be doing anything wrong—that URL may just be out of date.

Image Maps

An image map lets you use one image to link to multiple destinations. You insert the image in a PageMill document, then create "hotspots" on the image, each of which is associated with a different address. PageMill automatically creates the HTML-encoded map files for you.

There are two kinds of image maps:

◆ A *client-side* image map stores all hotspot and link information within the Web page document. When a user clicks a hotspot, the browser gets the link URL right from the Web page.

◆ A *server-side* image map stores all hotspot and link information in a separate image map file that is stored on the Web server. When a user clicks a hotspot, the browser must open and search through the corresponding image map file to get the link URL.

✔ Tips

■ Although client-side image maps are easier to create and use and offer quicker access to linked pages, they are not supported by older Web browsers.

■ A server-side image map may require a special program called a *Common Gateway Interface (CGI)* to operate. If you're not sure whether you need a CGI script to use a server-side image map, ask your System Administrator or Webmaster.

To create a client-side image map

1. Select an image file on the page.

2. Use drawing tools to add hotspots with links to the image.

3. Save the file.

✔ Tips

- Creating and editing client-side image maps is sometimes referred to as in-line editing because it's done on the page.

- I explain how to create hotspots later in this chapter and how to save files in **Chapter 1**.

To create a server-side image map

1. Set or check preferences for your server's image map format (**Figures 34a** and **34b**) and root folder (**Figure 35a** and **35b**).

2. Open an image on the page in the Image window.

3. Use drawing tools to add hotspots with links to the image.

4. Save the edited image.

5. Use the Inspector to set the image as an image map and specify a location for the image map file on the server.

✔ Tips

- I tell you about setting preferences in **Chapter 11**. If you're not sure how to set these options, ask your System Administrator or Webmaster.

- I explain how to save images in the Image window in **Chapter 5** and how to create hotspots and how to use the Inspector to set server-side image map options later in this chapter.

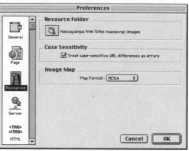

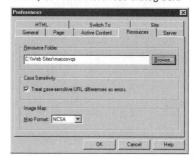

Figures 34a & 34b. The Resources section (Mac OS; above) and tab (Windows; below) of the Preferences dialog box.

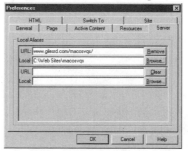

Figures 35a & 35b. The Server section (Mac OS; above) and tab (Windows; below) of the Preferences dialog box.

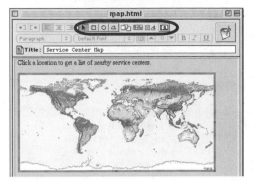

Figures 36a & 36b. Double-click an image to display its drawing tools for a client-side image map on Mac OS (above) and Windows (below).

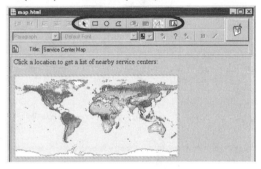

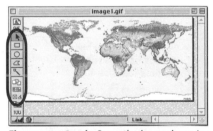

Figures 37a & 37b. Open the image in an Image window to display the drawing tools for a server-side image map on Mac OS (above) and Windows (below).

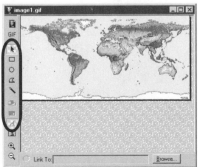

Hotspots

Hotspots are locations on an image that are linked to URLs. When a user clicks a hotspot on an image map, the destination URL is loaded into his browser.

Hotspots are created with drawing tools. The drawing tools are the same for both types of image maps. The only difference is where they appear:

◆ For client-side image maps, the drawing tools appear on the page window's toolbar (**Figures 36a** and **36b**).

◆ For server-side image maps, the drawing tools appear in the Image window (**Figures 37a** and **37b**).

To display the drawing tools for a client-side image map

Double-click the image you want to use as an image map.

A thick border appears around the image. The drawing tools appear on the toobar (**Figures 36a** and **36b**).

To display the drawing tools for a server-side image map

Hold down ⌘ (Mac OS) or Ctrl (Windows) while double-clicking the image you want to use as an image map.

or

Select the image you want to use as an image map, and then choose Edit > Image > Open Image Window or press ⌘D (Mac OS) or Ctrl D (Windows).

The image opens in the Image window (**Figures 37a** and **37b**). The drawing tools appear along the left side of the window.

To add hotspots to an image

1. Click the hotspot tool for the shape of the hotspot you want to draw:

   ◆ The Rectangle Hotspot tool draws 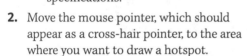 rectangular or square hotspots.

   ◆ The Circle Hotspot tool draws  round hotspots.

   ◆ The Polygon Hotspot tool draws 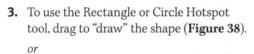 multisided hotspots to your specifications.

2. Move the mouse pointer, which should appear as a cross-hair pointer, to the area where you want to draw a hotspot.

3. To use the Rectangle or Circle Hotspot tool, drag to "draw" the shape (**Figure 38**).

   or

   To use the Polygon Hotspot tool, click to create polygon corners (**Figure 39**), then click on the starting point to close the polygon.

   When you complete the shape, it appears in blue with a number beneath it (**Figure 40**).

✔ Tips

■ To draw a square hotspot, click the Rectangle Hotspot tool and hold down (Shift) while you drag.

■ To change the size or shape of a hotspot, click it to select it and drag its resizing handles (**Figure 41**).

■ To move a hotspot, position the mouse pointer in the middle of the hotspot, press the mouse button down, and drag to a new position.

■ To delete a hotspot, click it to select it and press (Del), (Delete) (Mac OS), or (Backspace) (Windows).

■ The number under each hotspot corresponds to its stacking order. If two or more spots overlap, the one with the lowest number is the one that will be activated when the overlapping area is clicked.

Figure 38.
To use the Rectangle Hotspot tool, simply drag to "draw" the hotspot shape.

Figure 39.
To use the Polygon Hotspot tool, click at the polygon shape's corners. To close the shape, click on the starting point.

Figure 40. Here are 11 completed hotspots.

Figure 41.
A selected hotspot has resizing handles you can drag to resize it.

Figure 42.
One way to add a link to a selected hotspot is to drag an anchor icon onto it.

Figure 43.
The name of the link appears in blue on top of the hotspot.

Figure 44. Another way to add a link to a selected hotspot is to enter the link's URL in the Link To bar.

Figure 45. Here's what the image from **Figure 40** looks like with all hotspots linked. When you create a default link, its name or URL appears in the bottom left corner of the image.

To add a link to a hotspot by dragging

1. Click the hotspot to select it.
2. To link a page to a hotspot, drag the Page icon for the destination page onto the selected hotspot.

   or

   To link an anchor to a hotspot, drag the anchor for the destination onto the selected hotspot (**Figure 42**).

   or

   To link an image to a hotspot, drag the image icon from an Image view window onto the selected hotspot.

The name of the link appears in blue over the hotspot (**Figure 43**).

To add a link to a hotspot by typing

1. Click the hotspot to select it.
2. Activate the Link To bar by clicking in it or pressing [Enter] on the numeric keypad.
3. Type the URL for the destination (**Figure 44**) and press [Return] (Mac OS) or [Enter] (Windows).

The name of the link appears in blue over the hotspot (**Figure 45**).

To create a default link

1. Click on the image anywhere except on a hotspot so no hotspot is selected.
2. Activate the Link To bar by clicking in it or pressing [Enter] on the numeric keypad.
3. Type the URL for a default destination and press [Return] (Mac OS) or [Enter] (Windows) to complete the entry.

The name of the link appears in blue in the lower-left corner of the image (**Figure 45**). This is the destination that will be displayed if someone clicks the image but misses the hotspots.

To remove a link from a hotspot

1. Click the hotspot containing the link to select it.

2. Activate the Link To bar by clicking in it or pressing [Enter] on the numeric keypad.

3. Delete the contents of the Link To bar and press [Return] (Mac OS) or [Enter] (Windows) to complete the entry.

The name of the link disappears from the hotspot.

To change the stacking order of hotspots

1. Click the hotspot you want to change to select it (**Figure 46**).

2. Click the Shuffle Hotspot tool to display a menu of four stacking options (**Figures 47a** and **47b**):

   ◆ Bring To Front assigns number 1 to the hotspot, thus putting it on the top of the stack.

   ◆ Send To Back assigns the highest number to the spot, thus putting it on the bottom of the stack.

   ◆ Shuffle Forward lowers the number of the spot by one, thus bringing it up one layer.

   ◆ Shuffle Back raises the number of the spot by one, thus sending it back one layer.

When you make your selection, the numbers under each of the hotspots change as necessary (**Figure 48**).

✔ Tip

■ Stacking order is only important if the hotspots on an image map overlap.

Figure 46. In this example, one hotspot (#1) is overlapping two others, making it impossible to click either of the two smaller hotspots.

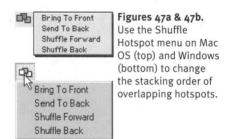

Figures 47a & 47b. Use the Shuffle Hotspot menu on Mac OS (top) and Windows (bottom) to change the stacking order of overlapping hotspots.

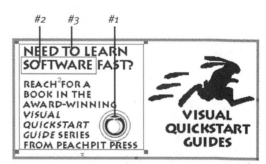

Figure 48. By moving the large hotspot to the back, the other two hotspots are accessible. The hotspot numbers change accordingly.

Figures 49a & 49b. The Hotspot Color menu on Mac OS (above) and Windows (right).

Figure 50. Here's the image from **Figure 45** with yellow hotspots...

Figure 51. ...and here's the image with hotspot labels turned off.

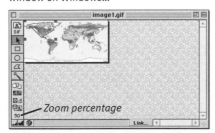

Figure 52. An enlarged image in the Image window on Windows...

Figure 53. ...and a reduced image in the Image window on Mac OS.

To change the hotspot color

1. Click the Hotspot Color icon to display a menu of colors (**Figures 49a** and **49b**).

2. Choose a color that contrasts from the dominant color of the image.

The color changes for all hotspots and URL text in the active Image window.

Figures 45 and **50** illustrate the same image with the default blue hotspot color (**Figure 45** and a bright yellow color (**Figure 50**).

✔ Tip

-   Because hotspot outlines are invisible on Web pages, changing hotspot color does not affect the appearance of images.

To toggle the display of hotspot labels

Click the Show Hotspot Label button.

The labels disappear (**Figure 51**).

✔ Tip

-   On Mac OS, the button's check box appears turned on when labels are displayed. On Windows, the button appears pushed in when labels are displayed.

To change the Image window's magnification

To enlarge the view of the image (**Figure 52**), click the Zoom In button.

or

To reduce the view of the image (**Figure 53**), click the Zoom Out button.

✔ Tips

-   You can only change magnification in the Image window.

-   On Mac OS, the zoom percentage is indicated above the two zoom buttons (**Figure 53**).

Additional Server-Side Image Map Settings

Server-side image maps require that you perform two additional steps after the image map has been created:

◆ Set the image's behavior as a map.

◆ Specify the image map (and possibly CGI) location.

To set an image as a map

1. If necessary, save the image and close the Image window for the image.

2. In the PageMill window, click the image to select it.

3. If necessary, display the Inspector and click its Object tab to display Image options (**Figures 54a** and **54b**).

4. Select the Map option in the Behavior area of the Inspector (**Figure 55**).

✔ Tip

■ You must select the Map radio button as instructed above for a server-side image map to function correctly. This option is turned on automatically for a client-side image map.

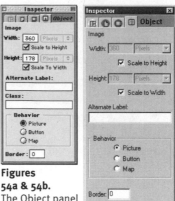

Figures 54a & 54b.
The Object panel of the Inspector for an image on Mac OS (left) and Windows (right).

Figure 55.
Select the Map option to set an image as a server-side image map. This is done automatically by PageMill for client-side image maps.

```
[ Link To : | http://www.gilesrd.com/images/world.map| ]
```
Figure 56. Enter the absolute URL of the image map file...

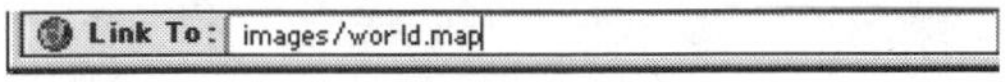

```
[ Link To : | images/world.map ]
```
Figure 57. ...or the relative URL of the image map file...

```
[ Link To : | http://www.gilesrd.com/cgi-bin/imagemap/world.map| ]
```
Figure 58. ...or the absolute URL of the CGI script and the image map file...

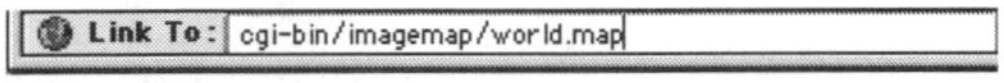

```
[ Link To : | cgi-bin/imagemap/world.map| ]
```
Figure 59. ...or the relative URL of the CGI script and the image map file.

To set the image map location

1. In the PageMill window, select the image.
2. Activate the Link To bar by clicking in it or pressing (Enter) on the numeric keypad.
3. Enter the URL for the image map file (**Figure 56**) and press (Return) (Mac OS) or (Enter) (Windows) to complete the entry.

✔ Tips

- You must set the image map location as instructed above for a server-side image map. Do not perform these steps for a client-side image map.
- The pathname entry varies depending on the Web server software. The most common options are:
  - ▲ Absolute URL of the image map file (**Figure 56**).
  - ▲ Relative URL of the image file (**Figure 57**).
  - ▲ Absolute URL of the CGI script name and image map (**Figure 58**).
  - ▲ Relative URL of the CGI script name and image map (**Figure 59**).
- If you're not sure what to enter as a pathname for the map, check with your System Administrator or Webmaster. Or find another image map that works and use its URL to guide you.
- If you do not set the correct location for the image map (and, if applicable, CGI script) a server-side image map will not work.

SETTING THE IMAGE MAP LOCATION

USING FRAMES

This frame contains a table of contents.   *This frame displays pages listed in the table of contents.*

Figure 1. Frames split a Web browser window into multiple sections, each of which can contain a different Web page.

Frames

The frames feature of HTML makes it possible to divide a Web browser window into multiple parts called *frames*. Each frame can contain a separate Web page and have its own scroll bars. By using frames, you can display more than one Web page at a time—in the same Web browser window. **Figure 1** shows an example.

✔ Tips

- Frames are often used in situations when the same information—like the table of contents shown in **Figure 1**—must appear in a certain position in every window.

- A link within a frame can be set so that its destination page opens in a specific frame of the window, in the window without frames, or in a new window. I provide general information about links in **Chapter 6** and information about using links with frames later in this chapter.

- Older Web browsers do not support frames. I explain how to edit a No Frames Message for browsers which cannot support frames at the end of this chapter.

Framesets

Information about how frames should appear within a Web browser window is stored in a special kind of Web page document called a frameset. You build a frameset by creating frames in a regular Web page document window. When you save the frameset, settings for each of the individual frames are saved within the frameset file.

PageMill offers two ways to create frames:

◆ Drag window borders to split the window horizontally, vertically, or both.

◆ Use commands under the Edit menu's Frame submenu (**Figures 11a** and **11b**) to split a selected frame horizontally, vertically, or both.

✔ Tips

■ A frameset can include any number of frames.

■ The more frames you include in a window, the less information can appear in that window due to the amount of space needed for scroll bars and frame borders. If you include too many frames in a window, the window will look cluttered and the frame contents may not display properly.

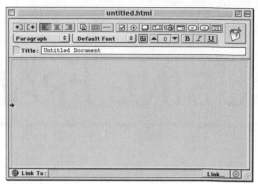

Figure 2. Position the mouse pointer on the left edge of the window.

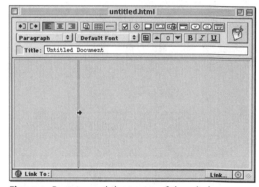

Figure 3. Drag toward the center of the window.

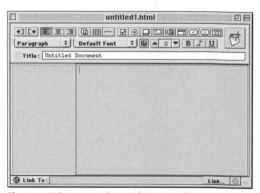

Figure 4. When you release the mouse button, the window splits.

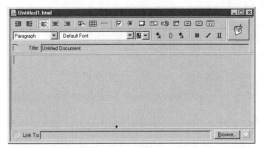

Figure 5. Position the mouse pointer on the bottom edge of the window.

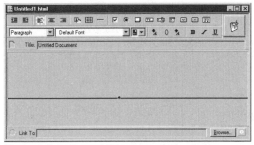

Figure 6. Drag toward the center of the window.

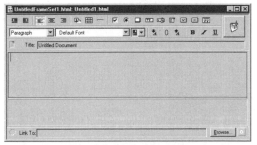

Figure 7. When you release the mouse button, the window splits.

To create a frame by dragging

1. Hold down (Option) (Mac OS) or (Ctrl) (Windows) and position the mouse pointer at the left, bottom, right, or top edge of the window. The mouse pointer should turn into a black arrow pointing into the document window (**Figures 2** and **5**.)

2. Press the mouse button down and drag in the direction of the arrow. A thick line indicating the frame edge moves along with the mouse (**Figures 3** and **6**).

3. When the thick line indicates the desired frame width (**Figure 3**) or height (**Figure 6**), release the mouse button. The frame border appears (**Figures 4** and **7**).

✔ Tips

- You can use the instructions above to split an existing frame. Simply hold down (Option) (Mac OS) or (Ctrl) (Windows) while positioning the mouse pointer on an outside edge of the frame. Drag when the arrow pointer appears.

- To create a frame that spans the entire width (**Figures 8** and **9**) or height of the window, hold down (⌃ ⌘)(Option) (Mac OS) or (Shift)(Ctrl) (Windows) while dragging as instructed above.

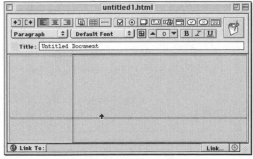

Figure 8. You can also drag...

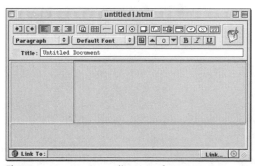

Figure 9. ...to create a split across frames.

CREATING FRAMES BY DRAGGING

To create a frame with Frame submenu commands

1. To split a window into two frames, position the insertion point inside the window (**Figure 10**).

2. To split the window or frame horizontally (**Figure 12**), choose Edit > Frame > Split Frame Horizontally from the Edit menu (**Figures 11a** and **11b**) or press Shift ⌃ ⌘ H (Mac OS) or Ctrl Shift H (Windows).

   or

   To split the window or frame vertically (**Figure 13**) choose Edit > Frame > Split Frame Vertically (**Figures 11a** and **11b**) or press Shift ⌃ ⌘ V (Mac OS) or Ctrl Shift V (Windows).

   The window splits accordingly (**Figures 12** and **13**).

✔ Tip

- You can use the instructions above to split an existing frame. Simply position the insertion point within the frame you want to split. Then choose Edit > Frame > Split Frame Horizontally or Edit > Frame > Split Frame Vertically (**Figures 11a** and **11b**) to split the frame.

Figure 10. Position the insertion point within the window or frame.

Figures 11a & 11b. The Frame submenu under the Edit menu on Mac OS (left) and Windows (below) offers commands for editing a frameset.

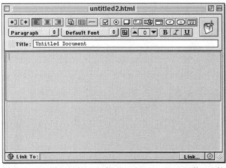

Figure 12. Choosing Split Frame Horizontally splits the window or frame in half horizontally.

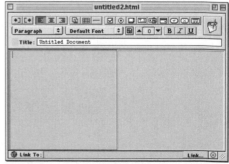

Figure 13. Choosing Split Frame Vertically splits the window or frame in half vertically.

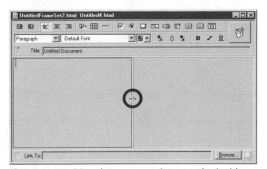

Figure 14. Position the mouse pointer on the inside border of the frame you want to remove.

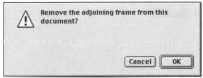

Figure 15. Drag the inside border to the outside border.

Figures 16a & 16b. A dialog box like this appears on Mac OS (above) and Windows (below) so you can confirm that you want to remove the frame.

To remove a frame

1. Position the mouse pointer on the inside border of the frame you want to remove. The mouse pointer turns into a two-headed arrow (**Figure 14**).

2. Press the mouse button down and drag to the outside border of the frame (**Figure 15**).

3. When you release the mouse button, a dialog box like the one in **Figures 16a** or **16b** appears. Click OK to remove the frame.

✔ Tips

- If the last thing you did was create a frame, you can choose Edit > Undo Create Frame or press (⌘ ⌘ Z) (Mac OS) or choose Edit > Undo or press (Ctrl Z) (Windows) to remove it. I tell you more about using the Undo command in **Chapter 2**.

- If you try to remove an unsaved frame, a dialog box like the one in **Figures 17a** or **17b** may appear. Click Save (Mac OS) or Yes (Windows) to save the frame before removing it. I tell you more about saving framesets and frames later in this chapter.

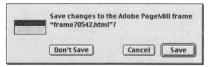

Figures 17a & 17b. If you try to remove an unsaved frame, a dialog box like this appears on Mac OS (above) and Windows (below).

Entering Information into Frames

Each frame in a frameset can contain a different Web page. There are two ways to specify what should appear in a specific frame:

◆ Enter text and objects in the frame just as you would any other Web page document. This creates a new Web page.

◆ Use commands under the Frameset submenu (**Figures 19a** and **19b**) to insert a new or existing Web page document into the frame.

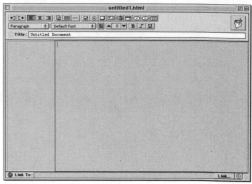

Figure 18. Position the insertion point in the frame in which you want to insert the page.

✔ Tips

■ I tell you how to enter, edit, and format text and objects in Web pages throughout this book. The same techniques apply when entering information into a frame.

■ If you try to insert a new or existing page into an unsaved frame, a dialog box like the one in **Figure 17a** or **17b** may appear. Click Save (Mac OS) or Yes (Windows) to save the frame's current contents before replacing it with another Web page. I tell you more about saving framesets and frames later in this chapter.

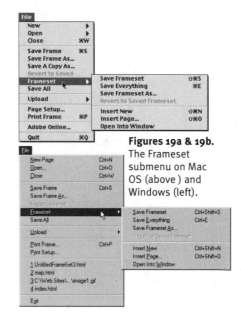

Figures 19a & 19b. The Frameset submenu on Mac OS (above) and Windows (left).

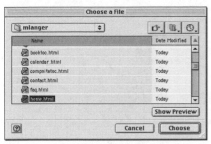

Figures 20a & 20b. Use the Choose a File dialog box on Mac OS (above) or Open dialog box on Windows (below) to open the page you want to insert.

Figure 21. The page opens in the selected frame.

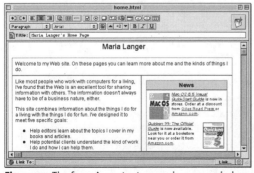

Figure 22. The frame's contents open in a new window.

To insert an existing page into a frame

1. Position the insertion point in the frame in which you want to insert the existing page (**Figure 18**).

2. Choose File > Frameset > Insert Page (**Figures 19a** and **19b**) or press Shift ⌃ ⌘ O (Mac OS) or Ctrl Shift O (Windows).

3. Use the Choose a File (Mac OS; **Figure 20a**) or Open (Windows; **Figure 20b**) dialog box that appears to locate and open the Web page you want to insert.

The page opens in the selected frame (**Figure 21**).

To work with a frame's contents in a separate window

1. Position the insertion point in the frame you want to open in its own window (**Figure 21**).

2. Choose File > Frameset > Open Into Window (**Figures 19a** and **19b**).

The page in the frame opens in its own window (**Figure 22**).

To create a new page in a frame

1. Position the insertion point in the frame in which you want to create a new page.

2. Choose File > Frameset > Insert New (**Figures 19a** and **19b**) or press Shift ⌃ ⌘ N (Mac OS) or Ctrl Shift N (Windows).

The contents of the frame are cleared out to make a new page.

Frame Options

The Inspector lets you set a variety of options for the frames you create:

◆ Give the frame a name that makes sense to you.

◆ Specify the frame width or height in pixels, as a percentage of window width or height, or relative to the other frames in the frameset.

◆ Set frame margin width and height.

◆ Specify whether scrollbars should appear in the frame.

◆ Set an anchor for the frame.

◆ Specify whether frames are resizable by users in their Web browsers.

✔ Tip

■ You can also change the width or height of a frame by dragging. I explain how later in this section of the chapter.

To set options for a frame

1. Position the insertion point in the frame for which you want to set options.

2. If necessary, display the Inspector and click its Frame tab to display Frame options (**Figures 23a** and **23b**).

3. Make changes in the Inspector as discussed throughout this part of the chapter.

To rename a frame

1. Enter a name in the Name box of the Inspector (**Figure 24**).

2. Press (Return) (Mac OS) or (Return) (Windows) to complete the entry.

3. A dialog box like the one in **Figures 25a** or **25b** may appear, warning you that renaming the frame can cause links to break. Click OK to rename the frame.

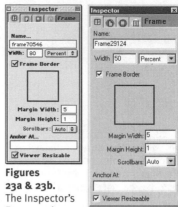

Figures 23a & 23b. The Inspector's Frame options on Mac OS (left) and Windows (right).

Figure 24. Enter the name you want to use in the Name box.

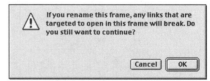

Figure 25. A dialog box like this appears on Mac OS (above) and Windows (below) when you rename a frame.

✔ Tip

■ To prevent links from breaking as **Figures 25a** and **25b** warn, it's a good idea to rename frames *before* creating links to them. I tell you about linking to target frames later in this chapter.

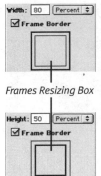

Frames Resizing Box

Figures 26 & 27.
If necessary, click in the Frames Resizing Box to display Width (top) or Height (bottom) options for a nested frame. As you can see here, the appearance of the Frames Resizing Box changes depending on which frame and option is selected.

Figures 28a & 28b.
The Width and Height menus in the Inspector on Mac OS (left) and Windows (right).

To resize a frame with the Inspector

1. If necessary, click a box in the Frames Resizing Box to display the Width (**Figure 26**) or Height (**Figure 27**) options for the frame you want to resize.

2. Choose an option from the Width or Height menu (**Figures 28a** and **28b**) in the Inspector:

   ◆ **Pixels** enables you to set width or height as an exact measurement.

   ◆ **Percent** enables you to set width or height as a percentage of the window size.

   ◆ **Relative** enables you to set width or height relative to other frames in the frameset. For example, in a three-column frameset, if you set one column to 200 pixels and the other two columns to 1 and 3 relative, the first column would be 200 pixels wide and the remaining width would be divided between the other two columns, with the third column three times the width of the second.

3. Enter a measurement in the Width or Height edit box (**Figures 26** and **27**).

4. Press [Return] (Mac OS) or [Return] (Windows) to complete the entry.

The frame size changes accordingly.

✔ Tips

■ Multiple boxes may appear in the Frames Resizing Box if the selected frame is a *nested frame*—a frame that is part of a split frame, like one of the two top frames in **Figure 9**.

■ If the total height or width of your entries is less than or greater than the size of the window, the frames are sized proportionally.

To resize a frame by dragging

1. Position the mouse pointer on the inside border of the frame whose width or height you want to change. The mouse pointer turns into a two-headed arrow (**Figure 29**).

2. Press the mouse button down and drag in a direction of the arrow to increase or decrease the size of the frame. A thick line indicating the frame edge moves along with the mouse (**Figure 30**).

3. When the thick line indicates the desired frame width (**Figure 30**) or height, release the mouse button. The frame resizes (**Figure 31**).

✔ Tip

■ When you resize a frame, the adjacent frame(s) may also resize. You can see this in **Figures 29** and **31**—when the left frame's width is increased, the right frame's width is automatically decreased.

Figure 29. Position the mouse pointer on the inside edge of the frame.

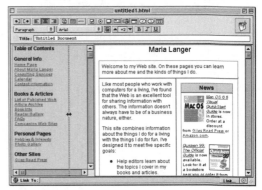

Figure 30. Press the mouse button down and drag.

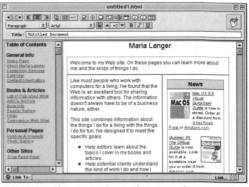

Figure 31. When you release the mouse button, the frame resizes.

Figure 32. Enter values in the Margin Width and Margin Height boxes.

Figure 33. In this example, the right frame's margin width and height are set to 20. Compare this illustration to the one in **Figure 31** to see how this differs from default values.

Figures 34a & 34b. The Scrollbars menu in the Inspector on Mac OS (left) and Windows (right).

To set frame margin width & height

1. To change the amount of space between the left and right edges of the frame and the contents of the frame, enter a value in the Inspector's Margin Width box (**Figure 32**).

   or

   To change the amount of space between the top and bottom edges of the frame and the visible contents of the frame, enter a value in the Inspector's Margin Height box (**Figure 32**).

2. Press (Return) (Mac OS) or (Return) (Windows) to complete the entry.

✔ Tips

- Margin height is set in pixels. The smallest acceptable value is 1.

- The default Margin Width setting is 5 and the default Margin Height setting is 1.

- **Figure 33** shows an example with a frame's Margin Width and Margin Height set to 20.

To set scrollbar display options

Choose an option from the Scrollbars menu in the Inspector (**Figures 34a** and **34b**):

- **Yes** displays both horizontal and vertical scrollbars all the time for the frame.

- **No** never displays the horizontal or vertical scrollbars for the frame.

- **Auto** displays a horizontal or vertical scrollbar (or both) only when needed. This is the default setting for all frames you create.

✔ Tip

- If a frame contains only a small amount of text or an object, you can specify a frame size in pixels and turn off scrollbars to create a fixed menu or navigation bar.

SETTING FRAME MARGINS & SCROLLBAR DISPLAY

To set a frame anchor

1. Follow the steps in **Chapter 6** to insert and rename an anchor (**Figure 35**).

2. In the Frame panel of the Inspector, enter the name of the anchor in the Anchor At box (**Figure 36**) and press ⌷Return⌷ (Mac OS) or ⌷Return⌷ (Windows) to complete the entry.

   or

   Drag the anchor from the frame into the Anchor At box in the Frame panel of the Inspector.

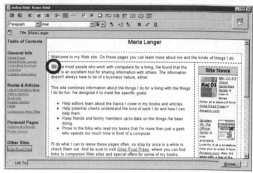

Figure 35. Insert and rename an anchor where you want the page to open in the frame.

✔ Tip

- When you set a frame anchor, the anchor appears at the top of the frame when the frameset first opens. This enables you to specify an exact page location to appear within a frame.

Figure 36. Enter the name of the anchor in the Anchor At box.

To specify whether a frame can be resized in a browser

Turn the Viewer Resizable check box in the Inspector (**Figure 37**) on or off as follows:

- To enable users to resize a frame while viewing the frameset with a Web browser, make sure the Viewer Resizable check box is turned on.

- To prevent users from resizing a frame while viewing the frameset with a Web browser, turn off the Viewer Resizable check box.

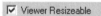

Figure 37. This check box setting determines whether a user can resize a frame while viewing it.

✔ Tips

- The Viewer Resizable check box is turned on by default.

- With the Viewer Resizable check box turned on, a user can resize a frame by dragging its border (**Figure 38**) in a Web browser window. Frame width changes made in a Web browser window are not saved.

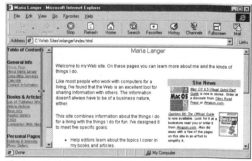

Figure 38. If the Viewer Resizable check box is turned on for a frame, a user can resize the frame by dragging its border in the browser window.

Target Frames

Most Web pages include links that, when clicked, display other Web pages. Unlike a regular Web page, however, a frameset has multiple frames in which a linked page can appear.

PageMill lets you specify a destination or *target frame* for any link in a frame. Your choices are:

- ◆ **Default**, which displays the linked page in the same window or frame as the link.

- ◆ **New window**, which creates a new browser window to display the linked page.

- ◆ **Parent frameset**, which displays the linked page with the "top-level" frameset—the main frameset for the window containing the link. This option applies when a frame contains another frameset.

- ◆ **Same frame**, which displays the linked page in the same frame as the link.

- ◆ **Same window**, which displays the linked page in the same window as the link.

Or you can select a specific frame in the current frameset to display the linked page.

✔ Tips

- ■ I tell you how to create and edit text and graphic links in **Chapter 6**. You should be familiar with what links are and how they work before attempting to create target frames.

- ■ You can also set a default or *base target* frame for all links on a page. This is much quicker than setting individual links if all or most links on a page should appear in the same target frame.

To set the base target frame for a page

1. Open the page for which you want to set the base target frame.

    or

    Click in the frame for which you want to set the base target frame.

2. If necessary, display the Inspector and click its Page tab to display Page options (**Figures 39a** and **39b**).

3. Click the Base Target menu to display its options (**Figure 40**).

4. Choose an option from the menu (**Figures 42** and **43**).

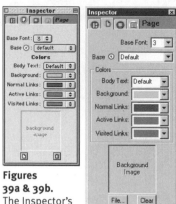

Figures 39a & 39b. The Inspector's Page options on Mac OS (left) and Windows (right).

✔ Tips

- The Base Target frame is the default target frame for all links on the page except those for which you have set a different target frame as instructed below.

- When you choose an option from the Base Target menu, your choice is written to the page file.

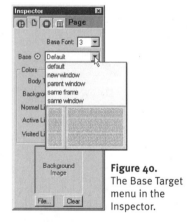

Figure 40. The Base Target menu in the Inspector.

To set a target frame for a link

1. Select the link for which you want to specify a target frame.

2. Position the mouse pointer on the Change Link Target button at the far right end of the Link To bar.

3. Click to display a target menu (**Figure 41**).

4. Choose an option from the menu (**Figures 42** and **43**).

Figure 41. You can display the target menu for a link by clicking the Change Link Target button.

✔ Tips

- When you choose an option from the target menu for a specific link, your choice is written to the frame file. There is no on-screen indication of the choice.

- Be sure to test your target frames before publishing the frameset on the Web. I tell you how to test pages in **Chapter 9**.

Figure 42. Select a location...

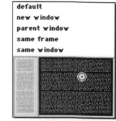

Figure 43. ...or select a specific frame in the current frameset.

SETTING TARGET FRAMES

Saving & Printing Framesets & Frames

When you work with framesets and frames, you're working with multiple documents at the same time:

◆ The frameset is the document that contains instructions regarding frame size and other settings.

◆ The frames are the documents that contain the Web page data that displays in the frames.

The File menu and its Frameset submenu (**Figures 19a** and **19b**) include commands to save framesets and frames and to print frames.

✔ Tips

■ PageMill will not allow you to close a frameset or frame without saving changes to it. If you try to close an unsaved frameset or frame, a dialog box like the one in **Figures 17a** or **17b** will appear, offering you a chance to save the frame.

■ A frameset document includes information about the Web pages that will appear in each frame. Before saving changes to a frameset, be sure that the Web pages you want to appear in each frame are displayed.

■ I tell you more about saving files in **Chapter 1**.

Figure 44. Enter a name for the frameset in the Title box.

To name a frameset

1. Enter a name for the frameset in the Title box near the top of the window (**Figure 44**).

2. Press ⌐Return⌐ (Mac OS) or ⌐Enter⌐ (Windows) to complete the entry.

✔ Tip

■ The frameset name is what appears in the title bar of a Web browser window when the frameset is displayed.

To save a frameset

1. Choose File > Frameset > Save Frameset (**Figures 19a** and **19b**) or press Shift Ğ ⌘ S (Mac OS) or Ctrl Shift S (Windows).

   If the frameset has already been saved at least once, changes you made to the frameset file are saved. You're finished.

   or

   If this is the first time you are saving the frameset, the Save (Mac OS; **Figure 45a**) or Save As (Windows; **Figure 45b**) dialog box appears. Follow the steps below.

2. Use the dialog box to open the disk location in which you want to save the frameset file.

3. Enter a name for the file in the Name (Mac OS) or File name (Windows) box.

4. Click Save.

   The frameset file is saved. The name you entered appears in its title bar.

✔ Tips

- The first time you save a frameset, the Save Frameset and Save Frameset As commands (**Figures 19a** and **19b**) do the same thing—open the Save (Mac OS) or Save As dialog box.

- Be sure to follow any file naming guidelines required by your server. If you're not sure what they are, ask the Webmaster or System Administrator.

- To save a previously saved frameset file with a new name or in a new disk location, use the Save Frameset As command.

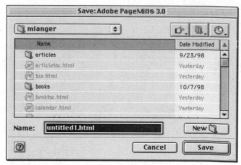

Figures 45a & 45b. Use the Save dialog box on Mac OS (above) or Save As dialog box on Windows (below) to save framesets or frame pages.

To save a frame

1. Position the insertion point anywhere in the frame you want to save.

2. Choose File > Save Frame (**Figures 19a** and **19b**) or press ⌃ ⌘ S (Mac OS) or Ctrl S (Windows).

   If the frame has already been saved at least once, changes you made to the frame's page file are saved. You're finished.

   or

   If this is the first time you are saving the frame, the Save (Mac OS; **Figure 45a**) or Save As (Windows; **Figure 45b**) dialog box appears. Follow the steps below.

3. Use the dialog box to open the disk location in which you want to save the frame's page file.

4. Enter a name for the file in the Name (Mac OS) or File name (Windows) box.

5. Click Save.

   The frame's page file is saved.

✔ Tips

- When you save a frame, you are really saving the page within the frame.

- The first time you save a frame, the Save Frame and Save Frame As commands (**Figures 19a** and **19b**) do the same thing—open the Save (Mac OS) or Save As dialog box.

- Be sure to follow any file naming guidelines required by your server. If you're not sure what they are, ask the Webmaster or System Administrator.

- To save a previously saved frame with a new name or in a new disk location, use the Save Frame As command.

To save all changed framesets & frames

1. Choose File > Frameset > Save Everything (**Figures 19a** and **19b**) or press ⌥ ⌘ E (Mac OS) or Ctrl E (Windows).

2. A Save (Mac OS; **Figure 45a**) or Save As (Windows; **Figure 45b**) dialog box appears for each frameset or frame page that has not yet been saved. Use it to select a destination folder and enter a name for the file. Then click Save. Repeat this step as necessary until all files have been saved.

To revert to the saved frameset or frame

1. To restore the frameset to the way it was the last time you saved it, choose File > Frameset > Revert to Saved Frameset.

   or

   To restore a frame to the way it was the last time you saved it, position the insertion point within the frame and choose File > Revert to Saved.

2. A dialog box appears, asking you to confirm that you want to revert to the last saved version of the file (**Figures 46a** and **46b**). Click Revert.

All changes you made to the frameset or frame since the last time it was saved are reversed.

✔ Tip

■ When you revert a frameset, you may see a dialog box like the one in **Figure 17a** or **17b** that asks whether you want to save changes to a frame. Click Save (Mac OS) or Yes (Windows) to save changes to the frame before reverting to the saved frameset.

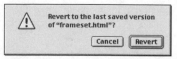

Figure 46a. A dialog box like this appears on Mac OS when you revert to a saved frameset...

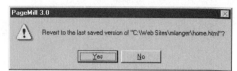

Figure 46b. ...and one like this appears on Windows when you revert to a saved frame.

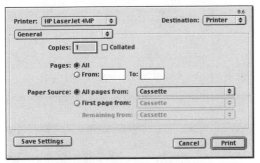

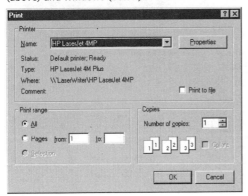

Figures 47a & 47b. The Print dialog box on Mac OS (above) and Windows (below).

To print a frame

1. Position the insertion point in the frame you want to print.

2. Choose File > Print Frame (**Figures 19a** and **19b**) or press ⌃⌘P (Mac OS) or Ctrl P (Windows).

3. In the Print dialog box that appears (**Figures 47a** and **47b**), set the number of copies, page range, and paper source.

4. On Mac OS, to print the page's background (which I tell you about in **Chapter 3**), be sure to turn on the Print Page Background check box. Depending on your printer, you may have to choose Adobe PageMill®3.0 from a pop-up menu at the top of the dialog box to switch to PageMill-specific printing options. (This is done in the Print Setup dialog box on Windows systems.)

5. Click Print (Mac OS) or OK (Windows) to print.

   The frame's page prints.

✔ Tips

■ Printing a frame is the same as printing a Web page.

■ You cannot print multiple frames in a frameset the way they appear on screen.

■ The way the Print dialog box appears (**Figures 47a** and **47b**) depends on your printer and the selected printer driver.

■ I tell you more about printing, including how to set page options, in **Chapter 1**.

The No Frames Message

As mentioned in the beginning of this chapter, older browsers cannot properly display frames. You can use the No Frames Message to tell users with browsers that don't support frames that the page they are viewing includes frames.

To edit the No Frames Message

1. Choose Edit > Frame > No Frames Message (**Figures 11a** and **11b**).

2. A No Frames Message window appears (**Figure 48**). Edit the contents of the window so it displays the text you want to appear (**Figure 49**).

3. When you finish making changes, click the No Frames Message window's close box to dismiss it.

Figure 50 shows an example of the way the No Frames Message in **Figure 49** appears when viewed in a browser that does not support frames.

✔ Tip

■   As shown in **Figures 49** and **50**, you can include links in the No Frames Message window. This is a great way to offer easy access to one or more alternate pages. I tell you how to add links in **Chapter 6**.

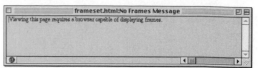

Figure 48. The default No Frames Message...

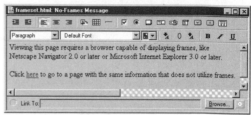

Figure 49. ...can be edited to include a custom message with links.

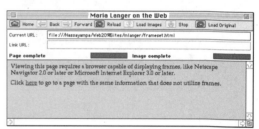

Figure 50. Here's the message from **Figure 49** viewed with an old America Online browser.

CREATING FORMS

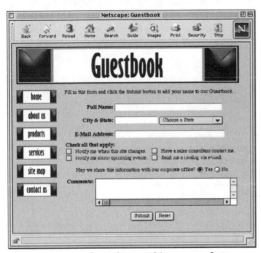

Figure 1. Here's a form that combines many form elements.

Forms

Forms are Web pages with special elements designed to gather information. You create a form by adding any combination of the following form elements to a Web page:

- ◆ *Check boxes*, which can be used to select multiple items from a list.
- ◆ *Radio buttons*, which let users choose from a variety of options.
- ◆ *Text areas*, which accept long passages of text.
- ◆ *Text fields*, which accept short strings of text.
- ◆ *Password fields*, which let users enter passwords.
- ◆ *Pop-up menus* and selection list fields, which let users choose from a variety of options.
- ◆ *Submit button*, which sends data on completed forms to be processed.
- ◆ *Reset button*, which clears all entries so the user can start over.
- ◆ *Hidden fields*, which can store predefined information that is used when processing the form.

Figure 1 shows an example of a form that uses many of these elements.

✔ Tip

- ■ To use a form, you need a program called a *Common Gateway Interface* (*CGI*). I tell you more about CGIs at the end of this chapter.

Creating Forms

With PageMill, you create forms by placing form elements, text, and images on a page.

◆ Form elements (**Figure 2**) collect input from the user. Each element must have a unique name and/or value that is recognized by the CGI with which the form will be used.

◆ Text labels or descriptions (**Figure 3**) identify the kind of information requested by each form object. Text can be formatted as desired. I tell you about entering and formatting text in **Chapters 2** and **3**.

◆ Graphic objects (**Figure 1**) and objects like horizontal rules add visual appeal to your forms. I tell you about working with graphic objects in **Chapter 4**.

✔ Tips

■ PageMill 3 enables you to include more than one form on a Web page. (Previous versions of PageMill allowed only one form per page.)

■ You can copy form elements within a form or from one form to another using the Copy and Paste commands or by holding down (Option) (Mac OS) or (Ctrl) (Windows) while dragging a selected object. I discuss copying techniques in **Chapter 2**.

■ To delete a form element, simply select it and press (Del), (Delete), or (Backspace) (Windows) or choose Edit > Clear.

■ Use the basic text and image entry, formatting, and editing techniques discussed in **Chapters 2** through **4** to modify and reorganize your forms as needed.

■ To align text and fields in a form, consider using the Preformatted format (**Figure 4**) or tables (**Figures 5** and **6**). I discuss the Preformatted format in **Chapter 3** and tables in **Chapter 5**.

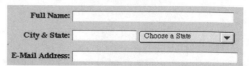

Figure 2. Form elements like the text fields and pop-up menu shown here gather information.

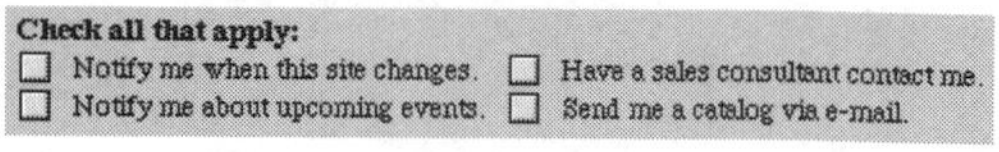

Figure 3. Without text labels beside each of these check boxes, how would the user know what to check?

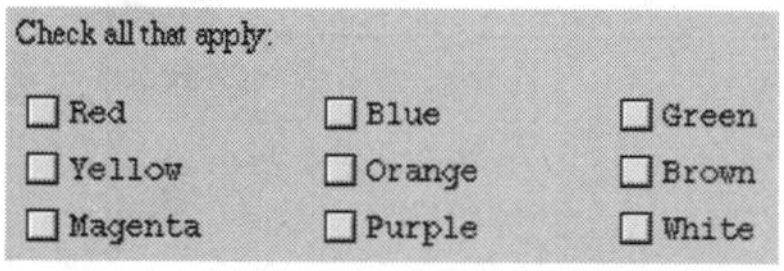

Figure 4. One way to align form elements is to use the Preformatted format, which features a monospaced typeface.

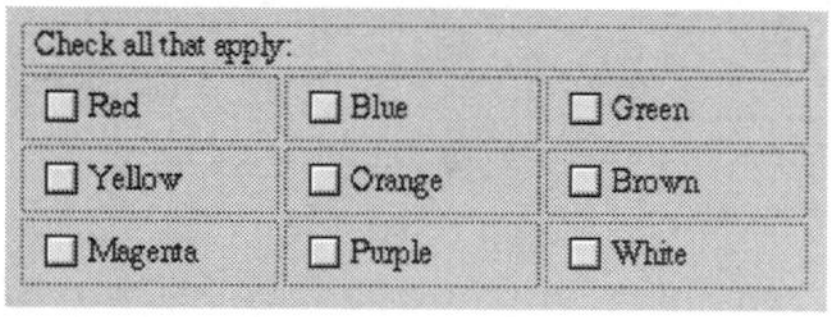

Figure 5. To align form elements, put them in a table.

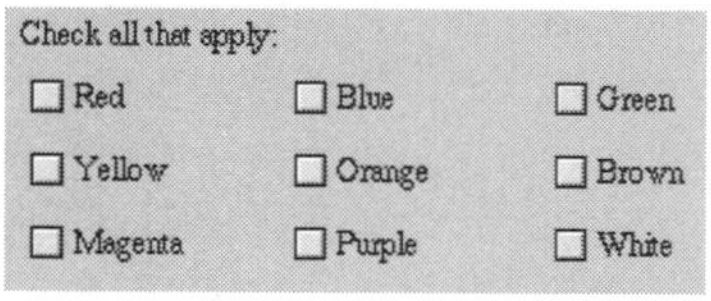

Figure 6. When the borderless table from **Figure 5** is viewed in Preview mode or with a Web browser, the form elements are neatly lined up.

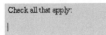

Figure 7. Position the insertion point where you want the check box to appear.

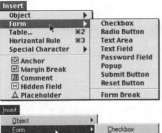

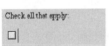

Figures 8a & 8b. The Form submenu under the Insert menu on Mac OS (left) and Windows (below) offers one way to insert form elements into a Web page document.

Figure 9. The check box appears at the insertion point.

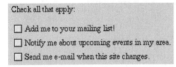

Figure 10. Finished check boxes.

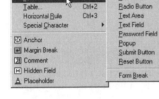

Figure 11. Click a check box to select it.

Figures 12a & 12b. The Inspector's Object panel showing Checkbox options on Mac OS (left) and Windows (right).

Check Boxes

Check boxes are used when you want to provide a list of options. Unlike radio buttons, which I discuss on the next page, a user can turn on any number of check boxes in a group.

To add a check box

1. Position the insertion point where you want the check box to appear (**Figure 7**).

2. Choose Insert > Form > Checkbox (**Figures 8a** and **8b**).

   or

   Click the Insert Checkbox button on the toolbar.

   A check box appears at the insertion point (**Figure 9**).

3. Type in a label or descriptive text for the check box.

4. Repeat steps 1 through 3 for each check box you want to add.

When you're finished, your check boxes might look something like the ones in **Figure 10**.

To specify check box settings

1. Select the check box for which you want to specify settings (**Figure 11**).

2. If necessary, display the Inspector and click its Object tab to display Checkbox options (**Figures 12a** and **12b**).

3. To name the check box, enter a name in the Name box.

4. To set a value for the check box, enter a value in the Value box.

5. To set the check box so it is turned on by default, turn on the Checked check box.

✔ Tip

■ The Name and Value you assign to a check box must meet the requirements of the CGI that will process the form. Consult the CGI documentation for specifics.

Radio Buttons

Radio buttons enable you to provide a list of options. Unlike check boxes, which I discuss on the previous page, a user must select one—and only one—radio button in a group.

To add a group of radio buttons

1. Position the insertion point where you want the first radio button to appear (**Figure 13**).

2. Choose Insert > Form > Radio Button (**Figures 8a** and **8b**).

   or

   Click the Insert Radio Button button on the toolbar.

   A radio button appears at the insertion point (**Figure 14**).

3. Type in a label or descriptive text for the radio button.

4. Click the radio button to select it (**Figure 15**).

5. Use the Copy and Paste commands to place a copy of the button where you want another radio button to appear.

   or

   Hold down (Option) (Mac OS) or (Ctrl) (Windows) and drag the first radio button to where you want another radio button to appear.

   A radio button appears where you duplicated the first radio button (**Figure 16**). Note that only one of the radio buttons is turned on.

6. Type in a label or descriptive text for the new radio button.

7. Repeat steps 4 through 6 for each radio button you want to add to the group.

When you're finished, your radio buttons might look something like the ones in **Figure 17**.

Figure 13. Position the insertion point where you want the radio button to appear.

Figure 14. The radio button appears at the insertion point.

Figure 15. Select the first radio button.

Figure 16. Duplicate or *clone* the selected radio button to create a second radio button in the group.

Figure 17. When you're finished making radio buttons for a group, only one will be selected.

✔ Tip

- You must copy or *clone* radio buttons as instructed here to create a group. If you simply insert a new radio button for each one, they will not be part of the same group.

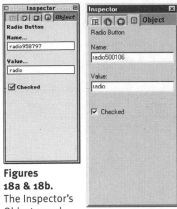

Figures 18a & 18b. The Inspector's Object panel showing Radio Button options on Mac OS (left) and Windows (right).

To specify radio button settings

1. Select the radio button for which you want to specify settings (**Figure 15**).

2. If necessary, display the Inspector and click its Object tab to display Radio Button options (**Figures 18a** and **18b**).

3. To name the radio button, enter a name in the Name box.

4. To set a value for the radio button, enter a value in the Value box.

5. To set the radio button so it is selected by default, turn on the Checked check box.

✔ Tips

- The Name and Value you assign to a radio button must meet the requirements of the CGI that will process the form. Consult the CGI documentation for specifics.

- All radio buttons in a group have the same name. If you change the name of one radio button in a group, be sure to change the names of the others so they match.

- To make radio buttons that you inserted individually (by clicking the Insert Radio Button button multiple times) into a group of radio buttons that work together, change their names so they're all the same.

CONFIGURING RADIO BUTTONS

Text Input Elements

Text input form elements collect typed input from users. There are three kinds of text elements, each of which are illustrated in **Figure 19**:

- ◆ A text area accepts multiple-line text entries. It is designed for lengthy input.

- ◆ A text field accepts a single line of text. It is designed for short input.

- ◆ A password field accepts a single line of text. It is specially designed for password entry since input is echoed back as bullet or asterisk characters.

To add a text input element

1. Position the insertion point where you want the object to appear. In most cases, this will be right after or under a typed-in label or descriptive text (**Figure 20**).

2. Insert the element you want:

   - ◆ To insert a text area, choose Insert > Form > Text Area (**Figures 8a** and **8b**) or click the Insert Text Area button on the toolbar.

   - ◆ To insert a text field, choose Insert > Form > Text Field (**Figures 8a** and **8b**) or click the Insert Text Field button on the toolbar.

   - ◆ To insert a password field, choose Insert > Form > Password Field (**Figures 8a** and **8b**) or click the Insert Password Field button on the toolbar.

   The object you inserted appears at the insertion point (**Figure 21**).

3. Repeat steps 1 and 2 for each input element you want to add.

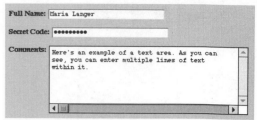

Figure 19. Here's an example of each of the three text input elements.

Figure 20. Position the insertion point where you want the element to appear.

Figure 21. The element appears at the insertion point.

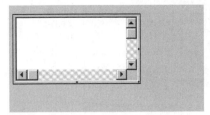

Figure 22. Click on the text input element to select it.

Figure 23. Drag one of its resizing handles.

Figure 24. When you release the mouse button, the text area resizes.

Figure 25. Click the text or password field to select it.

Figure 26. Drag its resizing handle.

Figure 27. When you release the mouse button, the field resizes.

To resize a text area by dragging

1. Click once on the text area to select it. A selection box and three resizing handles appear around it (**Figure 22**).

2. Position the mouse pointer on one of the resizing handles, press the mouse button down, and drag.

    ◆ To change the width of the text area, drag the right side resizing handle.

    ◆ To change the height of the text area, drag the bottom resizing handle.

    ◆ To change the width and height of the text area, drag the corner resizing handle.

    As you drag, an outline of the text area appears to indicate the final size (**Figure 23**).

3. When the text area is the desired size, release the mouse button. The text area resizes to your specifications (**Figure 24**).

To resize a text field or password field by dragging

1. Click on the text field or password field to select it. A selection box appears around it and one resizing handle appears on its right side (**Figure 25**).

2. Position the mouse pointer on the resizing handle, press the mouse button down, and drag to the left or right. As you drag, an outline of the field appears to indicate the final size (**Figure 26**).

3. When the field is the desired size, release the mouse button. The field resizes to your specifications (**Figure 27**).

RESIZING TEXT INPUT ELEMENTS BY DRAGGING

Chapter 8

To resize a text input element with the Inspector

1. Click once on the text area, text field, or password field to select it.

2. If necessary, display the Inspector and click its Object tab to display Text Area (**Figures 28a** and **28b**), Text Field (**Figures 29a** and **29b**), or Password Field (**Figures 30a** and **30b**) options.

3. Enter values in the Rows, Columns, Size, or Max Length box(es).

✔ Tips

- All sizes are expressed in characters. For example, a value of 10 means 10 characters of text.

- When you make a change to one of the size-related values in the Inspector, the size of the selected input object changes accordingly. The same holds true when you change the size of an object by dragging it—the values in the Inspector change accordingly.

- If you specify a Max Length value for a Text Field or Password Field, the field will not accept any more than the number of characters you specify.

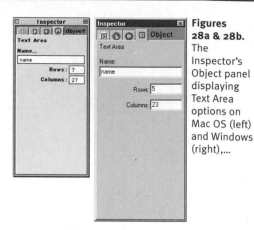

Figures 28a & 28b. The Inspector's Object panel displaying Text Area options on Mac OS (left) and Windows (right),...

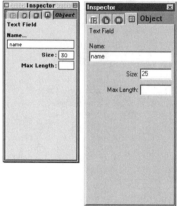

Figures 29a & 29b. ...Text Field options on Mac OS (left) and Windows (right),...

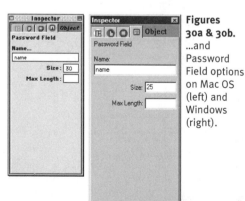

Figures 30a & 30b. ...and Password Field options on Mac OS (left) and Windows (right).

RESIZING TEXT ELEMENTS W/THE INSPECTOR

152

Figure 31. Double-click the element for which you want to provide a default value.

Figure 32. Enter the value you want to use as a default.

To specify a default value for a text input element

1. Double-click the object for which you want to specify a default value. A thick border appears around it and an insertion point appears inside it (**Figure 31**).

2. Enter the value you want to appear (**Figure 32**).

✔ Tip

■ Default text can be used when a field has a common response or when you want to provide hints on how text should be entered (**Figure 32**).

To name a text input object

1. Select the text input object you want to name (**Figures 22** and **25**).

2. If necessary, display the Inspector and click its Object tab to display Text Area (**Figures 28a** and **28b**), Text Field (**Figures 29a** and **29b**), or Password Field (**Figures 30a** and **30b**) options.

3. Enter a name in the Name box.

4. Press Return (Mac OS) or Return (Windows) to complete the entry.

✔ Tip

■ The Name you assign to a text input area must meet the requirements of the CGI that will process the form. Consult the CGI documentation for specifics.

Selection Fields

PageMill offers two types of selection fields:

◆ A pop-up menu, which enables the user to choose one option from a menu you provide.

◆ A list-selection field, which enables the user to choose one or more options from a scrolling list you provide.

To add a pop-up menu

1. Position the insertion point where you want the pop-up menu to appear. In most cases, this will be right after or under a typed-in label or descriptive text (**Figure 33**).

2. Choose Insert > Form > Popup (**Figures 8a** and **8b**).

   or

   Click the Insert Popup button on the toolbar.

   A pop-up menu appears at the insertion point (**Figure 34**).

To add a list-selection field

1. Follow steps 1 and 2 above.

2. Click once on the pop-up menu you created to select it (**Figure 35**).

3. If necessary, display the Inspector and click its Object tab to display Selection Field options (**Figures 36a** and **36b**).

4. Enter the number of menu items you want to appear in the scrolling list in the Items Visible edit box.

5. Press [Return] (Mac OS) or [Enter] (Windows) to complete the entry.

The pop-up list expands to show the number of items you specified. A scroll bar appears on the right side of the box (**Figure 37**). The field will now function as a list-selection field.

Figure 33. Position the insertion point where you want the pop-up menu to appear.

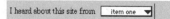

Figure 34. A pop-up menu with PageMill's default values appears at the insertion point.

Figure 35. Click a pop-up menu to select it.

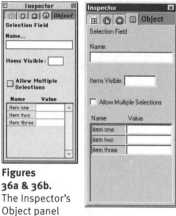

Figures 36a & 36b. The Inspector's Object panel displaying Selection Field options on Mac OS (left) and Windows (right).

Figure 37. The number of items you specified appears in a scrolling list.

Figure 38. Another way to turn a pop-up menu into a list-selection field is to drag its resizing handle.

✔ Tip

■ Another way to turn a pop-up list into a list-selection field is to select it and drag its bottom resizing handle (**Figure 38**).

Figure 39. Double-click a pop-up menu...

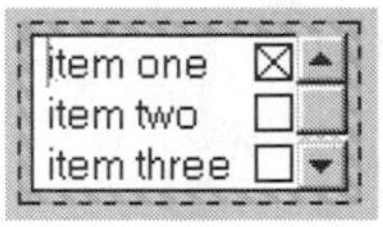

Figure 40. ...or list-selection field.

Figure 41. Enter the options you want to appear on the pop-up menu...

Figure 42. ...or list-selection field.

Figure 43. Here's the pop-up list from Figure 41...

Figure 44. ...and here's the list-selection field from Figure 42.

To specify selection field options

1. Double-click the pop-up menu or list-selection field for which you want to specify options. The menu or list opens to display the default options (**Figures 39** and **40**).

2. Select all the default options by dragging the mouse over them, choosing Edit > Select All, or pressing ⌘A (Mac OS) or Ctrl A (Windows).

3. Type in the values you want. Be sure to press Return (Mac OS) or Enter (Windows) after each one. When you're finished, your list might look like the one in **Figure 41** or **42**.

4. Click elsewhere in the document window to close the menu options (**Figures 43** and **44**).

✔ Tips

- The list expands to accept as many entries as you need to include.

- The width of the pop-up menu or list-selection field is determined by the number of characters in the longest entry for the field.

- You can also use this technique to edit the values in a pop-up menu or list selection field if you need to change them.

SPECIFYING SELECTION FIELD OPTIONS

To set a default selection field option

1. Double-click the pop-up menu or list-selection field for which you want to set a default option. The list opens to display the options (**Figures 41** and **42**).

2. To change the default option for a pop-up menu, drag the triangle into position beside the option you want (**Figure 45**).

   or

   To change the default option for a list-selection field, turn on the check box for the option you want (**Figure 46**).

3. Click elsewhere in the page window to close the menu options.

The entry you set as the default appears on the pop-up menu (**Figure 47**) or list-selection field (**Figure 48**).

✔ Tips

■ Although you can use this technique to set any option as the default, the default option in a pop-up menu or list-selection field is usually the first one.

■ You can set multiple default options for a list-selection field if the Allow Multiple Selections check box is turned on in the Inspector (**Figures 36a** and **36b**) for the field. I tell you about specifying selection field settings on the next page.

Figure 45. Drag the triangle into position beside the default option on a pop-up menu...

Figure 46. ...or turn on the check box beside the default option in a list-selection field.

Figure 47. The default pop-up menu option is the one that appears when the menu is closed.

Figure 48. The default list-selection field option is the one that is automatically selected when the field appears in a form.

Figure 49. Click to select the pop-up menu...

Figure 50. ...or list selection field.

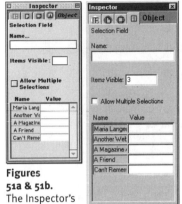

Figures 51a & 51b. The Inspector's Object panel displaying Selection Field options on Mac OS (left) and Windows (right).

To specify selection field settings

1. Select the pop-up menu or list-selection field for which you want to specify settings (**Figures 49** and **50**).

2. If necessary, display the Inspector and click its Object tab to display Selection Field options (**Figures 51a** and **51b**).

3. To name the field, enter a name in the Name box.

4. To allow users to select more than one option in a list-selection field, turn on the Allow Multiple Selections check box.

5. To set a value for a pop-up menu or list-selection field option, enter it in the Value box beside the selection field option.

✔ Tips

■ The Values you assign to Names for a pop-up menu or list-selection field must meet the requirements of the CGI that will process the form. Consult the CGI documentation for specifics.

■ You must turn on the Allow Multiple Selections check box before you can specify multiple default options. I explain how to specify default options on the previous page.

Hidden Fields

A hidden field is a special kind of field that the form user never sees. You use a hidden field to include information required by the CGI that remains the same for every processed form and is not entered by the user.

Figure 52. Position the insertion point where you want the hidden field to appear.

✔ Tips

■ It doesn't really matter where you place a hidden field, since it will never appear to the user. Just make sure you put it with the rest of the form's elements.

■ A form can contain as many hidden fields as required by the CGI that will process the form.

To add a hidden field

1. Position the insertion point among the fields on the form to which you want to add a hidden field (**Figure 52**).

2. Choose Insert > Hidden Field (**Figures 8a** and **8b**).

The hidden field appears as a purple H icon on the page (**Figure 53**).

To specify hidden field options

1. Click the hidden field icon to select it (**Figure 54**).

2. If necessary, display the Inspector and click its Object tab to display Hidden Field options (**Figures 55a** and **55b**).

3. To name the field, enter a name in the Name box.

4. To set a value for the field, enter it in the Value box.

✔ Tip

■ The Name and Value you assign to a hidden field must meet the requirements of the CGI that will process the form. Consult the CGI documentation for specifics.

Figure 53. A hidden field looks like a purple H in a box.

Figure 54. Click a hidden field to select it.

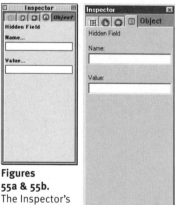

Figures 55a & 55b. The Inspector's Object tab displaying Hidden Field options on Mac OS (left) and Windows (right).

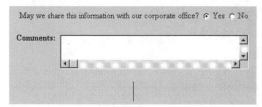

Figure 56. Position the insertion point where you want the button(s) to appear.

Figure 57. The Submit and Reset buttons are usually placed together at the bottom of a form.

Submit & Reset Buttons

Forms usually include two special buttons:

◆ The Submit button sends the information from the form to the CGI on the server.

◆ The Reset button clears all entries in the form so the user can start fresh.

✔ Tips

■ You should only have one Submit button on a form.

■ Submit and Reset buttons are normally placed together on a form.

■ In most cases, Submit and Reset buttons are placed at the bottom of a form, right after the last input area.

To add a Submit or Reset button

1. Position the insertion point where you want the button to appear (**Figure 56**).

2. Insert the button you want:

◆ To insert a Submit button, choose Insert > Form > Submit Button (**Figures 8a** and **8b**) or click the Insert Submit Button button on the toolbar.

◆ To insert a Reset button, choose Insert > Form > Reset Button (**Figures 8a** and **8b**) or click the Insert Reset Button button on the toolbar.

The button you inserted appears at the insertion point (**Figure 57**).

To change the label on a button

1. Double-click the button. A dark border appears around it and an insertion point appears inside it (**Figure 58**).

2. Edit the name of the button by selecting it and typing your changes (**Figure 59**). The button resizes to accommodate the text inside it.

3. Click elsewhere in the page window to accept your changes.

To use an image as a Submit button

1. Select the image you want to use as a Submit button (**Figure 60**).

2. If necessary, display the Inspector and click its Object tab to display Image options (**Figures 61a** and **61b**).

3. Select the Button option in the Behavior area of the Inspector.

The image is converted to a button. If the Border box in the Inspector is empty or set to a value greater than 0, a blue border appears around the image.

✔ Tip

■ I tell you more about working with images in **Chapter 4**.

Figure 58. Double-click the button to edit it.

Figure 59. As you enter new text to appear on the button, the button resizes to accommodate it.

Figure 60. Click the image you want to use as a Submit button to select it.

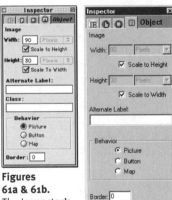

Figures 61a & 61b. The Inspector's Object tab displaying Image options on Mac OS (left) and Windows (right).

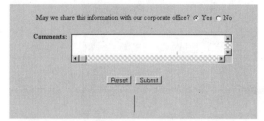

Figure 62. Position the insertion point where you want the Form Break to appear.

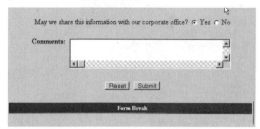

Figure 63. The Form Break ends one form so you can create a new one after it.

Putting Multiple Forms on a Page

PageMill 3 enables you to place more than one form on each Web page. You do this by placing a Form Break between each form on the page.

✔ Tips

- Putting more than one form on a page enables you to offer access to multiple CGIs on the same Web page.

- A Form Break does not appear in a Web browser.

To place multiple forms on a page

1. Follow the instructions throughout this chapter to create the first form you want on the page. Be sure to include any required hidden fields and a Submit and Reset button.

2. Position the insertion point on the line after the last form element (**Figure 62**).

3. Choose Insert > Form > Form Break (**Figures 8a** and **8b**) or click the Insert Form Break button on the toolbar.

    A form break appears on the page. It looks like a thick white (Mac OS) or blue (Windows) bar labeled *Form Break* (**Figure 63**).

4. Add elements for the next form after the form break.

5. Follow steps 2 through 4 for each additional form you want to add.

✔ Tip

- A Form Break defines each form's section of the Web page. You must group each form's elements within its section for the forms to work. For example, if a page contains two forms, you must put all of the first form's elements above the Form Break and all of the second form's elements below the Form Break.

CGIs

Forms work with programs called *CGIs* (*Common Gateway Interfaces*) that run on the Web server. When a user fills in a form and clicks the Submit button, the information gathered by the form is processed by the CGI. The CGI can do almost anything with the data, such as:

◆ Send the data to someone via e-mail.

◆ Add the data to a database maintained in another application.

◆ Use the data to form the basis of a database search, perform the search, and display the results.

◆ Use the data to create a Web page.

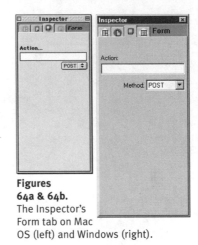

Figures 64a & 64b.
The Inspector's Form tab on Mac OS (left) and Windows (right).

✔ Tips

■ The CGI's functionality (not the form itself) determines how the data is used.

■ CGIs can be created with AppleScript (on Apple Servers) or other programming languages or purchased from third-party vendors.

To specify a CGI for a form

1. If the page contains more than one form, position the insertion point among the elements for the form for which you want to specify a CGI.

2. If necessary, display the Inspector and click its Form tab to display Form options (**Figures 64a** and **64b**).

3. Enter the pathname for the CGI in the Action box.

4. Choose Get or Post from the Method menu beneath the Action box (**Figures 65a** and **65b**).

✔ Tip

■ If you're not sure what to enter in the Inspector's Form tab, ask your Webmaster or System Administrator or consult the documentation that came with the CGI.

Figures 65a & 65b.
The Method menu in the Inspector's Form tab on Mac OS (left) and Windows (right).

TESTING & ENHANCING PAGES

9

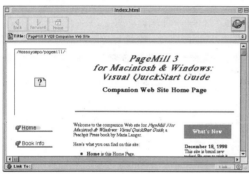

Figure 1. Use PageMill's Preview mode to find missing images...

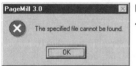

Figure 2.
...or incorrect URLs.

Figure 3. Open pages with several Web browsers to avoid surprises. In this example, an old version of AOL's browser failed to display form fields and buttons or animate a GIF.

Testing Pages

Even after you've put the finishing touches on your Web pages, they may not be ready for installation on your Web server. There's one last thing you need to do: test them.

The testing process should include the following procedures:

◆ Use PageMill's Preview mode to view pages and test all local links. This is how you can learn about missing images (**Figure 1**) or incorrect URLs on your site (**Figure 2**).

◆ Open the pages with a variety of Web browsers to make sure they look the way you expect them to. This is how you can avoid formatting and incompatibility surprises (**Figure 3**).

◆ Use your favorite Web browser to test remote links. This is how you can learn about incorrect URLs for pages that aren't on your site.

✔ Tip

■ In reality, the testing process never ends. Even if you never change a thing on your Web site, other sites change regularly. If your pages include external links, it's important that you test them regularly. That's the only way you can be sure that the linked pages are still available on an ever-changing Internet.

Testing Pages in Preview Mode

PageMill's Preview mode gives you an idea of how your Web pages will look when viewed with a Web browser (**Figures 4a**, **4b**, and **4c**). It also lets you test links and some multimedia elements, like animated GIFs and QuickTime movies.

✔ Tips

- Don't depend solely on PageMill's Preview mode to test your pages. Since the appearance of a Web page varies depending on the browser used to view it, it's a good idea to open your pages with one or more popular Web browsers—like Netscape Navigator and Microsoft Internet Explorer. I tell you more about testing pages with Web browsers later in this chapter.

- Although you can use Preview mode to manually test links, you can also use PageMill's site management features to automatically test links. I explain how in **Chapter 10**.

- As you uncover problems with your pages, you can switch back to Edit mode to fix them. The information throughout this book should help you solve any problems you might encounter.

- I tell you about links in **Chapter 6** and about multimedia objects in **Chapter 4**.

- You can set an option in the General area of the Preferences dialog box (**Figures 5a** and **5b**) to automatically open all pages in Preview mode. I tell you about setting Preferences in **Chapter 11**.

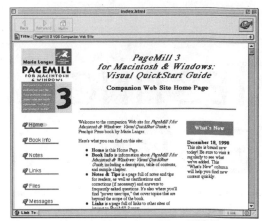

Figure 4a. The Mac OS version of PageMill offers a standard Preview mode,...

Figure 4b. While the Windows version offers a standard Preview mode...

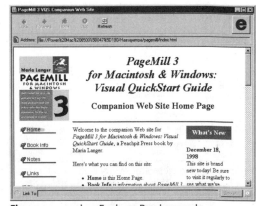

Figure 4c. ...and an Explorer Preview mode.

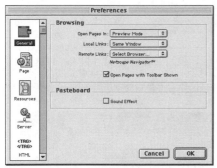

Figures 5a & 5b. The General options of the Preferences dialog box on Mac OS (above) and Windows (below).

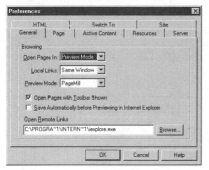

Figures 6a, 6b, 6c, & 6d. The Toggle Preview Mode button in Edit mode (far left), in Preview mode on Mac OS (left center), in Preview mode on Windows (right center), and in Explorer Preview mode on Windows (far right).

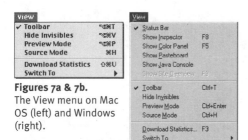

Figures 7a & 7b.
The View menu on Mac OS (left) and Windows (right).

Figure 8. Right-click the Toggle Preview Mode button on Windows to choose which Preview mode you want to view.

To view a page in Preview mode

In Edit mode, click the Toggle Preview Mode button (**Figure 6a**).

or

Choose View > Preview Mode (**Figures 7a and 7b**) or press Option ⌘ P (Mac OS) or Ctrl Enter (Windows).

The window switches to Preview mode (**Figures 4a** and **4b**).

✔ Tip

- The Toggle Preview Mode button looks like the one in **Figure 6a** only if the page is currently displayed in Edit mode. Once you're in Preview mode, the Toggle Preview Mode button changes to look like the one in **Figures 6b** (Mac OS) or **6c** (Windows).

To view a page in Explorer Preview mode (Windows only)

1. Right-click on the Toggle Preview Mode button to display a menu like the one in **Figure 8**.

2. Choose Internet Explorer.

The window switches to Explorer Preview mode (**Figure 4c**).

✔ Tip

- When in Explorer Preview mode, the Toggle Preview Mode button looks like the one in **Figure 6d**.

To check page appearance in Preview mode

Use the scroll bars to scroll through the page and examine it for problems. Some areas you should concentrate on are:

◆ **Text formatting and legibility.** Can you easily read the text? Is the formatting clean? Does the formatting add legibility or distract the reader?

◆ **Images and their borders (if any).** Do the images appear the way you intended? Is there haloing around images with transparent backgrounds? Are borders the desired thickness?

◆ **Multimedia objects like animated GIFs and QuickTime movies.** Do animated GIFs appear properly? Do QuickTime movies play properly?

◆ **Table and table cell dimensions and borders.** Do tables appear the way you intended? Are border, cell padding, and cell spacing measurements appropriate?

◆ **Frame layout and dimensions.** Do the correct Web pages appear in each frame? Are the frames sized appropriately for their contents? Do scrollbars appear when necessary?

✔ Tips

■ It's a good idea to resize the window once or twice to see how changes in window size affect word wrap, tables, and frames. **Figures 9** and **10** show examples.

■ In order to display QuickTime movies in Preview mode, you must have the Quick-Time plug-in properly installed. I tell you about QuickTime and the QuickTime plug-in in **Chapter 4**.

■ I tell you about text formatting in **Chapter 3**, about images and multimedia objects in **Chapter 4**, about tables in **Chapter 5**, and about frames in **Chapter 7**.

Figure 9.
Word wrap around images may look fine when viewed with one page width...

Figure 10. ...but not when viewed with another. The *Motorcycling* heading in this example could be forced to appear after the helicopter picture by inserting a margin break character at the end of the previous paragraph; see **Chapter 4** for details.

Figure 11. When you point to a link in Preview mode, the mouse pointer turns into a pointing finger and the link URL appears in the Link To bar at the bottom of the window.

Previous page *Next page* *Home page* *Menu of viewed pages*

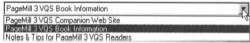

Figure 12a. Navigation buttons and a menu at the top of the Preview mode window enable you to move from one viewed page to another.

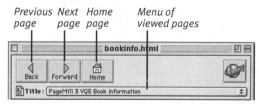

Figure 12b. Clicking the menu displays a list of the pages you have already viewed. Choose one to see it again.

Figures 13a & 13b. You can display a menu within a frame on Mac OS (left) and Windows (right) to navigate within a frame in Preview mode.

To check links in Preview mode

1. Position the mouse pointer on a link. The mouse pointer turns into a pointing finger and the URL for the link appears in the Link To bar at the bottom of the window (**Figure 11**).

2. Click the link once. One of two things will happen:

   ◆ If the link you clicked is a local link, the linked page appears in the Preview mode window.

   ◆ If the link you clicked is a remote link and you have access to the Internet, PageMill will launch your preferred Web browser, connect to the Internet, and display the linked page.

3. Repeat steps 1 and 2 to check all links.

✔ Tips

■ You can set options in the General area of the Preferences dialog box (**Figures 5a** and **5b**) to specify local and remote link viewing options. I tell you how to set preferences in **Chapter 11**.

■ You can use buttons (**Figure 12a**) and a menu (**Figure 12b**) at the top of the Preview mode window to move backward and forward through the pages you check.

■ To navigate forward and backward through links in a frameset:

   ▲ On Mac OS, position the mouse pointer in a blank area of the page window and press the mouse button down until a menu like the one in **Figure 13a** appears. Choose an option to navigate in the frame.

   ▲ On Windows, position the mouse pointer in a blank area of the page window and press the right mouse button. A menu like the one in **Figure 13b** appears. Choose an option to navigate in the frame.

Testing Pages with a Web Browser

As mentioned earlier in this chapter, PageMill's standard Preview mode is not the same as a Web browser. Only by viewing pages with specific browsers can you really see what the pages will look like to the people who view them.

Figures **14** through **17** show examples of the page from **Figure 4** when viewed with Netscape Navigator 4 and Microsoft Internet Explorer 4 on Mac OS and Windows. Note the differences.

✔ Tips

- The Explorer Preview mode available in the Windows version of PageMill displays Web pages the way they appear in Microsoft Internet Explorer version 4 (**Figure 4c**).

- You do not need an Internet connection to open and view a Web page file on your hard disk with a Web browser.

- By testing pages with older browsers, you can see how they display incompatible formatting options such as tables, horizontally aligned graphic objects, and frames.

- You must use a Web browser to view and test certain multimedia objects, like Shockwave files.

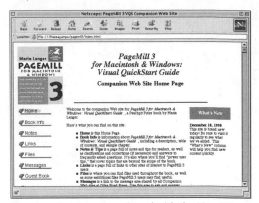

Figure 14. Here's a page viewed with the Mac OS version of Netscape Navigator 4...

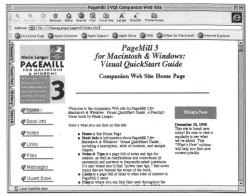

Figure 15. ...and the Mac OS version of Microsoft Internet Explorer 4.

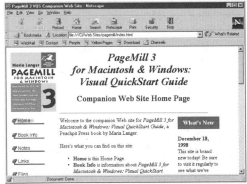

Figure 16. Here's the same page viewed with the Windows version of Netscape Navigator 4...

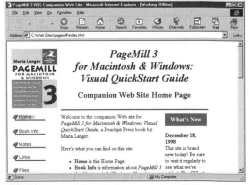

Figure 17. ...and the Windows version of Microsoft Internet Explorer 4.

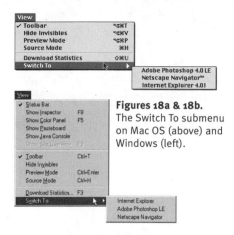

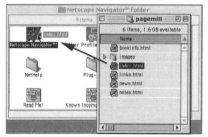

Figures 18a & 18b.
The Switch To submenu on Mac OS (above) and Windows (left).

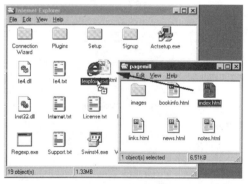

Figures 19a & 19b. Drag the page icon onto the browser program icon in the Mac OS Finder (above) or Windows desktop (below).

Figures 20a & 20b.
The Open Page command in Navigator on Mac OS (left) and the Open command in Explorer on Windows (right).

To open a page with a Web browser

1. From within PageMill, if necessary, activate the window containing the page you want to view with a Web browser.

2. Choose the browser you want to use to view the page from the Switch To submenu under the View menu (**Figures 18a** and **18b**).

or

In the Finder (**Figure 19a**) or Windows desktop (**Figure 19b**), drag the icon for the page you want to view on top of the icon for the Web browser with which you want to view it.

or

1. Launch the Web browser with which you want to view the page.

2. Use the Open or Open Page command under its File menu (**Figures 20a** and **20b**) to locate and open the page you want to view.

✔ Tips

■ To take advantage of the Switch to menu feature, you must configure it. Specify which programs should appear by setting Switch To area Preferences. I tell you how to set preferences in **Chapter 11**.

■ If you use either of the second two techniques to load a web page that you're currently working with in PageMill, be sure to save the page in PageMill before opening it with your Web browser.

To test appearance & links with a Web browser

1. To test appearance, use the scroll bars to scroll through the page and examine it for problems. Some areas you should concentrate on are:

    ◆   Text formatting and legibility.

    ◆   Images and multimedia objects.

    ◆   Compatibility issues affecting the display of text, tables, forms, and frames.

2. To test links, click each link to display linked pages.

✔ Tips

■   When testing appearance, it's a good idea to resize the window once or twice to see how changes in window size affect word wrap, tables, and frames.

■   Your browser can test local links without connecting to the Internet. If you try to test a remote link, however, your browser may attempt to connect to the Internet.

■   Each link that is successfully tested will turn purple or the custom color you may have specified for visited links.

■   If you discover problems with your pages, you can switch back to PageMill and use its Edit mode to fix them. Be sure to save changes to the page before using your browser's Reload or Refresh button to recheck the page—otherwise the unchanged version will load and you won't see your changes.

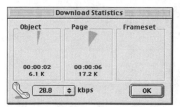

Figures 21a & 21b. The Download Statistics dialog box for an object selected on a page on Mac OS (above) and an object selected in a frame on Windows (below).

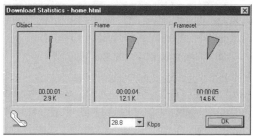

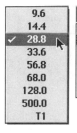

Figures 22a & 22b. The Kbps menu on Mac OS (left) and Windows (right).

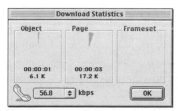

Figures 23a & 23b. Here are the same Download Statistics dialog boxes from **Figures 21a** and **21b**, but with different Kbps options selected.

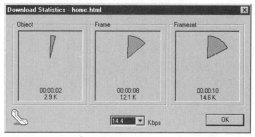

Download Statistics

Each element of each page or frameset must be downloaded from your Web site to a user's computer before the entire page is displayed. PageMill's Download Statistics feature provides information about the amount of time it will take users to download and display your pages.

To view Download Statistics

1. If necessary, activate the window containing the page whose Download Statistics you want to view.

2. Choose View > Download Statistics (**Figures 7a** and **7b**) or press (Shift)(⌃)(⌘)(U) (Mac OS) or (F3) (Windows).

   A window like the one in **Figure 21a** or **21b** appears. It provides size and download time information for a selected object (if applicable), the page (or frame), and the frameset (if applicable).

3. If desired, choose a connect speed from the kbps menu (**Figures 22a** and **22b**) to see download time information at a different speed (**Figures 23a** and **23b**).

4. When you are finished using the Download Statistics window, click OK to dismiss it.

✔ Tips

- For best results, try to keep your page sizes small and quick to download. Remember, not everyone has a direct connection to the Internet. Many people won't wait more than 10 or 15 seconds for a page to load.

- You can keep page size small (and download times low) by limiting the size and number of images and other multimedia objects in your pages.

VIEWING DOWNLOAD STATISTICS

Editing HTML

Underlying every Web page is programming code written using HTML (HyperText Markup Language) tags. PageMill automatically generates the HTML code for the pages you create. **Figures 24a** and **24b** show the HTML source code PageMill has written for the Web page that appears in **Figure 4** and elsewhere throughout this chapter.

PageMill offers several ways you can work with the HTML code it writes:

◆ Add comments that do not appear on the Web page but are encoded in the underlying HTML.

◆ Add placeholders that contain HTML code that is not checked or edited by PageMill.

◆ View and edit HTML code using PageMill's Source mode (**Figures 24a** and **24b**).

✔ Tips

■ Editing the HTML code that PageMill generates makes it possible to include formatting and features that cannot be automatically included by PageMill.

■ **Appendix D** provides a list of the HTML tags that PageMill supports, as well as some additional tags that might interest advanced PageMill users.

■ Although PageMill doesn't support every HTML tag, older browsers don't support all of them either. If you use PageMill to create your Web pages and don't add unsupported tags and extensions, you're more likely to produce pages that will appear relatively the same in all browsers.

■ You can use PageMill to open pages created by any HTML editor or Web publishing tool. If PageMill encounters tags it does not recognize, it displays a question mark in Edit mode.

Figures 24a & 24b. PageMill's Source mode lets you view and edit the HTML underlying a Web page. Here's the beginning of the code for the page in **Figure 4** (and throughout this chapter) on Mac OS (above) and Windows (below).

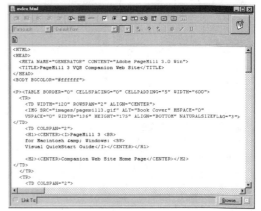

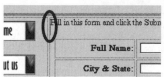

Figure 25. Position the insertion point where you want to place the comment.

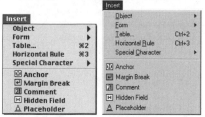

Figures 26a & 26b. The Insert menu on Mac OS (left) and Windows (right).

Figure 27. A comment icon appears at the insertion point.

Figure 28. Click the icon to select it.

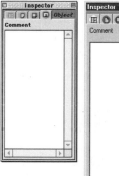 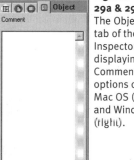

Figures 29a & 29b. The Object tab of the Inspector displaying Comment options on Mac OS (left) and Windows (right).

Figure 30. When you're finished entering your comment, it might look something like this.

To add a comment

1. In Edit mode, position the insertion point where you want to place the comment (**Figure 25**).

2. Choose Insert > Comment (**Figures 26a and 26b**).

   A comment icon appears at the insertion point (**Figure 27**).

3. Click the comment icon to select it (**Figure 28**).

4. If necessary, display the Inspector and click its Object tab to display Comment options (**Figures 29a and 29b**).

5. Enter your comment in the Comment box. When you're finished, it might look something like **Figure 30**.

✔ Tips

- As you can see in **Figure 30**, text does not automatically word wrap in the Comment scrolling window. You must press Return (Mac OS) or Enter (Windows) to begin a new line.

- To read or edit a comment, follow steps 3 through 5 above.

- Comments enable you to annotate or explain the HTML code, so it can be more easily understood by others.

ADDING COMMENTS

To add a placeholder

1. In Edit mode, position the insertion point where you want to place the placeholder (**Figure 31**).

2. Choose Insert > Placeholder (**Figures 26a** and **26b**).

   A placeholder icon appears at the insertion point (**Figure 32**).

3. Click the placeholder icon to select it (**Figure 33**).

4. If necessary, display the Inspector and click its Object tab to display Placeholder options (**Figures 34a** and **34b**).

5. Enter HTML code in the Placeholder box. When you're finished, it might look something like **Figure 35**.

✔ Tips

■ As you can see in **Figure 35**, text does not automatically word wrap in the Comment scrolling window. You must press Return (Mac OS) or Enter (Windows) to begin a new line.

■ You can click the page icon (Mac OS) or File button (Windows) beneath the placeholder image well in the Inspector (**Figures 34a** and **34b**) and use the dialog box that appears to select an image to appear in place of the default placeholder icon.

■ The placeholder icon (or any image you use to replace it) appears only in PageMill.

■ To read or edit the contents of a placeholder, follow steps 3 through 5 above.

■ Placeholders protect code from editing by PageMill's HTML checking routines. Use placeholders to insert JavaScript and HTML code that is not supported by PageMill.

■ For more information about using JavaScript in Web pages, check out *JavaScript for the World Wide Web: Visual QuickStart Guide, 2nd Edition* by Tom Negrino and Dori Smith.

Figure 31.
Position the insertion point where you want to place the placeholder.

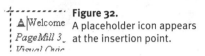

Figure 32.
A placeholder icon appears at the insertion point.

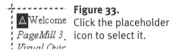

Figure 33.
Click the placeholder icon to select it.

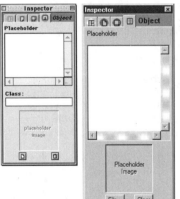

Figures 34a & 34b.
The Object tab of the Inspector displaying Placeholder options on Mac OS (left) and Windows (right).

Figure 35.
Here's an example of some JavaScript code in a placeholder.

ADDING PLACEHOLDERS

Figure 36. Here's the HTML from Figure 24a, edited to reference a style sheet supported by HTML 4.0, but not directly supported by PageMill. This is an example of how you can edit pages to add features PageMill cannot code for you.

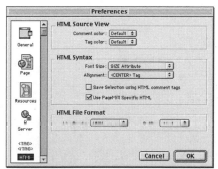

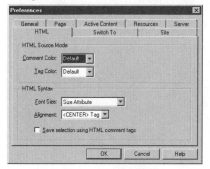

Figures 37a & 37b. HTML options in the Preferences dialog box on Mac OS (above) and Windows (below).

To view & edit HTML source

1. If necessary, activate the window containing the page for which you want to view HTML code and switch to Edit mode.

2. Choose View > Source Mode (**Figures 7a** and **7b**) or press ⌘H (Mac OS) or Ctrl H (Windows).

3. The HTML source code for the page appears in the window (**Figures 24a** and **24b**). Make changes as desired right in the window (**Figure 36**).

4. To return to Edit mode, choose View > Source Mode (**Figures 7a** and **7b**) or press ⌘H (Mac OS) or Ctrl H (Windows) again.

✔ Tips

- Save the page before editing HTML code, just in case something goes wrong during the editing process.

- To view the HTML source for a frame, click in the frame to activate it before switching to Source mode as instructed above.

- You cannot view the HTML source for a frameset from within PageMill. To view the HTML underlying a frameset, you must open its file with a text editor or word processor like SimpleText (Mac OS), Word-Pad (Windows), or Microsoft Word (Mac OS or Windows).

- The text that appears in HTML Source view is color coded to make it easier to read. You can change the color coding, as well as the HTML syntax for font size and alignment coding in the HTML area of the Preferences dialog box (**Figures 37a** and **38b**). I tell you how to set preferences in **Chapter 11**.

- For more information about writing and editing HTML, check out *HTML 4 for the World Wide Web: Visual QuickStart Guide* by Elizabeth Castro.

VIEWING & EDITING HTML SOURCE CODE

USING SITE MANAGEMENT TOOLS

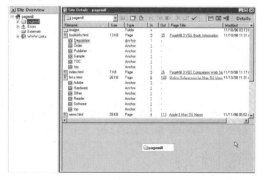

Figure 1. The Site window on Mac OS (above) and the Site Overview and Site Details windows on Windows (below).

Site Management Tools

PageMill's site management features enable you to perform the following tasks from within PageMill:

◆ Manage the files that make up a Web site. This includes changing file names, locations, and contents.

◆ Automatically check for broken local and remote links, as well as other errors.

◆ Upload site elements to a Web server using FTP (File Transfer Protocol).

Site management tasks are performed with buttons, commands, and other options that are only available when a Site window (Mac OS; **Figure 1a**) or Site Overview and Site Details window (Windows; **Figure 1b**) is open. This chapter explains how to open and use these windows and their features for a Web site.

✔ Tips

■ To use PageMill's site management tools, your Web site must be organized into a single *root folder* that contains all Web pages, images, and other site elements.

■ As you'll learn throughout this chapter, PageMill's site management tools offer additional ways to perform tasks covered elsewhere in this book.

Site Windows

The site windows (**Figures 1a** and **1b**) display information about an entire Web *site*—a folder full of related Web files. There are three parts to these windows:

◆ The **Site Overview** area (**Figure 2**) displays the folder hierarchy for the Web site, as well as errors and objects and links that are external to the Web site. On Mac OS, this area is on the left side of the Site window (**Figure 1a**). On Windows, this is a separate area on the left side of the screen (**Figure 1b**). You can use this area to move, copy, cut, unlink, and rename files.

◆ **List view** (**Figure 3**) displays the contents of the item selected in the Site Overview area. For site folder contents, it displays the titles, file sizes, modification dates, and number of links. On Mac OS, List view is on the upper-right side of the Site window (**Figure 1a**). On Windows, List view is in the top half of the Site Details window (**Figure 1b**). You can also use List view to move, copy, cut, unlink, and rename files.

◆ **Links view** (**Figure 4**) displays a graphical representation of the relationship between a selected file in the site folder and the files linked to or from it. On Mac OS, Links view is on the lower right side of the Site window (**Figure 1a**). On Windows, List view is in the bottom half of the Site Details window (**Figure 1b**).

Figure 2.
The Site Overview area displays the hierarchy of the site folder, as well as any errors and external items.

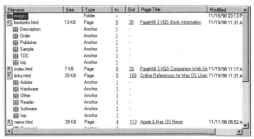

Figure 3. List view provides details about the items in a selected folder.

Figure 4. Links view displays a graphical representation of the relationship between files on the site.

Figure 5. On Mac OS, you open a site by choosing Open Site from the Open submenu under the File menu.

Figure 6. On Windows, you open a site by choosing Browse from the Load submenu under the Site menu.

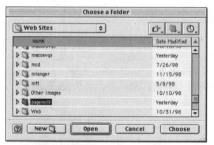

Figures 7a & 7b. Use the Choose a Folder dialog box on a Mac (above) or the Browse for Folder dialog box on Windows (left) to select and open the folder containing the site's files.

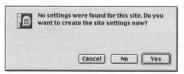

Figure 8. On Mac OS, this dialog box may appear when you open a site folder for the first time.

To open a site

1. Choose File > Open > Open Site (Mac OS; **Figure 5**) or Site > Load >Browse (Windows; **Figure 6**).

   or

   Press Option ⌃ ⌘ O (Mac OS only).

2. Use the Choose a Folder (Mac OS; **Figure 7a**) or Browse for Folder (Windows; **Figure 7b**) dialog box to locate the folder containing the site.

3. Select the folder and then click Choose (Mac OS) or OK (Windows).

4. On Mac OS, a window like the one in **Figure 8** may appear, offering to create site settings. For now, click No.

On Mac OS, a Site window opens (**Figure 1a**). On Windows, the Site Overview area appears with a Site Details window beside it (**Figure 1b**).

✔ Tips

- I tell you more about site settings later in this chapter.

- If site settings exist for the file (Mac OS) or the site has already been opened at least once, you can open it by choosing its name from the Open submenu (Mac OS; **Figure 9**) or Load submenu (Windows; **Figure 10**).

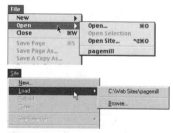

Figures 9 and 10. You may also be able to open a site by simply selecting its name from the Open submenu (Mac OS; top) or its path from the Load submenu (Windows; bottom).

OPENING A SITE

To create a new site on Mac OS

1. Choose File > New > New Site (**Figure 11**) or press Option ⌃ ⌘ N.

   The New Site dialog box appears (**Figure 13a**).

2. Enter a name for the site in the Name box.

3. Click the folder button to display the Choose a Folder (**Figure 7a**) dialog box.

4. To create a new site from scratch, create a new folder and select it.

   or

   To create a new site based on an existing folder, select the existing folder.

5. Click Choose in the Choose a Folder dialog box to choose the selected folder. Its pathname appears in the New Site dialog box.

6. Click Create in the New Site dialog box.

A Site window opens for the brand new (**Figure 15**) or existing (**Figure 1a**) site folder.

To create a new site on Windows

1. Choose Site > New (**Figure 12**).

   The New Site dialog box appears (**Figure 13b**).

2. Enter a name for the site in the Name box.

3. Click the Browse button to display the Open Site Folder (**Figure 14**) dialog box.

4. To create a new site from scratch, create a new folder and open it.

   or

   To create a new site based on an existing folder, open the existing folder.

5. Click OK in the Open Site Folder dialog box to choose the open folder. Its pathname appears in the New Site dialog box.

6. Click Create in the New Site dialog box.

A Site window opens for the brand new or existing (**Figure 1b**) site folder.

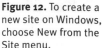

Figure 11. To create a new site on Mac OS, choose New Site from the New submenu.

Figure 12. To create a new site on Windows, choose New from the Site menu.

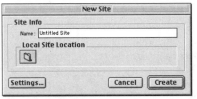

Figures 13a & 13b. The New Site dialog box on Mac OS (above) and Windows (below).

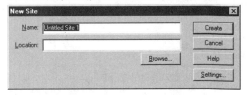

Figure 14. Use the Open Site Folder dialog box on Windows to open a folder containing a new site.

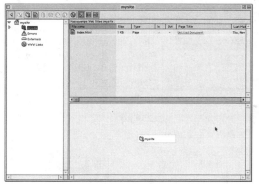

Figures 15. When you create a new site from scratch, PageMill creates a home page and lists it in the List view window for the site.

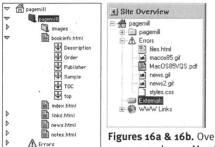

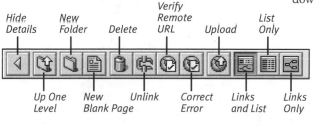

Figures 16a & 16b. Overview area examples on Mac OS (left) and Windows (above).

To expand & collapse Overview & Link view items

On Mac OS:

- To expand an item's view, click the right-pointing triangle beside the item.
- To collapse an item's view, click the down-pointing triangle beside the item.

On Windows:

- To expand an item's view, click the plus sign beside the item.
- To collapse an item's view, click the minus sign beside the item.

✔ Tip

- **Figures 16a** and **16b** show a combination of expanded and collapsed Overview list items on Mac OS and Windows.

To navigate in List view lists

- To see inside a folder, double-click the folder.
- To back out of the folder, click the Up One Level button (**Figures 17a** and **17b**) or use the menu at the top of the Site Detail window to choose a different folder (Windows only).

Hide Details *New Folder* *Delete* *Verify Remote URL* *Upload* *List Only*

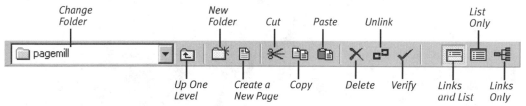

Up One Level *New Blank Page* *Unlink* *Correct Error* *Links and List* *Links Only*

Figures 17a & 17b. The toolbar at the top of the Site window (Mac OS; left) and Site Details window (Windows; below) offers a variety of buttons for working with site contents.

Change Folder *New Folder* *Cut* *Paste* *Unlink* *List Only*

Up One Level *Create a New Page* *Copy* *Delete* *Verify* *Links and List* *Links Only*

VIEWING SITE WINDOW ITEMS

To toggle the display of the Site Details area (Mac OS only)

◆ To hide the Site Details area, click the Hide Details button (**Figure 17a**), choose Window > Hide Site Details (**Figure 18**), or press Option ⌃ ⌘ D. The Site Details area disappears and the Hide Details button turns into a Show Details button (**Figure 19**).

◆ To display the Site Details area, click the Show Details button, choose Window > Show Site Details, or press Option ⌃ ⌘ D. The Site Details area reappears (**Figure 1a**).

To toggle the display of the Site Overview area (Windows only)

Click the triangle button at the top left of the Site Overview area. The Site Overview area collapses to a narrow bar (**Figure 20**) or expands to its usual size (**Figure 1b**).

To change the width of the Site Overview area

1. Position the mouse pointer on the right border of the Site Overview area. The mouse pointer turns into a double-headed arrow (**Figure 21**).

2. Press the mouse button down and drag:

   ◆ Drag to the left to make the Site Overview area narrower (**Figure 22**).

   ◆ Drag to the right to make the Site Overview area wider.

3. Release the mouse button. The width of the Site Overview area changes (**Figure 23**).

Figure 18.
The Hide Site Details command under the Window menu on Mac OS. This command turns into the Show Site Details command when the Site Details area is hidden.

Show Details button

Figure 19. The Site window on Mac OS with the Site Details area hidden.

Figure 20. The Site Overview area on Windows collapsed to a narrow bar.

Figure 21. Position the mouse pointer on the Site Overview area border,...

Figure 22. ...then press the mouse button down and drag.

Figure 23. When you release the mouse button, the Site Overview area resizes.

WORKING WITH SITE WINDOWS

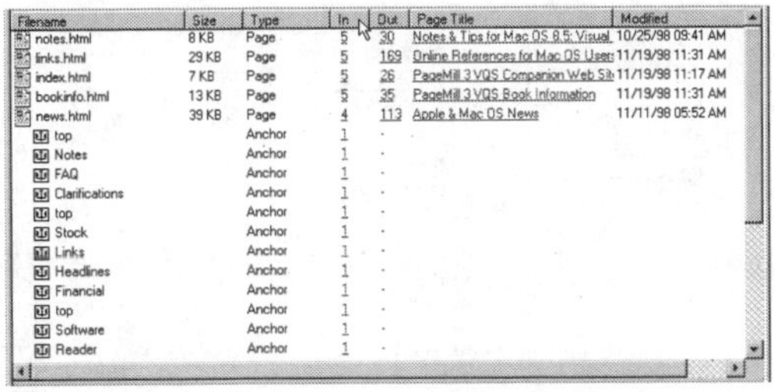

Figure 24. Clicking a column heading changes the List view sort order. In this example, items are sorted by the In column.

Figure 25. You close a site with the Close command under the File menu on Mac OS...

Figure 26. ...and with the Close command under the Site menu on Windows.

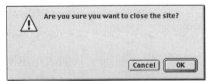

Figure 27. On Mac OS, a dialog box like this asks if you're sure you want to close the site.

To change List view sort order

Click the heading above the column by which you want to sort List view contents. The sort order changes (**Figure 24**).

To close the site

1. Close the site window(s):

   ◆ On Mac OS, click the site window's close box, choose File > Close (**Figure 25**), or press ⌃ ⌘ W.

   ◆ On Windows, choose Site > Close (**Figure 26**).

2. On Mac OS, a window like the one in **Figure 27** may appear. Click OK.

The site window(s) disappear.

✔ Tip

■ On Windows, closing the Site Details window is not the same as closing the site. The site remains open until you use the Close command on the Site menu.

WORKING WITH SITE WINDOWS

Managing Site Files

You can use the site windows to add, delete, rename, and move site elements. On Windows, you can also copy, cut, and paste site elements.

✔ Tip

- When you use PageMill's site management features to reorganize, add, and remove site elements, PageMill automatically places files in the correct folders or directories on your hard disk.

To add a Web page or folder

1. In List view area, open the folder in which you want to add a Web page or folder and select any item in it.

2. To add a Web page, click the New Blank Page (Mac OS) or Create a New Page (Windows) button on the toolbar (**Figures 17a** and **17b**).

   or

   To add a new folder, click the New Folder button on the toolbar (**Figures 17a** and **17b**).

   An untitled HTML document (**Figure 28**) or folder appears in the List view window with its name selected.

3. Enter a new name for the document or folder and press [Return] (Mac OS) or [Enter] (Windows).

✔ Tips

- After adding a Web page, you can add content to it by opening and editing it. I explain how later in this chapter.

- You can also add a Web page or any other site element by dragging its icon from a Finder window or Windows Explorer window into a folder in the Site Overview area (**Figure 29**). PageMill moves (Mac OS) or copies (Windows) the file to the folder you indicated within the site (**Figure 30**).

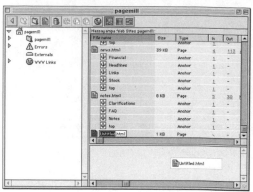

Figure 28. An untitled HTML document appears in the List view window.

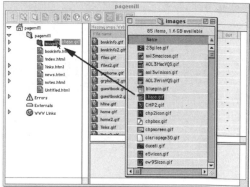

Figure 29. You can drag a file from a Finder window on Mac OS (as shown here) or a Windows Explorer window onto a folder in the Site Overview area to add it to the Web site.

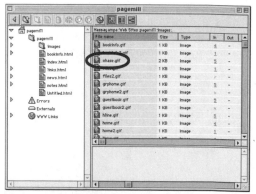

Figure 30. The file you drag in is moved (Mac OS) or copied (Windows) to the folder you specified and appears in the List view window.

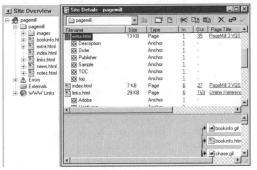

Figure 31. Select the element that you want to delete.

Figures 32a & 32b. A dialog box like this appears on Mac OS (above) or Windows (below) to confirm that you really do want to delete the file.

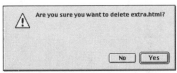

Figure 33. Drag an item onto the folder where you want to move it.

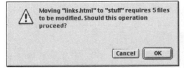

Figures 34a & 34b. A dialog box like this appears on Mac OS (left) and Windows (right) when you move a linked file.

To delete a site element

1. In the Site Overview or List view area, click once on the element you want to delete to select it (**Figure 31**).

2. Click the Delete button on the toolbar (**Figures 17a** and **17b**).

3. A dialog box like the one in **Figure 32a** or **32b** appears. Click Yes to delete the file.

✔ Tips

- Use the Delete button with care! When you use the Delete button to delete an item from a Web site, the item is permanently removed from the site and your hard disk.

- If a file you delete is referenced by another Web page on the site, deleting it will cause an error. Be sure to check errors after deleting any site element. I explain how to check for errors later in this chapter.

To move a site element

1. In the Site Overview or List view area, click once on the element you want to move to select it.

2. Drag the item onto a different folder in the Site Overview or List view area (**Figure 33**) and release the mouse button.

3. If the file is referenced by or includes links to other files, a dialog box like the one in **Figure 34a** or **34b** appears. Click OK.

The file is moved to the location you specified. Any links that required changing are modified accordingly.

✔ Tip

- You can copy rather than move an item by holding down (Option) (Mac OS) or (Ctrl) (Windows) while dragging it from one location to another.

To use the Copy, Cut, & Paste buttons (Windows only)

1. In the Site Overview or List view area, select the item you want to copy.

2. To copy the item, click the Copy button on the toolbar (**Figure 17b**).

   or

   To cut the item (thus removing it from its current location), click the Cut button on the toolbar (**Figure 17b**).

   The item is copied (**Figure 35**) or cut.

3. In the List view area, open the folder in which you want to paste the copied or cut item and select any item within it.

4. Click the Paste button on the toolbar (**Figure 17b**).

   The item is pasted into the location you specified (**Figure 36**).

✔ Tips

■ If you paste a copied item into the same location as the original, the words *Copy of* appear before the item name (**Figure 36**). Be sure to change the item name so it meets the requirements of your Web server software.

■ On Mac OS, you can copy an item by holding down (Option) while dragging it to the destination location as discussed on the previous page.

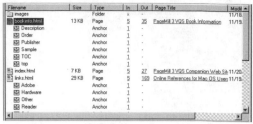

Figure 35. Select an item and click the Copy button to copy it.

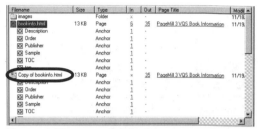

Figure 36. When you click the Paste button, the item you copied or cut appears in the List view area.

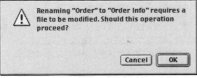

Figure 37.
Click an item's name to display an edit box around it. In this example, an anchor is being renamed.

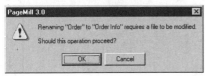

Figures 38a & 38b. A dialog box like this appears on Mac OS (above) and Windows (below) when you rename a referenced item.

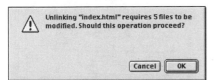

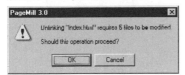

Figures 39a & 39b. A dialog box like this appears on Mac OS (above) and Windows (below) when you unlink a file.

To rename an item

1. In the Site Overview or List view area, select the item you want to copy.

2. Click on the item name. After a moment, a box appears around the name, enabling you to edit it (**Figure 37**).

3. Enter the new name and press (Return) (Mac OS) or (Enter) (Windows).

4. If the file is referenced by other files, a dialog box like the one in **Figure 38a** or **38b** appears. Click OK.

The file's name changes and, if necessary, any references to it in other files are changed accordingly.

To unlink an item

1. In the List or Link view area, select the item that you no longer want referenced by other items.

2. Click the Unlink button on the toolbar (**Figures 17a** and **17b**).

3. A dialog box like the one in **Figure 39a** or **39b** appears. Click OK.

All incoming links to the file are removed from the files that contain them.

✔ Tips

- Using the Unlink button removes incoming links to a file, not outgoing links. This means that other files no longer reference the unlinked file—it's not a destination file anymore. If the file is a Web page that includes links to other files, however, those links are preserved—it remains a source file.

- Unlinking a file does not remove the text or graphics to which the file was linked from the source document. It simply removes the link.

- For more information about links, consult **Chapter 6**.

RENAMING & UNLINKING ITEMS

Editing Web Pages

You can also use PageMill's site management tools to edit individual pages within a Web site:

◆ Open a page and make changes using the standard editing and formatting techniques discussed throughout this book.

◆ Create links and add images to Web pages by dragging elements from the List view area onto an open Web page.

◆ Use the Find and Replace commands and perform a spelling check on all pages in a site.

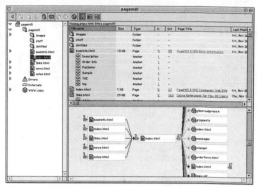

Figure 40. Double-clicking a page in a site window...

✔ Tip

■ Specific page editing techniques are discussed throughout this book. Consult the chapter dealing with the topic that interests you for more information about performing a specific editing task.

To open a Web page for editing

In the Site Overview or List view area, double-click the icon for the page you want to open (**Figure 40**).

The page opens in a regular PageMill window (**Figure 41**).

✔ Tip

■ You can also double-click an image file to open it in a PageMill Image window.

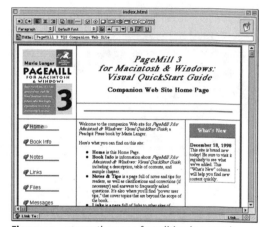

Figure 41. ...opens the page for editing in a regular PageMill window.

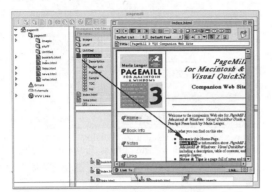

Figure 42. Drag the destination item onto a selection to create a link.

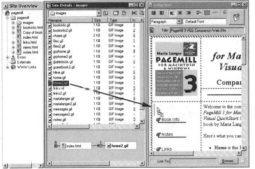

Figure 43. Drag an object into the Web page window to insert it.

To create a link with the site window

1. Open the Web page in which you want to create a link to another item on the site.

2. Arrange the site and Web page windows so you can see inside both of them.

3. Select the text or image to which you want to link the destination item.

4. Drag the icon for the destination item from the Site Overview or List view area in the site window to the selected text or image in the Web page (**Figure 42**).

When you release the mouse button, the link is created.

✔ Tip

■ When dealing with a large or complex Web site, you may find this method of creating links easier than the methods discussed in **Chapter 6**. Not only is this a completely visual approach to creating references, but PageMill will create error-free references automatically for you.

To insert an object with the site window

1. Open the Web page in which you want to insert another site object.

2. Arrange the site and Web page windows so you can see inside both of them.

3. Drag the icon for the object from the Site Overview or List view area in the site window to the Web page. As you drag, an insertion point indicates where the item will appear when you release the mouse button (**Figure 43**).

4. Release the mouse button to insert the item.

✔ Tip

■ For more information about inserting objects, consult **Chapter 4**.

To find & replace text, URLs, & objects throughout the site

PageMill's find and replace features can be used to locate and/or change information throughout a Web site. You use the Find dialog box (**Figures 44a** and **44b**) to specify your find and, if applicable, replacement information. Then use buttons within the Find dialog box or on the Edit (Mac OS) or Search (Windows) menu to locate and/or replace information as specified.

I discuss the find and replace features in detail in **Chapter 2**. They work the same way for an entire site. Just remember to choose an option from the Scope menu (**Figures 45a** and **45b**) at the bottom of the Find dialog box before beginning the search:

◆ **Entire Site** searches all pages in the site.

◆ **Site Selection** searches only the item(s) that are selected in the site window.

✔ Tips

■ I provide step-by-step instructions for using the find and replace features in **Chapter 2**.

■ To select multiple items in the site window, hold down ⌘ (Mac OS) or Ctrl (Windows) while clicking each item you want to select.

■ When you click the Replace All button in the Find dialog box, a warning dialog box like the one in **Figure 46a** or **46b** may appear. Click OK if you're sure you want to replace all instances of the Find text with the Replace with text.

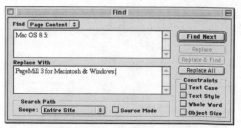
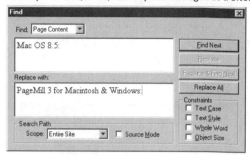

Figures 44a & 44b. Use the Find dialog box to find and replace text, links, and objects throughout a site.

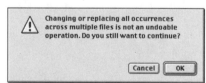

Figures 45a & 45b. The Scope menu on Mac OS (left) and Windows (right).

Figure 46a & 46b. A warning dialog box appears on Mac OS (above) and Windows (below) when you click the Replace All button.

FINDING & REPLACING THROUGHOUT THE SITE

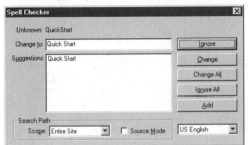

Figures 47a & 47b. The Spell Checker dialog box on Mac OS (above) and Windows (below).

To check spelling throughout the site

PageMill's spelling check features can be used to check spelling on Web pages throughout a site. You use the Spell Checker dialog box (**Figures 47a** and **47b**) to work with unknown words as PageMill finds them. PageMill automatically opens each Web page that contains an unknown word as it checks spelling.

I discuss the spelling check feature in detail in **Chapter 2**. It works the same way for an entire site. Just remember to choose an option from the Scope menu (**Figures 45a** and **45b**) at the bottom of the Spell Checker dialog box the first time it stops for an unknown word:

◆ **Entire Site** checks the spelling on all pages in the site.

◆ **Site Selection** checks the spelling on only the pages(s) that are selected in the site window.

✔ Tips

■ I provide step-by-step instructions for using the spelling checker in **Chapter 2**.

■ To select multiple pages in the site window, hold down ⌘ (Mac OS) or Ctrl (Windows) while clicking each item you want to select.

■ When you click the Change All button in the Spell Checker dialog box, a warning dialog box like the one in **Figure 46a** or **46b** may appear. Click OK if you're sure you want to replace all instances of the Unknown word with the Change to word.

Examining & Resolving Errors

The Errors icon in the Site Overview area represents a folder containing errors that were automatically found by PageMill. You can open this folder to examine and resolve the errors, thus correcting problems on the Web site.

Figure 48. Clicking the Errors icon displays a list of errors in the List view area.

✔ Tip

■ Most errors involve *broken links*—links to files that cannot be found.

To open the Errors folder

Click on the Errors icon in the Site Overview area. A list of errors appears in the List View area (**Figure 48**).

To examine an error

1. Click on the icon for the error you want to examine.

2. Consult the List and Links view areas to get more information about the error (**Figure 49**):

   ■ Broken links—files that cannot be found on the site—have red arrows leading to them from other files in the Links view window (**Figure 49**).

   ■ Unlinked files—files that are not referenced by other files on the site—have red *x* marks in the List view area.

   ■ Orphan files—files that are not referenced by other files and do not include references to other files on the site—have red *x* and blue - (dash) marks in the List view area.

Figure 49. Here's an example of a broken link. The arrow in the Links view area is red. (Since I haven't graduated to 2-color books yet, you'll have to take my word for it.)

✔ Tip

■ Unlinked and orphaned files may not be errors. But they could indicate files that you have forgotten to link to others on your site.

Figures 50a & 50b.
The Site Selection
submenu on Mac OS
(above) and Windows
(below) with a broken
link error selected.

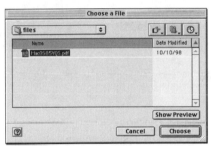

Figures 51a & 51b. The Choose a File dialog
box on Mac OS (above) and the Correct Error
dialog box on Windows (below).

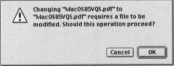

Figure 52a & 52b. This dialog box appears on Mac OS
(above) and Windows (below) when you change the
path (but not the file name) for a broken link's URL.

To resolve a broken link error by unlinking the file

1. In the List view area, click the item containing the error.

2. Choose Site > Site Selection > Unlink (**Figures 50a** and **50b**) or click the Unlink button on the Toolbar (**Figures 17a** and **17b**).

3. Click the OK button in the warning dialog box that appears (**Figures 39a** and **39b**).

PageMill removes all links to the file in the pages that reference it.

To resolve a broken link error by correcting the link reference

1. In the List view area, click the item containing the error.

2. Choose Site > Site Selection > Correct Error (**Figures 50a** and **50b**) or click the Correct Error button on the Toolbar (Mac OS only; **Figure 17a**).

3. Use the Choose a File (Mac OS; **Figure 51a**) or Correct Error (Windows; **Figure 51b**) dialog box that appears to locate, select, and open the missing file or a replacement file.

4. A dialog box like the one in **Figures 52a** or **52b** appears. Click OK.

PageMill updates the link to the file in all files that reference it.

RESOLVING ERRORS

Working with Externals

Externals are files on your hard disk or local network that are not within the Web site's root folder. These files may be properly referenced to files on the Web site, but because they are not within the site's root folder, they will not be uploaded to the Web server with the rest of the site's files. If you don't manually upload them to the proper location on your Web site, errors will result.

PageMill's Gather Externals command enables you to move all external files so they are included in the Web site's root folder. PageMill takes care of changing all the links to these files for you. Then, when you upload the site, these files are uploaded with the others.

✔ Tip

■ Externals with broken links should be listed in the Errors folder with other errors. I tell you about working with errors on the previous two pages.

To open the Externals folder

Click on the Externals icon in the Site Overview area. A list of volumes containing externals appears in the List View area (**Figure 53**).

✔ Tip

■ The List View area displays volumes containing externals as folders (**Figure 53**). You can double-click a folder to open it and see the external items within it. You can also open folders in the Overview area to see their contents (**Figure 54**); this can show you the complete path to the external file.

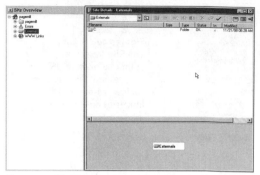

Figure 53. Clicking the Externals folder displays a list of volumes on which external items reside.

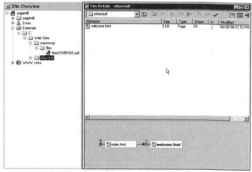

Figure 54. You can examine the folder hierarchy for external items in the Site Overview area. The contents of the folder you select are displayed in the List view area. (This technique works with all folders displayed in the Site Overview area, but can be especially useful for externals.)

OPENING THE EXTERNALS FOLDER

Figures 55a & 55b.
The Site menu on Mac OS (left) and Windows (right).

Figure 56. PageMill adds a Resources folder to the site and copies the externals to it. The externals are now part of the site and the Externals folder should be empty.

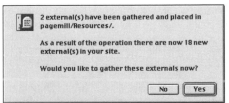

Figures 57a & 57b. A dialog box like this appears on Mac OS (above) and Windows (below) if gathering externals causes new externals to be added.

To copy externals to the site folder

Choose Site > Gather Externals (**Figures 55a** and **55b**).

A status dialog box appears briefly while PageMill copies the external files to a Resources folder within the site folder, which it creates if necessary. All links to those files are modified as required. When PageMill is finished, the files are within the site's root folder (**Figure 56**).

✔ Tips

■ If copying an external file would create additional externals (because of links in the files to other external files), a dialog box like the one in **Figure 57a** or **57b** appears. You can proceed one of two ways:

▲ Click Yes to gather the new externals immediately. The external files are copied to the Resources folder and links to them are changed as necessary.

▲ Click No to keep the new externals as externals. You can then review them in the Externals folder. Unlink the ones you don't want to include on the site and use the Gather Externals command to copy the others to the site.

■ You don't have to keep gathered externals in the Resources folder. You can move them to any other location on the site. Just drag them to the new location as instructed earlier in this chapter. PageMill changes links as necessary for you.

WWW Links

WWW Links or *remote links* are links to URLs outside your site—usually other locations on the Web. PageMill's site management features help you keep track of these links by listing them and offering the Verify Remote URLs command to test them automatically.

✔ Tips

- To use the Verify Remote URLs command, you must have a connection to the Internet.

- PageMill cannot verify mailto links.

- Use the Verify Remote URLs command regularly to make sure all remote links are still valid. Due to the ever-changing nature of the Internet, remote links "break" frequently. Failure to fix or remove broken links can make your site seem out-of-date.

To open the WWW Links folder

Click on the WWW Links icon in the Site Overview area. A list of remote links appears in the List View area (**Figure 58**).

To verify remote links

Choose Site > Verify Remote URLs (**Figures 55a** and **55b**) or click the Verify Remote URL button (Mac OS; **Figure 17a**) or Verify button (Windows; **Figure 17b**).

PageMill connects to the Internet and begins checking each of the URLs in the WWW Links folder. The word *Verifying* and an animated arrow appear in the toolbar (**Figure 59**).

✔ Tips

- Although you can continue working on other things while PageMill verifies URLs, doing so may slow down the verification process.

- To cancel remote link verification, choose Site > Cancel Remote URL Verification. (This command is only available while URLs are being verified.)

Figure 58. Clicking the WWW Links icon displays a list of remote links.

Figure 59. As PageMill verifies remote URLs, it displays an animation in the toolbar and changes the icons and status of the URLs it checks.

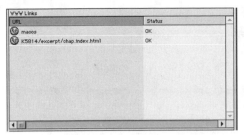

Figure 60. Double-clicking a remote link folder icon displays the links within its domain.

Figure 61. Although PageMill couldn't successfully verify this URL today, I had no trouble opening it with my Web browser.

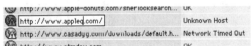

Figure 62. Fixing an error in a remote URL may be as easy as editing it in the List view area. On completing this entry, PageMill will automatically update the link on any pages that reference it.

To review verified links

Look at the icon and Status column entry for a URL (**Figure 59**) to learn its status:

◆ A plain globe or plain globe with folder icon and OK in the Status column means the link has been successfully verified.

◆ An exclamation point on the icon means the link could not be verified. PageMill may display a message in the Status area to explain why the link could not be verfied.

◆ A question mark on the icon and in the Status column means the link has not yet been checked.

✔ Tips

■ A folder icon on a WWW Link entry indicates that there are multiple URLs for that domain. If one of these icons displays an exclamation point, double-click it to see the individual URLs within it (**Figure 60**).

■ You can manually check a URL that could not be verified by PageMill by double-clicking its icon. PageMill launches your Web browser, which then attempts to load the page (**Figure 61**). In some instances, you'll find that links that could not be verified by PageMill but have no message in the Status column are still valid.

To fix a broken remote link

Edit the URL for the link to correct it in the List view area (**Figure 62**).

or

Use the Unlink button to unlink the URL.

or

Open the page on which the URL is referenced, delete the link, and save the page.

✔ Tip

■ I explain how to do all of these things throughout this chapter.

Site Settings

PageMill uses site settings to record information about the location of your Web site on the Internet and your site management preferences. You can create or modify site settings at any time.

✔ Tip

■ You can also create site settings when you first open a Web site on Mac OS or when you create a new site on either Mac OS or Windows.

To open the Edit or Add Site Settings dialog box

1. Choose Site > Show Settings (**Figures 55a** and **55b**). The Site Settings dialog box appears (**Figures 63a** and **63b**).

2. To edit existing settings, select the name of the settings you want to edit and click the Edit button. The Edit Site Settings dialog box appears (**Figure 64a** and **64b**).

    or

    To create new settings, click the add button. The Add Site Settings dialog box appears (**Figure 65a** and **65b**).

✔ Tips

■ You can click the Duplicate button in the Site Settings dialog box (**Figures 63a** and **63b**) to duplicate the selected settings. Then edit the duplicate as desired.

■ You can click the Remove button in the Site Settings dialog box (**Figures 63a** and **63b**) to remove the selected settings if you no longer need them. You cannot, however, remove the settings for an open site.

■ As you can see in **Figures 64** and **65**, the Edit Site Settings and Add Site Settings dialog boxes are virtually identical in appearance and functionality.

**Figures
63a & 63b.**
The Site Settings dialog box on Mac OS (left) and Windows (below).

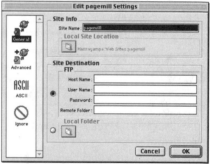

**Figures
64a & 64b.**
The General options of the Edit Site Settings dialog box on Mac OS (above) and Windows (left).

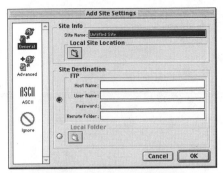

Figures 65a & 65b. The Add Site Settings dialog box on Mac OS (above) and Windows (left).

Host Name :	ftp.gilesrd.com
User Name :	mlanger
Password :	••••
Remote Folder :	/home/mlanger/pagemill/

Figure 66. Here's an example of what the FTP settings might look like.

To specify site name, location, & FTP information

1. In the Edit Site Settings or Add Site Settings dialog box, click the General icon (Mac OS) or General tab (Windows) to display its options (**Figures 64a** and **64b**).

2. Enter a name for the site in the Site Name box.

3. Enter the Local Site Location (Mac OS) or Local Folder (Windows) by clicking the folder button (Mac OS) or the Browse button (Windows) and using the dialog box that appears to select the site's root folder on your hard disk.

4. On Mac OS, select the FTP or Local Folder radio button.

   If you select Local Folder, skip ahead to step 6.

5. Enter FTP information for accessing your Web server in the Host Name, User Name, Password, and Remote Folder boxes. You can get this information from your System Administrator or Internet Service Provider. **Figure 66** shows an example.

   On Windows, skip ahead to step 7.

6. If you selected Local Folder in step 4, click the folder button beside it and use the dialog box that appears to select the site's folder on the Web server, which can be your computer or another computer accessible via network.

7. Click OK to save your settings.

✔ Tips

- FTP information is used to upload your site to the Web server.

- On Windows, to have PageMill memorize your password, turn on the Save Password check box. On Mac OS, PageMill automatically memorizes your password.

To specify transfer settings

1. In the Edit Site Settings or Add Site Settings dialog box, click the Advanced icon (Mac OS) or Advanced tab (Windows) to display its options (**Figures 67a** and **67b**).

2. Select an option in the Transfer Settings area:

   ◆ **Upload All Files** (Mac OS) or **Always** (Windows) instructs PageMill to upload all files in the local folder.

   ◆ **Upload Modified Files** (Mac OS) or **Newer Files** (Windows) only uploads files that are newer than the corresponding files on the Web server. This option can result in quicker uploads than the other two options.

   ◆ **Synchronize** (Mac OS) or **Synchronize Files** (Windows) compares the local files to the files on the Web server and makes sure the newer files are copied to both locations. If you select this command, turn on the Warn me of files to delete when Synchronizing check box to be notified of files to be deleted as a result of a synchronization.

3. Click OK to save your settings.

✔ Tips

■ Choosing Synchronize (Mac OS) or Synchronize Files (Windows) in step 2 can change or delete files on your hard disk, as well as the Web server.

■ On Windows there are two additional advanced options:

   ▲ Connection lets you set the number of times PageMill attempts to connect to the server and the amount of time it should wait for a connection before displaying an error.

   ▲ Port Settings lets you set the port number to which the upload should occur.

   If you do not understand the purpose of these options, do not change them.

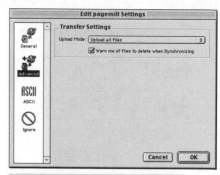
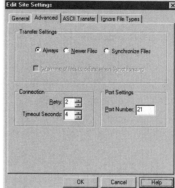

Figures 67a & 67b. The Advanced options of the Edit Site Settings dialog box on Mac OS (above) and Windows (left).

SETTING ADVANCED SITE OPTIONS

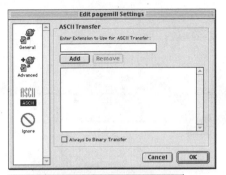

Figures 68a & 68b. The ASCII Transfer options of the Edit Site Settings dialog box on Mac OS (above) and Windows (left).

Figures 69a & 69b. The Ignore File Types options of the Edit Site Settings dialog box on Mac OS (above) and Windows (left).

To specify ASCII Transfer settings

1. In the Edit Site Settings or Add Site Settings dialog box, click the ASCII (Mac OS) or ASCII Transfer tab (Windows) to display its options (**Figures 68a** and **68b**).

2. To use ASCII tranfer to upload files with a specific file extension, enter the extension in the box at the top of the window and click the Add button. The extension appears in the list below it. Repeat this step for each extension.

3. To disable ASCII transfer, turn on the Always Do Binary Transfer check box.

4. Click OK to save your settings.

✔ Tip

■ ASCII and Binary transfer are two different transfer modes recognized by Web servers. If you're not sure whether these options apply to you, ask your System Administrator or Internet Service Provider.

To ignore specific file types

1. In the Edit Site Settings or Add Site Settings dialog box, click the Ignore (Mac OS) or Ignore File Types tab (Windows) to display its options (**Figures 69a** and **69b**).

2. To prevent files with a specific file extension from being uploaded to the Web server, enter the extension in the box at the top of the window and click the Add button. The extension appears in the list below it. Repeat this step for each extension.

3. To enable this feature, turn on the Always Ignore Files check box.

4. Click OK to save your settings.

✔ Tip

■ This feature enables you to store files not used within Web pages in your site's root folder without uploading them to the Web server.

SETTING OTHER SITE OPTIONS

Site Statistics

PageMill can provide some information about the documents that make up an entire site. This information is known as site statistics.

✔ Tip

■ For information about the size and download times for a Web page or frameset and its contents, use the Download Statistics command, which I discuss in **Chapter 9**.

To view site statistics

1. Choose Site > Show Statistics (**Figures 55a** and **55b**).

2. In the Site Statistics dialog box that appears, choose a menu option (Mac OS) or click a tab (Windows) for the type of statistics that interest you:

    ◆ **Site Content** (**Figure 70**) indicates the number of pages, images, Java files, sounds, Adobe PDF documents, and other elements used on your site.

    ◆ **Site Resources** (**Figure 71**) indicates the number of site files, errors, external files, and WWW links used on your site.

3. When you are finished reviewing site statistics, click the OK button to dismiss the dialog box.

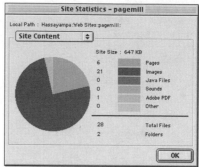

Figure 70. The Site Content area of the Site Statistics dialog box on Mac OS. It displays the same information on Windows.

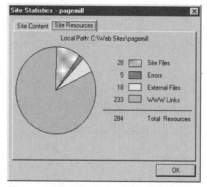

Figure 71. The Site Resources area of the Site Statistics dialog box on Windows. It displays the same information on Mac OS.

Figure 72. A dialog box like this appears in Windows if you did not instruct PageMill to save your password.

Figures 73a & 73b. PageMill displays a status dialog box like this on Mac OS (above) and Windows (below) as it uploads site files to the Web server.

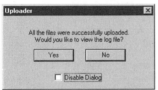

Figure 74. On Windows, a dialog box like this asks if you want to view a log file for the FTP session.

Uploading Files

PageMill's built-in FTP features can upload Web page files for you automatically. All you need is a connection to the Internet. PageMill does the rest, based on the information you provided in the site settings.

✔ Tip

- I explain how to set options for site settings earlier in this chapter. You must enter correct basic site settings information (**Figures 64a** and **64b**) before you can use PageMill to upload your site to the Internet.

To upload a site

1. With the site window(s) active, choose Site > Upload (**Figures 55a** and **55b**), press [Option] [⌃ ⌘ U] (Mac OS only), or click the Upload button on the toolbar (Mac OS only; **Figure 17a**).

2. On Windows, if you did not turn on the Save Password check box in site settings (**Figure 64b**), a dialog box like the one in **Figure 72** appears. Enter a password and click OK.

3. PageMill displays a status dialog box while it uploads files to the Web server (**Figures 73a** and **73b**). Wait until it is finished.

4. On Windows, a dialog box like the one in **Figure 74** appears when the upload is complete. If you click Yes, your Web browser launches to display a log file that lists the files transferred to the Web server.

✔ Tip

- You can display an FTP log for Mac OS by selecting the settings file name in the Site Settings dialog box (**Figure 63a**) and clicking the View Log button. The log appears in a window within PageMill.

To upload specific site elements

1. In the List view area of the site window, select the site elements that you want to upload to the Web server (**Figure 75**).

2. Choose Site > Site Selection > Upload (**Figures 76a** and **76b**).

3. Follow steps 2 through 4 on the previous page.

✔ Tip

- To select multiple site elements, hold down Shift (Mac OS) or Ctrl (Windows) while clicking each one.

To upload a page or frameset

Follow the steps above to select and upload a single page or frameset file.

or

1. Open the page you want to upload.

2. To upload a page, choose File > Upload > Page (**Figures 77a** and **77b**).

   or

   To upload a frameset, choose File > Upload > Frameset (**Figures 77a** and **77b**).

3. Follow steps 2 through 4 on the previous page.

To upload an object

Follow the steps at the top of this page to select and upload a single object.

or

1. Open the page containing the object you want to upload.

2. Select the object you want to upload.

3. Choose File > Upload > Object (**Figures 77a** and **77b**).

4. Follow steps 2 through 4 on the previous page.

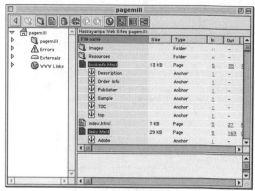

Figure 75. Select the items you want to upload.

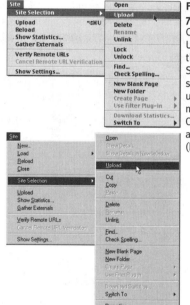

Figures 76a & 76b. Choosing Upload from the Site Selection submenu under the Site menu on Mac OS (above) and Windows (below).

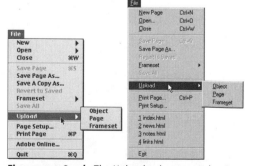

Figures 77a & 77b. The Upload submenu under the File menu on Mac OS (left) and Windows (right).

UPLOADING SPECIFIC ELEMENTS

Setting Preferences

11

PageMill's Preferences

PageMill's Preferences dialog box lets you set the way PageMill works:

◆ **General** preferences (**Figures 2a** and **2b**) control browsing options and Pasteboard sound.

◆ **Page** preferences (**Figures 4a** and **4b**) control the appearance and format of pages, warnings, and file formats.

◆ **Resources** preferences (**Figures 5a** and **5b**) set the PageMill resource folder and image map format.

◆ **Server** preferences (**Figures 7a** and **7b**) enable you to maintain local aliases for remote Web servers.

◆ **HTML** preferences (**Figures 8a** and **8b**) set HTML source view colors and syntax options.

◆ **Switch To** preferences (**Figures 9a** and **9b**) customize the Switch to submenu under the View menu.

◆ **Java** preferences (Mac OS only; **Figure 12a**) control the operation of Java within PageMill.

◆ **Active Content** preferences (Windows only; **Figure 12b**) control the operation of ActiveX Controls and Java within PageMill.

Continued on next page...

PREFERENCES

Continued from previous page.

◆ **Site** preferences (**Figures 13a** and **13b**) control the operation of PageMill's site management features.

◆ **Proxy** preferences (Mac OS only; **Figure 14**) enable you to set up proxy information for operation behind a firewall.

◆ **Launch** preferences (Mac OS only; **Figure 15**) enable you to match applications to file types for launching applications from within PageMill.

✔ Tips

■ Since some preferences affect pathnames used within files, it's a good idea to review and set preferences before you create Web pages with PageMill.

■ Many preference settings apply to pages you create after closing the Preferences dialog box—not to pages that are open when you change settings.

To open the Preferences dialog box

Choose Edit > Preferences (**Figures 1a** and **1b**) or press ⌥ ⌘ K (Mac OS) or F2 (Windows).

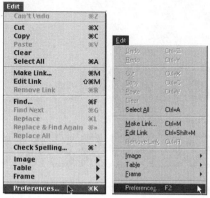

Figures 1a & 1b. Choosing Preferences from the Edit menu on Mac OS (left) and Windows (right).

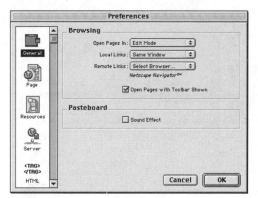

Figures 2a & 2b. The General options in the Preferences dialog box on Mac OS (above) and Windows (below).

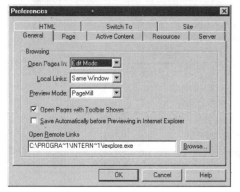

Figure 3. On Mac OS, you can disable the viewing of remote links by choosing Disabled from the Remote Links menu.

To set General preferences

1. In the Preferences dialog box, click the General icon (Mac OS; **Figure 2a**) or General tab (Windows; **Figure 2b**).

2. Set options as desired:

    ◆ Use the Open Pages In menu to select the mode in which you want pages to open: Edit, Preview, or Source.

    ◆ Use the Local Links menu to specify whether links browsed with PageMill should open in the same window or a new window.

    ◆ Use the Preview Mode menu (Windows only) to set the default Preview mode to PageMill Preview mode or Explorer Preview mode.

    ◆ Use the Remote Links (Mac OS) or Open Remote Links (Windows) area to set the Web browser to open remote links.

    ◆ Turn on the Open Pages with Toolbar Shown check box to display the toolbar in document windows.

    ◆ Turn on the Save Automatically before Previewing in Internet Explorer check box (Windows only) to save documents before previewing them in Explorer Preview mode.

    ◆ Turn on the Sound Effect check box (Mac OS only) to play a page-flipping sound effect when you change Pasteboard pages.

3. Click OK to save your settings.

✔ Tip

■ On Mac OS, to disable remote link viewing, choose Disabled from the Remote Links menu (**Figure 3**).

To set Page preferences

1. In the Preferences dialog box, click the Page icon (Mac OS; **Figure 4a**) or Page tab (Windows; **Figure 4b**).

2. Set options as desired:

   ◆ Use the menus in the Appearance area to set default text, background, and link colors for the Web pages you create.

   ◆ Use the Background Image well and its controls to specify a default background image for the Web pages you create.

   ◆ Turn on the Confirm Find or Spell changes which are not undoable check box (Mac OS only) to be warned about Find or Check Spelling command tasks that cannot be undone.

   ◆ Turn on the Confirm frame name changes check box (Mac OS only) to be warned about errors that could occur when changing a frame name.

   ◆ Use the Line Breaks menu (Windows only) to choose a line break format for your Web server: Macintosh, UNIX, or DOS.

   ◆ Use the Suffix menu (Windows OS only) to choose the default file suffix for pages you create: .htm or .html.

3. Click OK to save your settings.

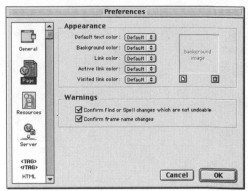

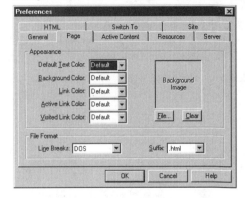

Figures 4a & 4b. The Page options in the Preferences dialog box on Mac OS (above) and Windows (below).

✔ Tips

■ I provide step-by-step instructions for setting page colors in **Chapter 3** and background images in **Chapter 4**.

■ Setting default colors and backgrounds is a great way to enhance consistency among the pages you create.

■ If you're not sure how to set the Line Break and Suffix options, ask your System Administrator or Internet Service Provider.

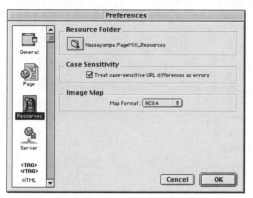

Figures 5a & 5b. The Resources options in the Preferences dialog box on Mac OS (above) and Windows (below).

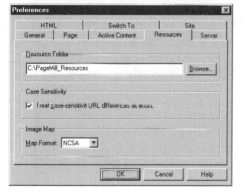

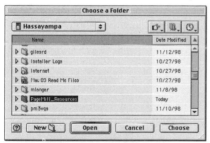

Figures 6a & 6b.
The Choose a Folder dialog box on Mac OS (above) and Browse for Folder dialog box on Windows (left).

To set Resources preferences

1. In the Preferences dialog box, click the Resources icon (Mac OS; **Figure 5a**) or Resources tab (Windows; **Figure 5b**).

2. Set options as desired:

   ◆ Click the button in the Resources Folder area (Mac OS) or the Browse button (Windows) and use the Choose a Folder (Mac OS; **Figure 6a**) or Browse for Folder (Windows; **Figure 6b**) dialog box that appears to select and choose the location for images and other resources saved by PageMill.

   ◆ Turn on the Treat case-sensitive URL differences as errors check box (Mac OS only) to have PageMill flag capitalization inconsistencies (such as *index.html* vs. *Index.HTML*) as errors.

   ◆ Use the Map Format menu to choose a format for server-side image maps you create: NCSA or CERN.

3. Click OK to save your changes.

✔ Tips

■ As advised in **Chapter 4**, you should set the Resource Folder before creating Web pages. Images converted and saved by PageMill will be saved into this folder.

■ As advised in **Chapter 6**, you should set the Map Format before creating server-side image maps.

■ If you're not sure how to set the Map Format option, ask your System Administrator or Internet Service Provider.

SETTING RESOURCES PREFERENCES

To set Server preferences

1. In the Preferences dialog box, click the Server icon (Mac OS; **Figure 7a**) or Server tab (Windows; **Figure 7b**).

2. On the first empty entry link, click beside the globe icon (Mac OS) or in the URL box (Windows) to position an insertion point. Then enter the domain name and directory for the Web site.

3. Click the folder icon (Mac OS) or Browse button (Windows) on the line beneath the URL entry. Use the Choose a Folder (Mac OS; **Figure 6a**) or Browse for Folder (Windows; **Figure 6b**) dialog box that appears to locate and choose the folder on your hard disk that will mirror the Web server directory.

4. Repeat steps 2 and 3 for each local alias you want to identify.

5. Click OK to save your settings.

✔ Tip

■ Set local aliases for any Web pages you create and save on a local hard disk that will later be copied or uploaded to a Web server. This ensures that the correct pathnames are used for local links and object resources when the files are uploaded to the Web server.

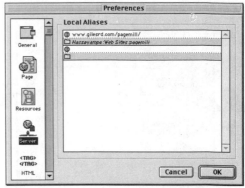

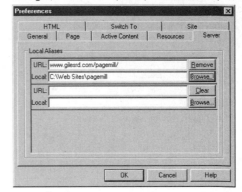

Figures 7a & 7b. The Server options in the Preferences dialog box on Mac OS (above) and Windows (below).

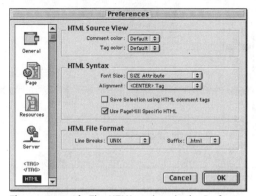

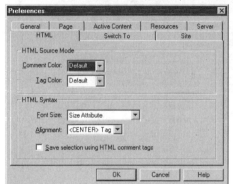

Figures 8a & 8b. The HTML options in the Preferences dialog box on Mac OS (above) and Windows (below).

To set HTML preferences

1. In the Preferences dialog box, click the HTML icon (Mac OS; **Figure 8a**) or HTML tab (Windows; **Figure 8b**).

2. Set options as desired:
    ◆ Use the Comment Color and Tag Color menus to set the color of HTML comments and tags in Source mode.

    ◆ Use the Font Size menu to choose the HTML tag used to specify font sizes: SIZE Attribute or <BIG> and <SMALL> tags.

    ◆ Use the Alignment menu to choose the HTML tag used to specify alignment: <CENTER> Tag, <DIV> Tag, or <P> Tag.

    ◆ Turn on the Save Selection using HTML comment tags check box to "comment out" a selection when saving an HTML file. With this option turned on, anything that is selected when you save a Web page file does not appear in a Web browser.

    ◆ Turn on the Use PageMill Specific HTML (Mac OS only) to include special HTML tags recognized only by PageMill in the Web page files you create.

    ◆ Use the Line Breaks menu (Mac OS only) to choose a line break format for your Web server: Macintosh, UNIX, or DOS.

    ◆ Use the Suffix menu (Mac OS only) to choose the default file suffix for pages you create: .htm or .html.

3. Click OK to save your settings.

✔ Tip

■ Changing options in the HTML Syntax area may affect how Web pages you create are formatted with different browsers. For best compatibility, leave these options set to their defaults: SIZE Attribute and <CENTER> Tag.

To customize the Switch To submenu

1. In the Preferences dialog box, click the Switch To icon (Mac OS; **Figure 9a**) or Switch To tab (Windows; **Figure 9b**).

2. Add a Switch To submenu program:

   ◆ On Mac OS, click the tiny application icon at the bottom of the list of applications. Then use the Choose a File dialog box that appears (**Figure 10a**) to locate and choose an application.

   ◆ On Windows, enter the name of the program in the first empty Name box. Then click the Browse button on the Path line beneath the name entry and use the Select Program dialog box that appears (**Figure 10b**) to locate and select a program.

3. Repeat step 2 for each program you want to add.

4. Click OK to save your changes.

The program you added appears on the Switch To submenu (**Figures 11a** and **11b**).

✔ Tip

■ To remove a program from the Switch To submenu, click the trash can (Mac OS; **Figure 9a**) or Remove button (Windows; **Figure 9b**) beside its name.

Figures 9a & 9b. The Switch To options in the Preferences dialog box on Mac OS (above) and Windows (below).

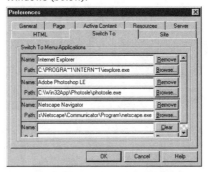

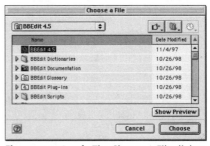

Figures 10a & 10b. The Choose a File dialog box on Mac OS (above) and Select Program dialog box on Windows (below).

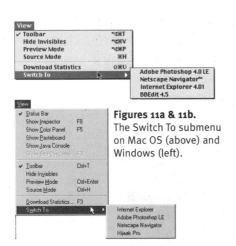

Figures 11a & 11b. The Switch To submenu on Mac OS (above) and Windows (left).

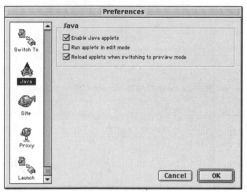

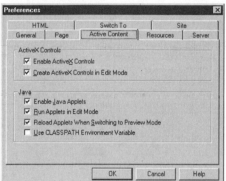

Figures 12a & 12b. The Java options in the Preferences dialog box on Mac OS (above) and the Active Content options in the Preferences dialog box on Windows (below).

To set Java & ActiveX preferences

1. In the Preferences dialog box, click the Java icon (Mac OS; **Figure 12a**) or Active Content tab (Windows; **Figure 12b**).

2. Set options as desired:

   ◆ On Windows only, turn on the Enable ActiveX Controls check box to allow ActiveX to work in PageMill.

   ◆ On Windows only, turn on the Create ActiveX Controls in Edit Mode check box to allow ActiveX to work in Edit mode. (With this check box turned off, ActiveX works only in Preview mode.)

   ◆ Turn on the Enable Java Applets check box to allow Java to work in PageMill.

   ◆ Turn on the Run Applets in Edit Mode check box to allow Java to work in Edit mode. (With this check box turned off, Java works only in Preview mode.)

   ◆ Turn on the Reload Applets when Switching to Preview Mode check box to instruct PageMill to reload Java applet code when previewing pages.

   ◆ On Windows only, turn on the Use CLASSPATH Environment Variable check box to instruct a Java applet to look elsewhere for additional code to run. (Keep this option turned off unless the Java applet documentation instructs you to do otherwise.)

3. Click OK to save your settings.

✔ Tip

■ I discuss how to insert objects such as Java Applets and ActiveX Controls in **Chapter 4**. Creating Java applets and ActiveX Controls is far beyond the scope of this book.

To set Site preferences

1. In the Preferences dialog box, click the Site icon (Mac OS; **Figure 13a**) or Site tab (Windows; **Figure 13b**).

2. Set options as desired:

   ◆ On Mac OS only, turn on the Open recent site when PageMill is launched check box to have PageMill automatically open the most recently opened site when it launches.

   ◆ Enter a name for the site resources folder in the Site Resources Folder Name box.

   ◆ Turn on check boxes in the Warnings (Mac OS) or Options (Windows) area to specify which alerts and other options should be enabled while working with PageMill's site management features. These options are self-explanatory.

   ◆ On Windows only, select an option for the Default Details Mode, which sets the appearance of the Site Details window. Your options are: List and Link view, List view only, and Link view only.

3. Click OK to save your settings.

✔ Tips

■ These options control the way PageMill's site management features work. I discuss these features in **Chapter 10**. If you do not use the site management features, you don't need to set these options.

■ Don't confuse the Site Resources folder with the PageMill Resources folder. The Site Resources folder, which I discuss in **Chapter 10**, is used when gathering externals using PageMill's site management features. The PageMill Resources folder, which I discuss in **Chapter 4**, is used by PageMill to save images and other objects you paste or drag into PageMill documents.

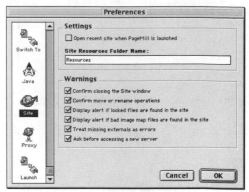
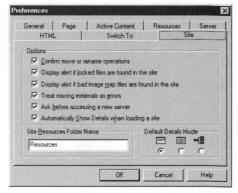

Figures 13a & 13b. The Site options in the Preferences dialog box on Mac OS (above) and Windows (below).

SETTING SITE PREFERENCES

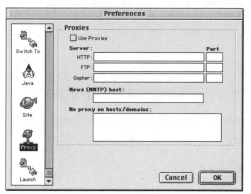

Figure 14. The Proxy options in the Preferences dialog box on Mac OS.

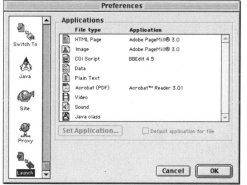

Figure 15. The Launch options in the Preferences dialog box on Mac OS.

To set Proxy preferences (Mac OS only)

1. In the Preferences dialog box, click the Proxy icon (**Figure 14**).
2. Turn on the Use Proxies check box.
3. Enter Proxy information in the appropriate edit boxes.
4. Click OK to save your settings.

✔ Tip

■ It is only necessary to set these options if your organization's network works with a proxy server. If you're not sure whether these options apply to you, ask your System Administrator. If you do need to set Proxy settings, your System Administrator can provide all the information you need.

To set Launch preferences (Mac OS only)

1. In the Preferences dialog box, click the Launch icon (**Figure 15**).
2. Select the icon for the file type for which you want to assign an application.
3. Click the Set Application button.
4. Use the Choose a File dialog box (**Figure 10a**) to locate and choose a program to open that type of file.
5. Repeat steps 2 through 4 for each file type for which you want to assign an application.
6. Click OK to save your settings.

✔ Tip

■ When you double-click a file in one of PageMill's site windows, the file opens using the application you specified for it in Launch preferences. I tell you about working with site windows in **Chapter 10**.

MENUS & SHORTCUT KEYS

Menus & Shortcut Keys

This appendix illustrates PageMill's menus and provides a list of shortcut keys you can use with PageMill.

To use a shortcut key, hold down the modifier key(s) while pressing the letter, number, or punctuation key corresponding to the command. I tell you more about using menus and shortcut keys in **Chapter 1**.

✔ Tip

■ PageMill's menus vary in appearance depending on the type of window open and the item selected within that window. It's impossible to illustrate all possible menu appearances without doubling the length of this book. Instead, I illustrate what the menu looks like most often. You can see variations for specific tasks throughout this book.

Modifier Keys

Key Name	Mac OS Key	Windows Key
Command	⌘ ⌘	n/a
Control	Control	Ctrl
Shift	Shift	Shift
Option	Option	n/a
Alt	n/a	Alt

File Menu

Command	Mac OS Keystroke	Windows Keystroke
New Page		Ctrl N
Open		Ctrl O
Close	⌘ W	Ctrl W
Save Page	⌘ S	Ctrl S
Save Frame	⌘ S	Ctrl S
Print Page	⌘ P	Ctrl P
Print Frame	⌘ P	Ctrl P
Quit	⌘ Q	

New submenu (Mac OS only)

New Page	⌘ N
New Site	Option ⌘ N

Open submenu (Mac OS only)

Open	⌘ O
Open Site	Option ⌘ O

Frameset submenu

Save Frameset	Shift ⌘ S	Ctrl Shift S
Save Everything	⌘ E	Ctrl E
Insert New	Shift ⌘ N	Ctrl Shift N
Insert Page	Shift ⌘ O	Ctrl Shift O

Upload submenu

(no shortcuts)

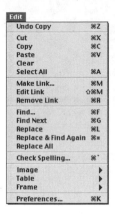

Edit Menu

Command	Mac OS Keystroke	Windows Keystroke
Undo	⌃ ⌘ Z	Ctrl Z
Redo		Ctrl Y
Cut	⌃ ⌘ X	Ctrl X
Copy	⌃ ⌘ C	Ctrl C
Paste	⌃ ⌘ V	Ctrl V
Select All	⌃ ⌘ A	Ctrl A
Make Link	⌃ ⌘ M	Ctrl M
Edit Link	Shift ⌃ ⌘ M	Ctrl Shift M
Remove Link	⌃ ⌘ R	Ctrl R
Find	⌃ ⌘ F	
Find Next	⌃ ⌘ G	
Replace	⌃ ⌘ L	
Replace & Find Again	⌃ ⌘ =	
Check Spelling	⌃ ⌘ `	
Preferences	⌃ ⌘ K	F2

Image submenu

	Mac OS Keystroke	Windows Keystroke
Open Image Window	⌃ ⌘ D	Ctrl D

Table submenu

	Mac OS Keystroke	Windows Keystroke
Select More	⌃ ⌘ 9	Ctrl 9
Select Less	Option ⌃ ⌘ 9	Ctrl Shift 9

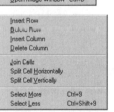

Frame submenu

	Mac OS Keystroke	Windows Keystroke
Split Frame Horizontally	Shift ⌃ ⌘ H	Ctrl Shift H
Split Frame Vertically	Shift ⌃ ⌘ V	Ctrl Shift V

EDIT MENU

View Menu

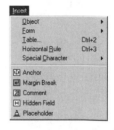

Command	Mac OS Keystroke	Windows Keystroke
Show/Hide Inspector		F8
Show/Hide Color Panel		F5
Toolbar	Option ⌘ T	Ctrl T
Hide Invisibles	Option ⌘ V	
Preview Mode	Option ⌘ P	Ctrl Enter
Source Mode	Option ⌘ H	Ctrl H
Download Statistics	Shift ⌘ U	F3

Insert Menu

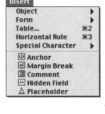

Command	Mac OS Keystroke	Windows Keystroke
Table	⌘ 2	Ctrl 2
Horizontal Rule	⌘ 3	Ctrl 3

Object submenu

	Mac OS	Windows
Other File	⌘ 1	Ctrl 1

Form submenu

(no shortcuts)

Special Character submenu

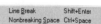

Command	Mac OS Keystroke	Windows Keystroke
Line Break	Shift Return	Shift Enter
Nonbreaking Space	⌘ Spacebar	Ctrl Spacebar

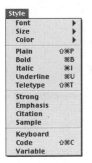

Style Menu

Command	Mac OS Keystroke	Windows Keystroke
Plain	Shift ⌃ ⌘ P	Ctrl Shift P
Bold	⌃ ⌘ B	Ctrl B
Italic	⌃ ⌘ I	Ctrl I
Underline	⌃ ⌘ U	Ctrl U
Teletype	Shift ⌃ ⌘ T	Ctrl Shift T
Code	Shift ⌃ ⌘ C	Ctrl Shift C

Font submenu

Note: The fonts that appear on this menu are fonts properly installed in your system. The fonts on your Font submenu will vary from the illustrations here.

(no shortcuts)

Size submenu

	Mac OS Keystroke	Windows Keystroke
Increase Font Size	Shift ⌃ ⌘ >	Ctrl Shift >
Decrease Font Size	Shift ⌃ ⌘ <	Ctrl Shift <

Color submenu

(no shortcuts)

STYLE MENU

Format Menu

Command	Mac OS Keystroke	Windows Keystroke
Paragraph	⌃ ⌘ 0	Ctrl Shift 0

Indent submenu

Indent Left	⌃ ⌘ [	Ctrl [
Indent Right	⌃ ⌘]	Ctrl]

Align Text submenu

(no shortcuts)

Align Object submenu

(no shortcuts)

Heading submenu

Smallest	Option ⌃ ⌘ 6	Ctrl Shift 6
Smaller	Option ⌃ ⌘ 5	Ctrl Shift 5
Small	Option ⌃ ⌘ 4	Ctrl Shift 4
Large	Option ⌃ ⌘ 3	Ctrl Shift 3
Larger	Option ⌃ ⌘ 2	Ctrl Shift 2
Largest	Option ⌃ ⌘ 1	Ctrl Shift 1

List submenu

(no shortcuts)

Search Menu (Windows only)

Command	Mac OS Keystroke	Windows Keystroke
Find		Ctrl F
Find Next		Ctrl G
Replace		Ctrl L
Replace & Find Again		Ctrl =
Check Spelling		F7

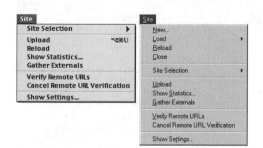

Site Menu

Command	Mac OS Keystroke	Windows Keystroke
Upload	Option ⌃ ⌘ U	

Load submenu (Windows only)

(no shortcuts)

Site Selection submenu

(no shortcuts)

Window Menu

Command	Mac OS Keystroke	Windows Keystroke
Show/Hide Inspector	Option ⌃ ⌘ I	
Show/Hide Color Panel	Option ⌃ ⌘ C	
Show/Hide Pasteboard	Option ⌃ ⌘ B	
Show/Hide Java Console	Option ⌃ ⌘ J	
Show/Hide Site Details	Option ⌃ ⌘ D	

Help Menu

(no shortcuts)

On the Web submenu (Windows only)

(no shortcuts)

TOOLBAR REFERENCE

B

Toolbars

PageMill makes extensive use of toolbars, which offer buttons for accessing commonly used commands. In this appendix, I provide labeled illustrations of each of PageMill's toolbars.

Page Window Toolbars

The Page window toolbars vary slightly depending on what is selected within the window.

Standard toolbar (Mac OS)

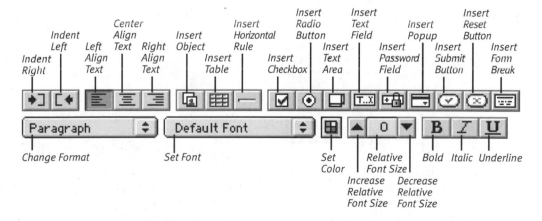

225

Standard toolbar (Windows)

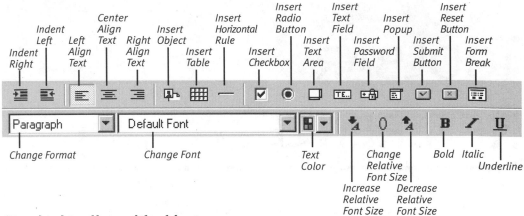

Indent Right · Indent Left · Left Align Text · Center Align Text · Right Align Text · Insert Object · Insert Table · Insert Horizontal Rule · Insert Checkbox · Insert Radio Button · Insert Text Area · Insert Text Field · Insert Password Field · Insert Popup · Insert Submit Button · Insert Reset Button · Insert Form Break

Change Format · Change Font · Text Color · Increase Relative Font Size · Change Relative Font Size · Decrease Relative Font Size · Bold · Italic · Underline

Standard toolbar with object alignment buttons (Mac OS)

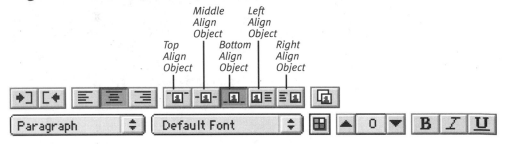

Top Align Object · Middle Align Object · Bottom Align Object · Left Align Object · Right Align Object

Standard toolbar with object alignment buttons (Windows)

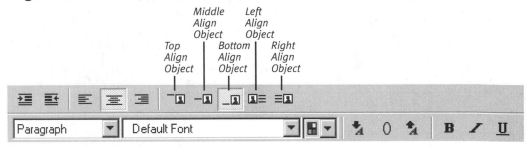

Top Align Object · Middle Align Object · Bottom Align Object · Left Align Object · Right Align Object

Standard toolbar with image editing buttons (Mac OS)

Selector Tool
Rectangle Hotspot
Circle Hotspot
Polygon Hotspot
Shuffle Hotspot
Hotspot Color
Show Hotspot Label
Open Image Window

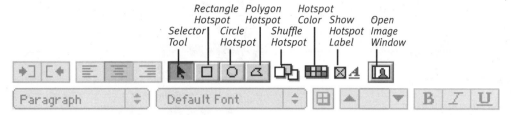

Standard toolbar with image editing buttons (Windows)

Selector Tool
Rectangle Hotspot
Circle Hotspot
Polygon Hotspot
Shuffle Hotspot
Hotspot Color
Show Hotspot Label
Open Image Window

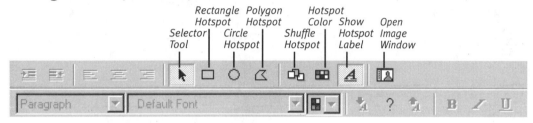

Standard toolbar with table editing buttons (Mac OS)

Insert Column
Delete Column
Insert Row
Delete Row
Join Cells
Split Cell Vertically
Split Cell Horizontally

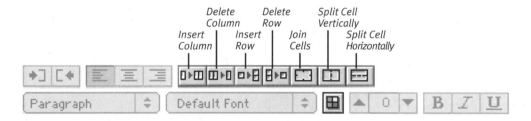

Standard toolbar with table editing buttons (Windows)

Insert Column
Delete Column
Insert Row
Delete Row
Join Cells
Split Cell Vertically
Split Cell Horizontally

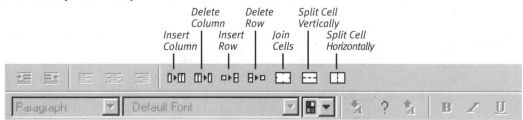

Image Window Toolbar

Mac OS

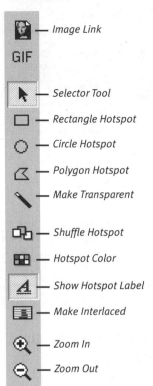

— Image Link

— Selector Tool

— Rectangle Hotspot

— Circle Hotspot

— Polygon Hotspot

— Make Transparent

— Shuffle Hotspot

— Hotspot Color

— Show Hotspot Label

— Make Interlaced

— Zoom In

Zoom Out

Windows

— Image Link

— Selector Tool

— Rectangle Hotspot

— Circle Hotspot

— Polygon Hotspot

— Make Transparent

— Shuffle Hotspot

— Hotspot Color

— Show Hotspot Label

— Make Interlaced

— Zoom In

— Zoom Out

Site Details Window Toolbar

Mac OS

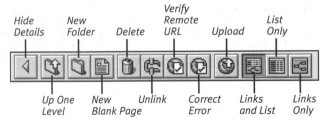

Hide Details | New Folder | Delete | Verify Remote URL | Upload | List Only

Up One Level | New Blank Page | Unlink | Correct Error | Links and List | Links Only

Windows

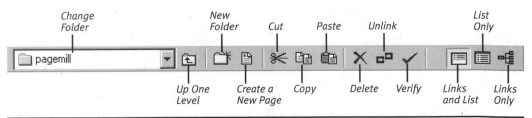

Change Folder | New Folder | Cut | Paste | Unlink | List Only

pagemill

Up One Level | Create a New Page | Copy | Delete | Verify | Links and List | Links Only

INSPECTOR REFERENCE

The Inspector

The Inspector offers a number of panels filled with options to change Frame, Page, Form, and Object settings.

To display the Inspector, choose Window > Show Inspector (Mac OS) or View > Show Inspector (Windows). You can also use the Show/Hide Inspector shortcut key: Option ⌃ ⌘ I (Mac OS) or F8 (Windows). The available panels vary depending on what is selected in the document window.

This appendix provides an illustrated guide to the Inspector's options. I provide additional information for using the Inspector throughout this book.

Frame Panel Options

Frame panel options, which are discussed in **Chapter 7**, let you specify settings for a selected frame.

 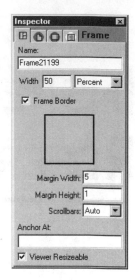

- **Name.** Use this box to give the frame a name.

- **Width/Height.** Use this box to set the width or height of a frame. The menu beside it lets you specify whether the width or height should be in pixels, as a percentage of the window size, or relative to other frames in the frameset.

- **Frame Border.** Use this check box to indicate whether the frame should have a border.

- **Margin Width/Margin Height.** Use these boxes to set the number of pixels between the edge of the frame and its contents.

- **Scrollbars.** Use this menu to specify whether the window should have scroll bars all the time, none of the time, or only when needed.

- **Anchor At.** Use this box to specify an anchor on the page which should be used when the page is opened into a frame.

- **Viewer Resizable.** Use this check box to specify whether the frame can be resized by a user viewing the page with a Web browser.

FRAME OPTIONS

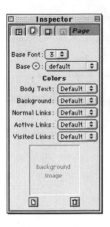

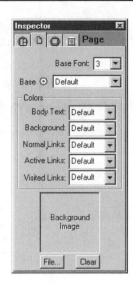

Page Panel Options

Page panel options, which are discussed in **Chapters 3**, **4**, and **7**, let you change the appearance of an active page and its text.

◆ **Base Font.** Use this menu to select a default relative font size for all the non-heading text on the page.

◆ **Base Target.** Use this menu to select a default target frame for links on the page when the page is viewed in a frameset.

◆ **Body Text.** Use this menu to change the color of text on the page that is not a link. The default color is black.

◆ **Background.** Use this menu to change the page background. The default color is gray.

◆ **Normal Links.** Use this menu to change the color of links that have not been visited. The default color is blue.

◆ **Active Links.** Use this menu to change the color of links as they are clicked. The default color is red.

◆ **Visited Links.** Use this menu to change the color of links that have been visited. The default color is purple.

◆ **Background Image.** Drag an image into this "well" to use it as a background image.

◆ **File Icon** (Mac OS)/**File Button** (Windows). Click this button to display a dialog box you can use to select an image for a background image.

◆ **Trash Icon** (Mac OS)/**Clear Button** (Windows). Click this button to remove a background image.

Form Panel Options

Form panel options, which are discussed in **Chapter 8**, let you properly associate a CGI with a form.

◆ **Action.** Use the box to enter the pathname for a CGI to launch on completion of a form on the page. Use the menu (labeled *Method* on Windows) to select the method of exchanging information with the server: GET or POST. Enter information only if the page includes a form. If you are not sure what to enter, ask your System Administrator or Internet Service Provider

Object Panel

The Object panel displays options for the selected object. Its appearance, therefore, changes based on what is selected.

Image options

Image options, which are discussed in **Chapter 4**, let you set options for an image.

◆ **Width.** Use this box to specify an image width. Use the menu beside it to specify whether the measurement is in pixels or a percentage of the page width. This box and menu will only function if the Scale to Height check box is turned off.

◆ **Scale to Height.** Turn on this check box to change the image width in proportion to its height.

◆ **Height.** Use this box to specify an image height. Use the menu beside it to specify whether the measurement is in pixels or a percentage of the page height. This box and menu will only function if the Scale to Width check box is turned off.

◆ **Scale to Width.** Turn on this check box to change the image height in proportion to its width.

◆ **Alternate Label.** Use this box to enter alternate text for the image. The text you enter will appear in text-based browsers or in graphic browsers that have the auto load image option turned off.

◆ **Behavior.** Select one of the options—Picture, Button, or Map—to specify how the image is to be used on the page. The default selection is Picture.

◆ **Border.** Enter a measurement, in pixels, to change the width of an image border. By default, this box is empty. Entering 0 in this box removes any border from an image, even if it is used as a button, map, or link.

IMAGE OPTIONS

233

Media options

Media options, some of which are discussed in **Chapter 4**, let you set the size, name, and value for multimedia objects like QuickTime movies.

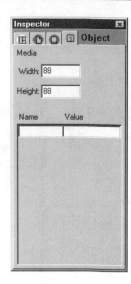

- ◆ **Height/Width.** Use these boxes to enter a height and width for the media element.

- ◆ **Name.** Use this box to enter a name for a media element.

- ◆ **Value.** Use this box to enter a value for a media element.

Horizontal Rule options

Horizontal Rule options, which are discussed in **Chapter 4**, let you change the appearance of a selected horizontal rule.

- ◆ **Width.** Use this box to enter a width for the horizontal rule. Use the menu beside it to select whether the measurement should be in pixels or as a percentage of the page width. The default value is 100 percent.

- ◆ **Size.** Use this box to enter a thickness, in pixels, for the horizontal rule. By default, this box is empty.

- ◆ **No Shade.** Use this check box to turn a horizontal rule's three-dimensional shade effect on or off. With this check box turned on, the rule appears as a plain line.

Break options

Margin Break options, which are discussed in **Chapter 4**, let you set the alignment for a margin break.

♦ **Alignment.** Select an option—Left, Right, or All—to set whether the break affects text at the left margin, the right margin, or both margins.

Table options

Table options, which are discussed in **Chapter 5**, let you change settings for a selected table.

♦ **Width Constraint.** Use this box to enter a width for the table. Use the menu beside it to specify whether the width you enter is in pixels or a percentage of the page width.

♦ **Height Constraint.** Use this box to enter a height for the table. Use the menu beside it to specify whether the height you enter is in pixels or a percentage of the page height.

♦ **Caption.** Turn on the check box to create a caption for the table. Then select an option to place the caption above or below the table.

♦ **Border.** Use this box to set a border width, in pixels, for the table.

♦ **Cell Spacing.** Use this box to set the amount of space, in pixels, between table cells.

♦ **Cell Padding.** Use this box to set the amount of space, in pixels, between the edge of each table cell and the text within it.

BREAK & TABLE OPTIONS

Table Cell options

Table cell options, which are discussed in **Chapter 5**, let you set options for selected cells.

◆ **Width Constraint.** Use this box to set the maximum width for a table cell. Use the menu beside it to specify whether the width is in pixels or a percentage of the table width.

◆ **Height Constraint.** Use this box to set the maximum height for a table cell. Use the menu beside it to specify whether the height is in pixels or a percentage of the table height.

◆ **Header Cell.** Use this check box to determine whether a cell should be formatted as a header cell. Header cells are bold and center-aligned.

◆ **No Wrap.** Use this check box to turn word wrap on or off within a cell.

◆ **Vertical Align.** Select one of these options—Top, Middle, Bottom, or Baseline—to specify the vertical alignment of text within a cell. The default setting is Middle.

◆ **Horizontal Align.** Select one of these options—Left, Center, or Right—to specify the horizontal alignment of text within a cell. The default setting is Left.

◆ **Background.** Use this menu to change the color of a cell's background.

Anchor options

Anchor options, which are discussed in **Chapter 6**, let you change the name of an anchor.

◆ **Name.** Use this box to enter a name for the anchor.

Checkbox options

Checkbox options, which are discussed in **Chapter 8**, let you change the name, value, and default status of a selected check box. The name and value may be dependent on the CGI that will be used with the form, so check CGI documentation when changing these options.

- ◆ **Name.** Use this box to give the check box a name.
- ◆ **Value.** Use this box to enter a value for the check box.
- ◆ **Checked.** Use this check box to determine whether the check box is turned on by default.

Radio Button options

Radio Button options, which are discussed in **Chapter 8**, let you change the name, value, and default status of a selected radio button. The name and value may be dependent on the CGI that will be used with the form, so check CGI documentation when changing these options.

- ◆ **Name.** Use this box to give the radio button a name. Each radio button in a group must have the same name.
- ◆ **Value.** Use this box to enter a value for the radio button.
- ◆ **Checked.** Use this check box to determine whether the radio button is selected by default. The default setting for this option is turned on for the last button in a group and turned off for all other buttons in the group. If you change this option for one radio button in a group, it will automatically change for one other button in the group since only one button in a group can be selected at a time.

CHECKBOX & RADIO BUTTON OPTIONS

237

Text Area options

Text Area options, which are discussed in **Chapter 8**, let you change the name and size of a selected text area. The name may be dependent on the CGI that will be used with the form, so check CGI documentation when changing this option.

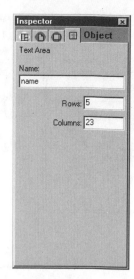

- ◆ **Name.** Use this box to give the text area a name.

- ◆ **Rows.** Use this box to enter the number of text rows that should appear within the text area. The default value is 7.

- ◆ **Columns.** Use this box to enter the number of character columns that should appear within the text area. The default value is 27.

Text Field options

Text Field options, which are discussed in **Chapter 8**, let you change the name, size, and maximum length of a selected text field. The name may be dependent on the CGI that will be used with the form, so check CGI documentation when changing this option.

- ◆ **Name.** Use this box to give the text field a name.

- ◆ **Size.** Use this box to enter the length, in characters, of the text field. The default value is 30.

- ◆ **Max Length.** Use this box to enter the maximum length, in characters, of an entry in the text field. By default, this box is empty.

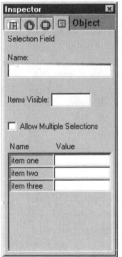

Password Field options

Password Field options, which are discussed in **Chapter 8**, let you change the name, size, and maximum length of a selected password field. The name may be dependent on the CGI that will be used with the form, so check CGI documentation when changing this option.

◆ **Name.** Use this box to give the password field a name.

◆ **Size.** Use this box to enter the length, in characters, of the password field. The default value is 30.

◆ **Max Length.** Use this box to enter the maximum length, in characters, of password field entry. By default, this box is empty.

Selection Field options

Selection Field options, which are discussed in **Chapter 8**, let you change the name, appearance, and functionality of a selected pop-up menu or selection-list field. The name and values may be dependent on the CGI that will be used with the form, so check CGI documentation when changing these options.

◆ **Name.** Use this box to give the pop-up menu or selection-list field a name.

◆ **Items Visible.** Use this box to enter the number of items you want to appear in the selection-list field. This determines the vertical size of the list. By default, this box is empty; leaving it empty displays the object as a pop-up menu.

◆ **Allow Multiple Selections.** Use this check box to determine whether the selection-list field should allow more than one selection. By default, this check box is turned off.

◆ **Value.** Use these boxes to assign values to each item in a pop-up menu or list-selection field. By default, these boxes are empty.

Hidden Field options

Hidden Field options, which are discussed in **Chapter 8**, let you change the name and value of a selected hidden field. The name and value may be dependent on the CGI that will be used with the form, so check CGI documentation when changing these options.

- ◆ **Name.** Use this box to enter a name for the hidden field.
- ◆ **Value.** Use this box to enter a value for the hidden field.

Submit Button options

Submit Button options, which are discussed in **Chapter 8**, let you change the name of a selected submit button. The name may be dependent on the CGI that will be used with the form, so check CGI documentation when changing this option.

- ◆ **Name.** Use this box to give the selected submit button a name.
- ◆ **Label.** Use this box to enter the text you want to appear on the button.

Reset Button options

Reset Button options, which are discussed in **Chapter 8**, enable you to specify a label for a selected reset button. The name may be dependent on the CGI that will be used with the form, so check CGI documentation when changing this option.

◆ **Label.** Use this box to enter the text you want to appear on the button.

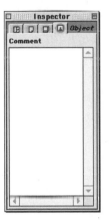

Comment options

Comment options, which are discussed in **Chapter 9**, let you enter comments in your Web page that do not appear in Web browser windows.

◆ **Comment.** Use this box to enter any comments you want to include in your Web page document but not display in a browser window.

RESET BUTTON & COMMENT OPTIONS

Placeholder options

Placeholder options, which are discussed in **Chapter 9**, let you enter raw HTML code that is not checked or edited by PageMill.

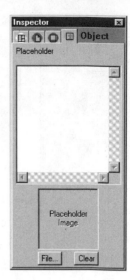

◆ **Placeholder.** Use this box to enter the HTML code you want protected from PageMill's error checking and editing functions.

◆ **Placeholder Image.** Drag an image into this "well" to have it appear as a placeholder image.

◆ **File Icon** (Mac OS)/**File Button** (Windows). Click this button to display a dialog box you can use to locate and select a placeholder image.

◆ **Trash Icon** (Mac OS)/ **Clear Button** (Windows). Click this button to discard the placeholder image.

HTML
REFERENCE

HTML

HyperText Markup Language (HTML) is a Web formatting language that uses special codes called markup tags to indicate formatting and special elements within a Web page. Web browser software such as Netscape Navigator, Microsoft Internet Explorer, and the Web browser that is part of America Online interpret HTML tags to display HTML documents as Web pages with formatted text and graphics.

PageMill 3 supports version 3.2 of HTML, as well as several extensions to HTML that are recognized by Netscape, Internet Explorer, and some other browsers. This appendix provides a list of HTML 3.2 markup tags and extensions.

This appendix is intended as a reference for PageMill users, not as an HTML tutorial. For step-by-step, fully illustrated instructions for using HTML, look for *HTML 4 for the World Wide Web: Visual QuickStart Guide* by Elizabeth Castro, which is also published by Peachpit Press. For the latest information about HTML and standards, check *http://htmlhelp.com/*.

HEAD Section Elements

<HEAD>...</HEAD>	Defines the HEAD section of the document.
<TITLE>...</TITLE>	Defines the page title.
<DOCTYPE>	Defines the document type.[2]
<ISINDEX>	Enables primitive searching.[2]
<META>	Provides meta information for the document.[2]
<LINK>	Indicates relationships between documents on a site.[2]
<BASE>	Indicates the location of the document.[2]
<SCRIPT>...</SCRIPT>	Specifies an inline script.[1]
<STYLE>...</STYLE>	Specifies style information.[1]
<MULTICOL>	Divides a page into multiple columns.[4]

BODY Section Elements

<BODY>...</BODY>	Defines the BODY section of the document.
<!--...-->	Specifies a comment.[3]
<!--NOEDIT-->...<!--/NOEDIT-->	
	Specifies HTML code to be ignored by PageMill.[3]

Text formatting

<B>...</B>	Applies bold formatting to text.
<I>...</I>	Applies italic formatting to text.
<U>...</U>	Underlines text.
<TT>...</TT>	Displays text with a monospaced font.
<FONT>...</FONT>	Changes the color and/or size of font characters.
<BIG>...</BIG>	Enlarges the font size of text.[2]
<SMALL>...</SMALL>	Reduces the font size of text.[2]
^{...}	Displays text as a superscript.[2]
_{...}	Displays text as a subscript.[2]
<STRIKE>...</STRIKE>	Displays text with a strikethrough font.
<EM>...</EM>	Emphasizes text.
<STRONG>...</STRONG>	Strongly emphasizes text.
<DFN>...</DFN>	Displays text as the definition of a term.
<CODE>...</CODE>	Displays text as a code fragment.
<SAMP>...</SAMP>	Displays text as a sample.
<KBD>...</KBD>	Displays text as keyboard input.
<VAR>...</VAR>	Displays text as a variable.
<CITE>...</CITE>	Displays text as a citation.
<BLINK>...</BLINK>	Flashes text on and off.[4]
<MARQUEE>...</MARQUEE>	
	Scrolls text across the browser window.[4]
<WBR>	Inserts optional hyphen for line break.[4]

Paragraph formatting

<P>...</P>	Defines a paragraph of text.
 	Inserts a line break within a paragraph.
<NOBR>...</NOBR>	Prevents line break in text.[4]
<DIV>...</DIV>	Aligns a section of a document.
<CENTER>...</CENTER>	Centers a section of a document.

BODY SECTION ELEMENTS

\<PRE>...\</PRE>	Displays preformatted (monospaced) text.
\<BLOCKQUOTE>...\</BLOCKQUOTE>	
	Displays text as an indented quotation.
\<ADDRESS>...\</ADDRESS>	
	Displays text as address information.
\<UL>...\</UL>	Defines an unordered (bulleted) list.
\<OL>...\</OL>	Defines an ordered (numbered) list.
\<DIR>...\</DIR>	Defines a directory list.
\<MENU>...\</MENU>	Defines a menu list.
\<LI>...\</LI>	Defines a list item.
\<DL>...\</DL>	Defines a definition list.
\<DT>...\</DT>	Defines a definition term.
\<DD>...\</DD>	Defines a definition.
\<H1>...\</H1>	Displays text as a level 1 (largest) heading.
\<H2>...\</H2>	Displays text as a level 2 (larger) heading.
\<H3>...\</H3>	Displays text as a level 3 (large) heading.
\<H4>...\</H4>	Displays text as a level 4 (small) heading.
\<H5>...\</H5>	Displays text as a level 5 (smaller) heading.
\<H6>...\</H6>	Displays text as a level 6 (smallest) heading.

Multimedia objects

\<IMG>	Inserts an image.
\<LOWSRC>	Specifies a low-resolution proxy image to load before a high-resolution image loads.[4]
\<SPACER>	Inserts a space that acts like a transparent GIF.[4]
\<HR>	Inserts a horizontal rule.
\<EMBED>	Inserts a multimedia object.[3]
\<NOEMBED>	Specifies alternative content if multimedia object cannot be displayed.[4]
\<APPLET>...\</APPLET>	Specifies a Java applet.
\<PARAM>	Specifies parameters for a Java applet.
\<TEXTFLOW>...\</TEXTFLOW>	
	Specifies alternative text if a Java applet cannot be played.

BODY SECTION ELEMENTS

245

Links

\<A>...\</A>	Identifies a hyperlink.
\<MAP>...\</MAP>	Identifies a client-side image map.
\<AREA>	Defines a hotspot in an image map.

Tables

\<TABLE>...\</TABLE>	Defines a table.
\<TR>...\</TR>	Defines a table row.
\<TD>...\</TD>	Defines a table cell.
\<TH>...\</TH>	Defines a header cell.
\<CAPTION>...\</CAPTION>	
	Defines a table caption.

Forms

\<FORM>...\</FORM>	Identifies a form.
\<INPUT>...\</INPUT>	Identifies an input field or button.
\<TEXTAREA>...\</TEXTAREA>	
	Identifies a text area field.
\<SELECT>...\</SELECT>	Identifies a selection list.
\<OPTION>...\</OPTION>	Defines selection list options.

Frames

\<FRAMESET>...\</FRAMESET>	
	Defines a frameset.[3]
\<FRAME>	Specifies a frame.[3]

Notes

[1] Supported in PageMill 3 through the use of a placeholder.

[2] Supported in PageMill 3 by editing HTML code in Source view.

[3] Extension to HTML 3.2; fully supported by PageMill 3.

[4] Extension to HTML 3.2; supported in PageMill 3 by editing HTML code in Source view.

INDEX